DOG HIKING NEW ENGLAND

45 Dog-Friendly Trails in Maine, New Hampshire, Vermont, Massachusetts, Connecticut and Rhode Island

HELVETIQ publishing is being supported by the Swiss Federal Office of Culture with a structural grant for the years 2026–2028.

Dog Hiking New England

45 Dog-Friendly Trails in Maine, New Hampshire, Vermont, Massachusetts, Connecticut and Rhode Island

Authors and photographers: © Jill McMahon and Kristen Valenti
Cover design: Ajša Zdravković
Illustrations, typesetting and layout: Elżbieta Kownacka
Editor: Angela Wade
Proofreader: Theresa Cameron

ISBN: 978-3-03964-121-5
First edition: 2026
Printed in China

We are grateful to Livia Waser for her work on Dog Hiking Switzerland.

Mittlere Strasse 4
4056 Basel
Switzerland

DOG HIKING NEW ENGLAND

45 Dog-Friendly Trails in Maine, New Hampshire, Vermont, Massachusetts, Connecticut and Rhode Island

By Jill McMahon and Kristen Valenti

TABLE OF CONTENTS

IMPORTANT INFORMATION

HOW WE SELECTED THE HIKES

With decades of experience hiking in New England, we created this guide with our own trail-loving dogs and understand how hiking together can forge stronger bonds.

We chose hikes not too far from major areas that are worth it for you both. We discovered quiet loops, water to swim in, open summits, off-leash trails, and plenty of hidden gems—and we're sharing our favorites with you! These 45 carefully selected hikes, across all six states, were chosen for their beauty, accessibility and dog-friendly policies.

Recognizing that each dog is different in ability and energy, we've included scenic hikes for dogs of all ages and challenging terrain for more adventurous pups. We spoke to locals while out on these trails to deliver the best insider knowledge to you. Our hope is that these trails help you and your dog explore and find joy in the simple act of hiking together. Have fun!

HIKE PREPARATION

Being well prepared is a must when hiking with dogs, no matter the hike's length or difficulty. You'll need a good daypack to hold gear for both you and your dog. Here are some items to consider for a safe and enjoyable hike.

1. **Navigation:** The AllTrails GPX files we used for the maps are for reference only. A paper map and compass, and knowing how to use them, are the most reliable navigation tools. Phone batteries can die, and there's no guarantee when using technology in the wilderness. Packing a backup charger helps, but be prepared to hike without your phone.

2. **Clothing:** Layering is key for hiking in New England, as weather can change quickly and temperatures fluctuate significantly with elevation. It's important to have rain and wind gear, plus extra layers of insulation, including a hat and gloves. Wear a moisture-wicking base layer and wool or wool-blend socks, which stay warm even if they get wet. For hiking in snow and cold temperatures, consider packing a dog vest and booties for extra warmth.

3. **Food:** Packing adequate, high-calorie food will provide enough fuel to sustain energy levels during an active hike. Dogs need extra calories while hiking, just like we do, and you may even feed them a larger portion at mealtimes on hike days. Carry extra snacks in case you find yourselves away from home longer than planned.

4. **First aid:** Carrying a first aid kit and having basic first-aid knowledge is crucial, since injuries can happen on any hike. Every kit should include moleskin for blisters, tweezers for tick removal, and bandages and biodegradable soap for cleaning wounds. The American Red Cross offers first-aid online training and an app: redcross.org/take-a-class/first-aid/cat-dog-first-aid

5. **Lights:** Packing a headlamp (plus spare batteries) for you and a collar light for your dog is a must for hikes of all durations. Hikes can take longer than planned, and getting caught in the dark is always a possibility—especially on a sunset hike.

6. **Sun protection:** Apply sunscreen before a hike and pack it with you—exposed trails can quickly lead to sunburn. Pack a broad-brimmed hat and sunglasses, too.

7. **Insect protection:** Ticks and black flies are a challenge in this region. Tick season starts in March and ends in November. Black flies are present from mid-May to late June, although this can last longer in Maine. Applying permethrin to clothing and gear will provide a layer of protection against ticks, black flies and mosquitoes. Permethrin is considered safe for dogs, but never apply it to their fur, skin or face—it should only be used on gear. The most reliable protection against ticks is a thorough check after every hike.

8. **Sanitation:** Proper waste disposal protects water sources, wildlife and the beauty of natural spaces. If you need to pee or poop in the woods, go at least 200 feet away from any trail or water source. Burying human waste in a six-inch-deep cathole allows for natural decomposition. Dog waste and toilet paper should be carried out, so pack those plastic dog poop-bags. Washing hands with biodegradable soap is better than alcohol-based hand sanitizer, which doesn't kill most fecal germs.

9. **Fire starter and shelter:** If you're on a difficult hike in challenging terrain, carry matches in a waterproof container, along with some fast-burning birch bark as a potential heat source. Warmth is invaluable if you and your dog are lost. Plus, pack a space blanket or small tarp for shelter in case of an emergency overnight stay.

10. **Hydration:** Remember to pack ample water for you and your dog, relative to the hike distance and weather conditions. The recommendation for moderate hikes is a pint of water per hour for humans and eight ounces per hour for dogs. For hot temperatures and strenuous hikes, double these amounts. Bring a collapsible bowl so your dog can drink easily.

CREATING THE MAPS

Maps in this book were created using AllTrails. With a paid AllTrails membership, you can download maps ahead of time and access them offline without an internet connection. Once downloaded, you'll be able to open that map via AllTrails and use the app's built-in GPS tracking to follow your location in real time—even without cell service.

The app will show you where you are on the trail, so you can easily tell if you're on track, need to make a turn, or should retrace your steps. It's a great way to explore with peace of mind, knowing you're on the right path.

HIKING WITH YOUR DOG

Hiking with dogs is endlessly rewarding and can provide both of you with an incredible bonding experience. These tips can help make it even better.

1. **Research each hike beforehand:** Before setting out on any hike, take into consideration your pet's health and fitness level, and the trail distance, elevation gain and difficulty. Be aware of potential obstacles, like rock scrambles or wooden ladders.

2. **Start with short, simple hikes:** If you're both new to hiking, work up to longer hikes by first building endurance and getting comfortable with different types of terrain.

3. **Avoid hiking in unsafe temperatures:** Anything below 20 or above 80 degrees F is considered unsafe for hiking with dogs. Even temperatures above 65 degrees can be risky for larger or older dogs, depending on the terrain. Consider hiking during cooler times of the day.

4. **Understand your dog's limits:** Pack plenty of snacks and water, take frequent breaks, seek shade, and pay attention to signs of distress or injury, such as excessive panting, drooling, lethargy, shivering, or disorientation.

5. **Maintain vaccinations and tick prevention:** Heartworm and flea/tick prevention are crucial for hiking dogs. Always check your dog for ticks after each hike, especially on their bellies, legs, ears, and face.

6. **ID tag:** Include your name and phone number in case you get separated.

7. **Obedience training:** Make sure your dog knows basic commands, like "come" and "stay," and walks easily on a leash.

LEASH LAWS

In New England, leash laws differ by state, but the majority of hiking trails require dogs be leashed or at the very least under voice command. In this book, we've noted a small handful of trails that are approved off-leash areas—they're clearly marked in each relevant chapter.

You can also refer to the land manager's website for the most up-to-date information. Regardless of the leash laws, be ready to leash your dog when you come across another dog or hiker on trail; not everyone is fond of dogs, so this is for everyone's comfort.

WEATHER AND SEASONS

The weather in New England can be unpredictable and it's important to re-check the forecast before setting out on a hike. Always be prepared for wind, rain and snow on hikes with higher elevation—even in the summer. Before heading out, check the National Weather Service for an accurate forecast: forecast.weather.gov.

Late spring and early fall are ideal times to hike, thanks to milder temperatures and smaller crowds compared to the summer, although each season has its own appeal. In spring, highlights include blooming wildflowers, flowing streams and fewer insects, despite the increased chance of rain and mud. Fall offers vibrant foliage and crisp air. Summer provides extra daylight for longer hikes and opportunities for swimming in mountain ponds, streams and waterfalls. Seasoned hikers with the right gear enjoy the quiet solitude and snow-covered trees during winter hikes. Always check for trail updates in winter, as access roads might be closed.

TRAIL ETIQUETTE

1. **Stay on trail:** This will reduce erosion and damage to fragile flora. If there's mud on the trail, walk through it, not around it. Try to keep your dog on trail, too.

2. **Limit group sizes:** Groups larger than ten people can be hard on the environment and a negative experience for other hikers. When hiking in a large group, consider splitting into smaller groups and choosing meetup spots along the way and after the hike.

3. **Leave no trace:** Leave rocks, plants and other discoveries undisturbed. Always take plastic bags (and plenty of dog-poop bags) to pack out your garbage.

4. **Respect wildlife:** Observe wildlife from a distance and never feed wild animals. Keep dogs on a leash when encountering other animals on a hike.

5. **Yield to other hikers.** Uphill hikers have the right-of-way, and people hiking with dogs should always yield, regardless of the direction they're hiking. Move entirely off the trail to give other hikers space to pass.

6. **Be considerate of others:** Hike quietly, kindly greet other hikers, and offer to help when needed.

7. **Park responsibly:** If the trailhead is full when you arrive, consider returning later or on another day, or look for an alternative legal space.

HUNTING SEASON

New England hunting seasons vary from state to state. During hunting season, always wear orange safety clothing and put your dog in an orange safety vest. Check these sites for hunting laws specific to each state:

State	Agency	Website
Maine		
	Department of Inland Fisheries and Wildlife	maine.gov/ifw/hunting-trapping/hunting/laws-rules/season-dates-bag-limits.html
New Hampshire		
	Fish and Game	wildlife.nh.gov/hunting-nh/dates-and-seasons
Vermont		
	Fish & Wildlife Department	vtfishandwildlife.com/hunt/hunting-and-trapping-seasons
Massachusetts		
	Division of Fisheries and Wildlife	mass.gov/hunting-regulations
Connecticut		
	State Department of Energy and Environmental Protection	portal.ct.gov/deep/hunting/ct-hunting-and-trapping
Rhode Island		
	Department of Environmental Management	dem.ri.gov/natural-resources-bureau/fish-wildlife/wildlife-hunting

PUBLIC TRANSPORT

If you're car-free, or want a car-free adventure, each state has its own rules about dogs and public transport. Always check the specific transit website before you travel. Be mindful of crowds, as some passengers may be uncomfortable around dogs, and try not to block seats or aisles. Service dogs are always permitted.

PARKING

Each hike explains how to get to the trailhead by car and where to park.

FURTHER RESOURCES

For hiking accommodation, BringFido is a pet-friendly hotel and dog travel directory: bringfido.com.

For more information by state, check these sites:

Maine

	Hiking	mainetrailfinder.com
	Visitor amenities	mainetourism.com

New Hampshire

	Hiking	trailfinder.info
	Visitor amenities	visitnh.gov

Vermont

	Hiking	trailfinder.info
	Visitor amenities	vermontvacation.com

Massachusetts

	Hiking	mass.gov/orgs/department-of-conservation-recreation
	Trustees of Reservations	thetrustees.org
	Visitor amenities	visitma.com

Connecticut

	Hiking	cttrailfinder.com
	Visitor amenities	ctvisit.com

Rhode Island

	Hiking	exploreri.org
	Visitor amenities	visitrhodeisland.com

MAP AND HIKE INDEX

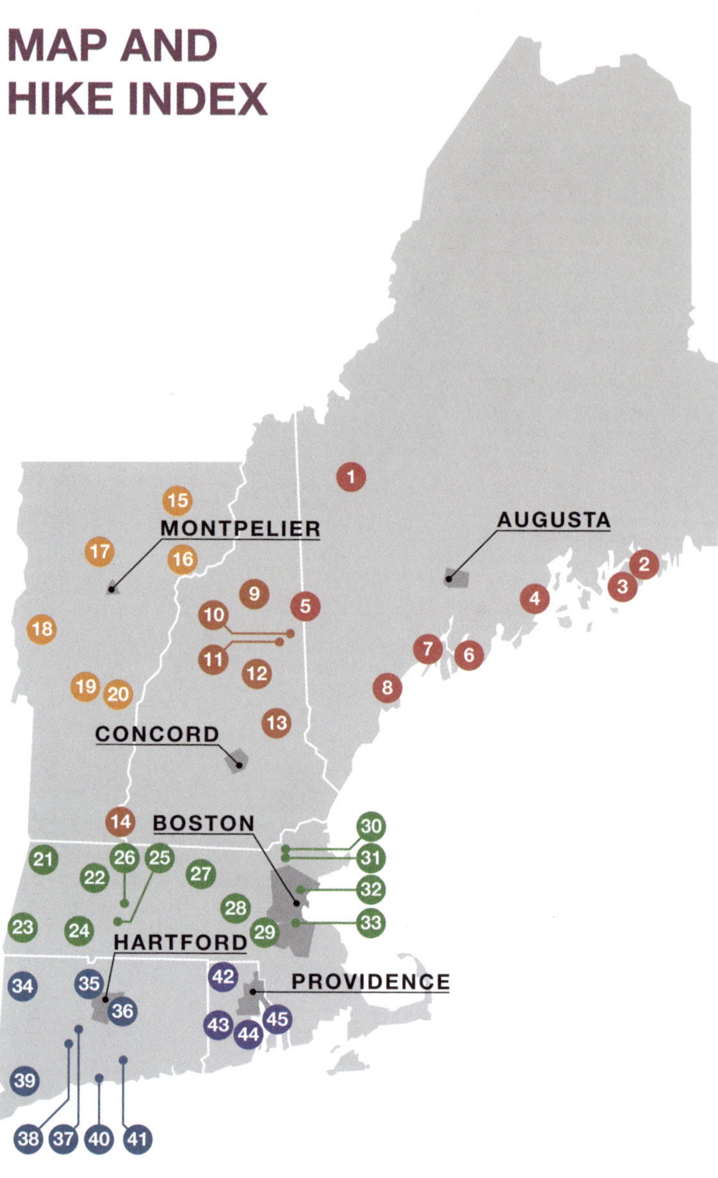

MAINE

NEW HAMPSHIRE

VERMONT

MASSACHUSETTS

CONNECTICUT

RHODE ISLAND

MAINE

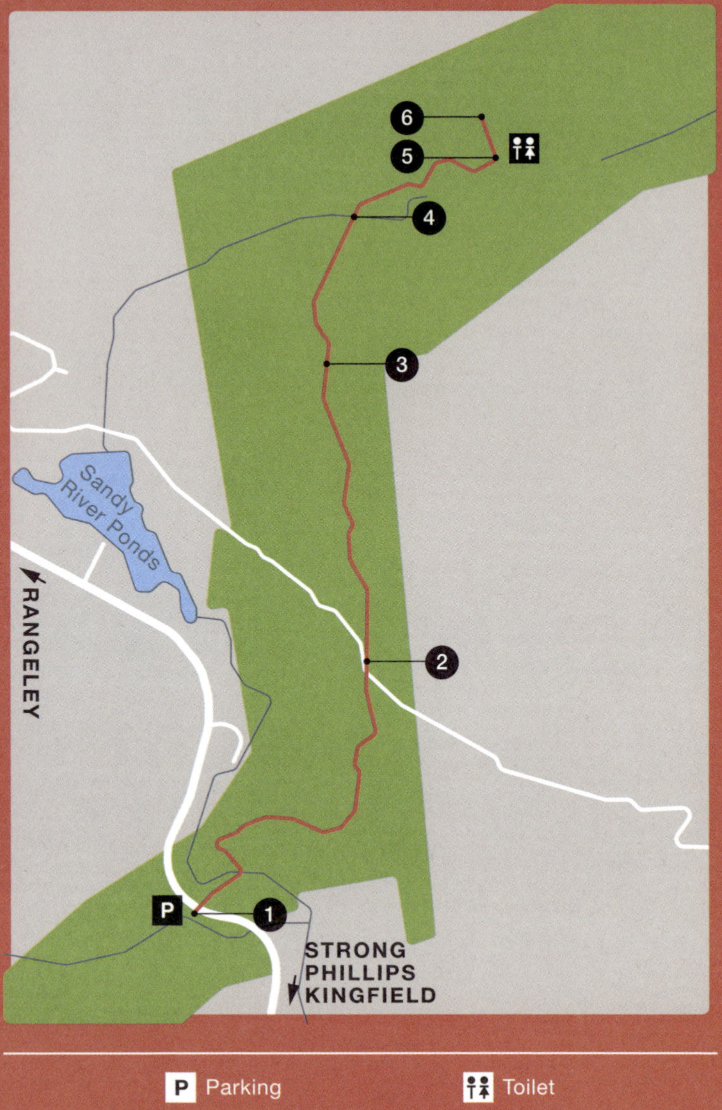

6
5
4
3
Sandy River Ponds
RANGELEY
2
P
1
STRONG
PHILLIPS
KINGFIELD
P Parking
Toilet

ft
2500
2000
1500
1000
500
0
0.0
0.5
1.0
1.5
2.0
2.5
3.0
3.5
3.8 mi

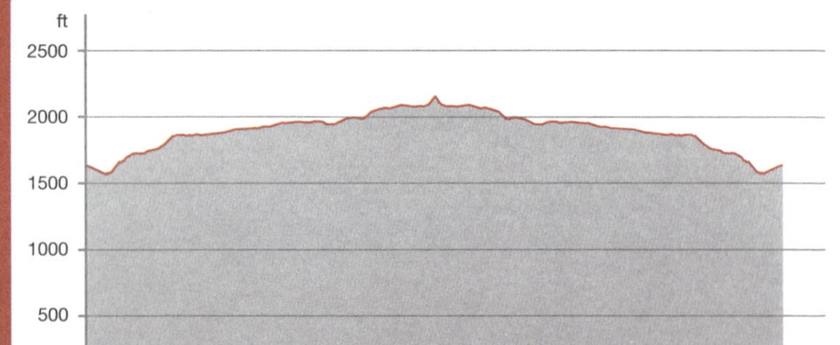

PIAZZA ROCK

THE COLOSSAL STONE CANOPY

SANDY RIVER, ME

LENGTH
3.8 miles
(in and out)

TIME & MONEY
1 hour 45 minutes;
free

ELEVATION GAIN
607 feet

DIFFICULTY
Easy to moderate

CONDITIONS
Year-round;
stream crossings,
shady

HIGHLIGHTS
Piazza Rock,
caves

ESSENTIALS

- **Find the trailhead:** From Rangeley, head southeast on ME-4 S/Main Street toward Lake Street. After 9.5 miles, take a right into the parking lot.
- **Land manager:** Maine Appalachian Trail Club, PO Box 7564, Portland, ME 04112; (304) 535-6331; info@matc.org matc.org

WHY YOU'LL LOVE IT

- Water features for hydration
- Mossy, shady forest
- Unique geological features and caves to explore

The jaw-dropping reward at the outer end of this hike evokes wonder for nature's majestic monuments. Soak in a serene path before reaching this geological marvel—a massive slab of stone jutting out from a pile of supporting boulders, like a roof overhang straight out of *The Flintstones*.

The parking area for Piazza Rock is located nine miles south of Rangeley's center off Route 4. From the spacious lot marked with a wooden AT sign, cross the busy road to pick up the Appalachian Trail.

The hike begins with an easy descent to Sandy River, then crosses a short footbridge over a narrow channel bordered by stone walls.

Beyond this point, the trail veers left and climbs a short, steep section. Besides the brief ascent to Piazza Rock, this is the most challenging part of the hike. The rest is fairly easy, making this hike suitable for all skill levels. With a lean-to located near the top, this is a fun introductory hike on the Appalachian Trail, given the intriguing rock formations and caves to explore at the top.

Along the peaceful, meandering route, there are numerous stream crossings that your dog will love. At 1.8 miles, reach the final stream, marked by a sign for the AT with caves to the right; turn left towards

Piazza Rock. This short spur, indicated by blue blazes, follows the stream and then bears left, leading to the remarkably large stone slab. Beneath Piazza Rock lies a flat boulder, perfect for enjoying a snack while marveling at the geological wonder floating above like a hovering spaceship.

For more adventure, explore the caves and boulders supporting Piazza Rock. Although your dog won't be able to climb through the narrow crevice leading to the top of the rock, there are easier ways to reach it via more gradual side trails to the left. The higher perspective will reward you with views of the top side of Piazza Rock and the gorgeous area of moss-covered forest surrounding it.

To visit Piazza Rock lean-to and privy on your return trip, go left after rejoining the Appalachian Trail from Piazza Rock spur. Continue 0.2 miles north of the shelter if you'd like to see more boulder caves. Or take a right from the spur trail, heading south and back to the start.

TURN-BY-TURN DIRECTIONS

1. From the parking lot, cross the fast-moving Route 4 with caution, then begin on the white-blazed Appalachian Trail as it leads down to Sandy River.
2. At 0.7 miles, cross over the dirt Beech Hill Road, then pick up the Appalachian Trail on the other side.
3. At 1.3 miles, arrive at a stream crossing where your dog can cool off and have a drink.
4. At 1.5 miles, pass the trail registration box on the right before crossing another stream.
5. At 1.8 miles, reach the final stream, then go left, following the sign for the blue-blazed Piazza Rock spur.
6. At 1.9 miles, reach Piazza Rock. Enjoy exploring, then return the way you came.

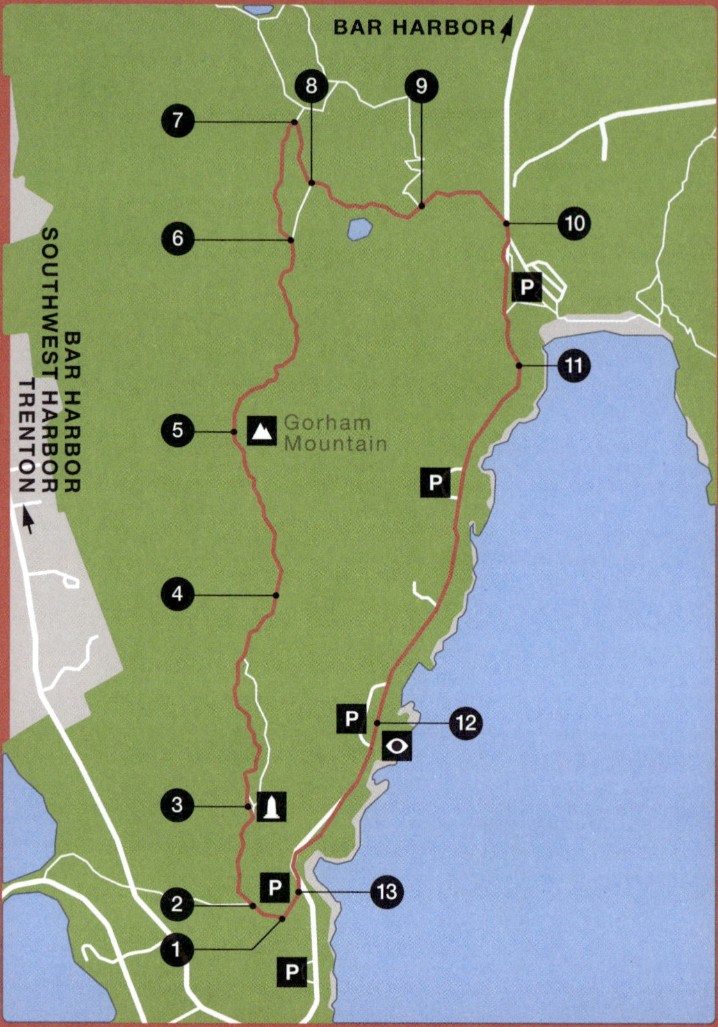

BAR HARBOR
BAR HARBOR
SOUTHWEST HARBOR
TRENTON
Gorham Mountain
1
2
3
4
5
6
7
8
9
10
11
12
13
P

P Parking | Waldron Bates Memorial | Mountain | Viewpoint

ft
2500
2000
1500
1000
500
0
0.0
0.5
1.0
1.5
2.0
2.5
3.0
3.2 mi

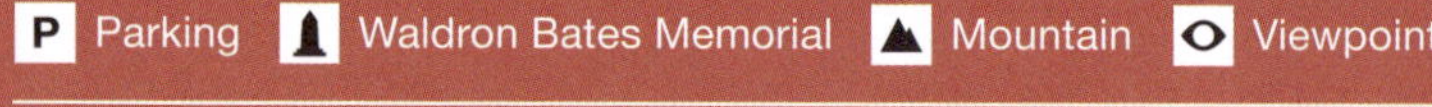

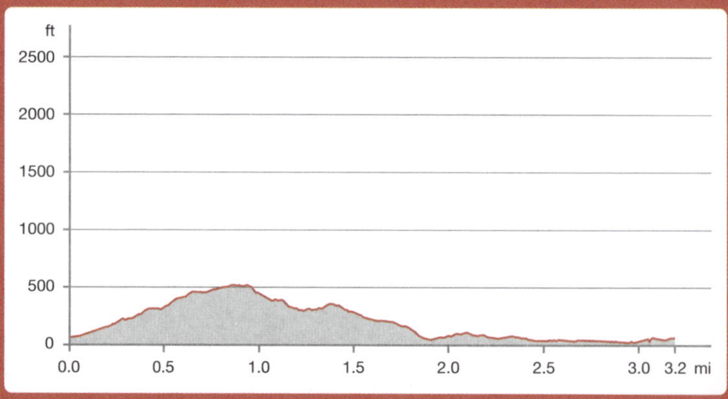

GORHAM MOUNTAIN TRAIL

SWEEPING VIEWS OF ACADIA NATIONAL PARK

BAR HARBOR, ME

2

LENGTH

3.2 miles (loop)

TIME & MONEY

1 hour 30 minutes; fee to enter Acadia National Park

ELEVATION GAIN

561 feet

DIFFICULTY

Moderate

CONDITIONS

Open mid-April to November; rocky, sunny

HIGHLIGHTS

Ocean views, Thunder Hole

ESSENTIALS

- **Find the trailhead:** From Main Street in downtown Bar Harbor, head south, then turn left onto Schooner Head Road. After 79 feet, turn right to stay on Schooner Head Road. After 2.5 miles, turn right. After 0.1 miles, turn left onto Park Loop Road. After 1.6 miles, turn right into the parking lot.

- **Land manager:** National Park Service, Acadia National Park, PO Box 177, Bar Harbor, ME 04609; (207) 288-3338; acadia_information@nps.gov
nps.gov/acad

WHY YOU'LL LOVE IT

- Panoramic views of and from Mount Desert Island
- Varied terrain with options for all dog sizes
- Well-marked trails leading to popular natural landmarks

Climb to an open summit with panoramic views of Acadia National Park, then wander along the gentle Ocean Path to Thunder Hole. In late summer, fuel your hike with wild Maine blueberries found along the trail.

Renowned for its rugged coastline, granite peaks, island scenery, and recreational paths, Acadia National Park welcomes millions of visitors annually. Gorham Mountain, the 23rd tallest in the park, is situated in the southeast corner of Mount Desert Island. Its location offers views of popular park attractions such as Cadillac Mountain, The Beehive, Sand Beach, and Thunder Hole, as well as views to neighboring Schoodic Peninsula on a clear day.

Thunder Hole is a shallow sea cave where giant waves crash into a narrow chamber between towering rock walls, producing a thunderous sound. To maximize your chances of hearing the roar of the waves, it's best to visit one to two hours before high tide. In the 1960s, walkways with handrails were built here, and in the early 1990s, it was renovated to include an accessible ramp with switchbacks. Across the road from Thunder Hole, there are restrooms and a gift shop offering snacks.

The large parking area for this trail is located off Park Loop Road, a scenic 27-mile drive around the east side of the island that provides access to many of the popular destinations in the park. The trailhead can be found in the southwest corner of the parking lot, marked by a large stump with Gorham Mountain Trail carved into it.

Start with a gradual climb up a stream bed with granite slabs before reaching Waldron Bates Memorial, a bronze plaque on a massive boulder at the junction of Gorham Mountain and Cadillac Cliffs trails. From 1900 to 1909, Bates served as chairman of the Path Committee of Bar Harbor Village Improvement Association, during which 25 miles of trails, including Gorham Mountain, were developed under his guidance.

Beyond this point, the trail becomes steeper with some stairs and rock scrambling. If you visit in late July or August, wild Maine blueberries lining the trail will fuel your climb. At just over half a mile, you reach what is known as the false summit of Gorham Mountain, offering open views of Otter Point to the south and Sand Beach to the northeast. Further ahead is the true summit with panoramic views of Mount Desert Island, including Cadillac Mountain. After descending to the Bowl Trail, you're at Park Loop Road. Turn right toward Sand Beach.

From June 15 to September 8, dogs aren't allowed on Sand Beach, but you can view the beach from the top of the stairs. At the south end of Sand Beach parking lot, connect with Ocean Path. This trail, composed mainly of flat, packed gravel and concrete, runs along the rocky coast and includes numerous spurs that lead to ocean cliffs with stunning views.

After 2.5 miles, take the granite staircase leading down to Thunder Hole. This spot can be crowded, so it's best to time your visit for early morning or sunset. Beyond this point are the picturesque Monument Cove and Otter Cliffs before you arrive at a large boulder that marks the trailhead and parking area for Gorham Mountain Trail.

TURN-BY-TURN DIRECTIONS

1. From the trailhead, follow a stream bed to the junction with Otter Cove Trail.
2. At 0.1 miles, take a right to follow Gorham Mountain Trail, marked by blue blazes.
3. At 0.2 miles, pass Waldron Bates Memorial and continue straight on Gorham Mountain Trail, ignoring Cadillac Cliff Trail to the right.
4. At 0.6 miles, enjoy an overlook to Sand Beach and Newport Cove to the east.
5. At 0.9 miles, reach the summit of Gorham Mountain, then bear left, following blue blazes.
6. At 1.2 miles, go left toward Gorham Mountain Trail, avoiding a cut-through to the right.
7. At 1.5 miles, connect with Bowl Trail, heading right toward Park Loop Road/Sand Beach.
8. At 1.6 miles, arrive at a T-Junction with Gorham Mountain Trail and go left toward Sand Beach, continuing on Bowl Trail.
9. At 1.8 miles, pass Beehive Trail on the left, continuing straight.
10. At 1.9 miles, cross Park Loop Road and bear right, connecting with Ocean Path. Look out over Sand Beach or continue straight.
11. At 2.2 miles, reach the first of many spur trails leading down to the ocean cliffs.
12. At 2.9 miles, explore Thunder Hole on the left.
13. At 3.2 miles, take a right toward Gorham Mountain, crossing Park Loop Road to reach the trailhead parking.

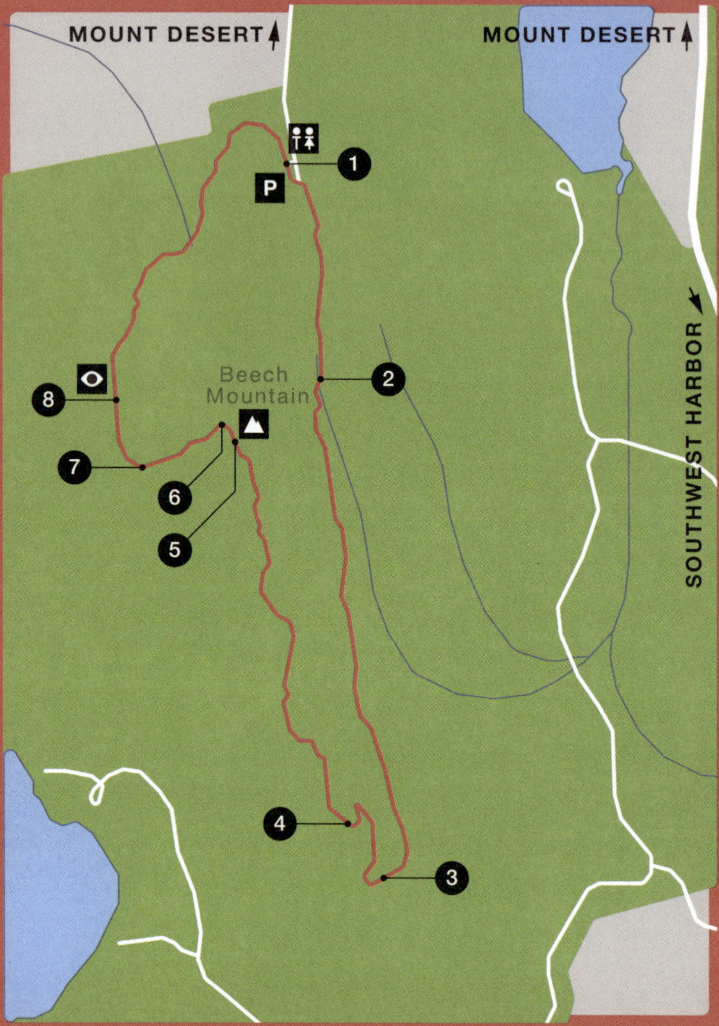

MOUNT DESERT
MOUNT DESERT
SOUTHWEST HARBOR
Beech Mountain
P
1
2
3
4
5
6
7
8

P Parking   Toilet   Mountain   Viewpoint

ft
2500
2000
1500
1000
500
0
0.0
0.5
1.0
1.5
2.0
2.5 mi

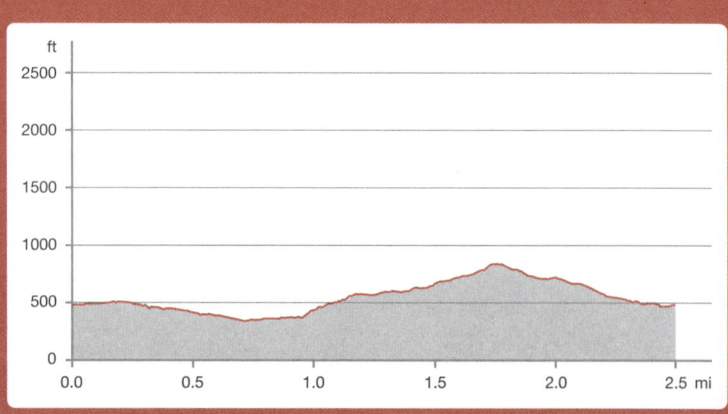

BEECH MOUNTAIN

MOSSY WOODLANDS TO SWEEPING VIEWS

SOUTHWEST HARBOR, ME

3

LENGTH

2.5 miles (loop)

TIME & MONEY

1 hour;
fee to enter Acadia National Park

ELEVATION GAIN

499 feet

DIFFICULTY

Moderate

CONDITIONS

Year-round; stone stairs, open ledge

HIGHLIGHTS

Views, fire tower, less crowded

ESSENTIALS

- **Find the trailhead:** From Mount Desert Street in downtown Bar Harbor, continue straight onto ME-233 W/Eagle Lake Road. After 5.8 miles, turn right onto ME-198 N/ME-3 E. After 1.4 miles, turn left onto ME-102 S. After 0.9 miles, turn right onto ME-102 N. After 0.3 miles, turn left onto Beech Mountain Road and follow it for 3.1 miles to the trailhead parking on the right.
- **Land manager:** National Park Service, Acadia National Park, PO Box 177, Bar Harbor, ME 04609; (207) 288-3338; acadia_information@nps.gov nps.gov/acad/index.htm

WHY YOU'LL LOVE IT

- Lush woods filled with moss
- Open views at several points
- Well-maintained trails and outhouses

Hike through a moss-covered forest to a fire tower with stunning views in Maine's national park. Due to its location in Southwest Harbor, this mountain is less crowded than other popular hiking areas in Acadia.

Acadia National Park on Mount Desert Island offers rocky coastline views, endless summits and diverse wildlife. Beech Mountain is located on the west side of the island in Southwest Harbor, known as the "quiet side," where visitors can experience the park's natural beauty without the large crowds. The mountain is sandwiched between Echo Lake and Long Pond, providing spectacular views from both sides.

The summit includes one of the few remaining fire towers in the area, with 360-degree views of the ocean and surrounding mountains. Constructed by Civilian Conservation Corps, this historic fire tower was originally made out of wood and was in use from 1941 to the mid-50s. Due to deterioration, the tower was replaced with steel in 1962 and was no longer manned after 1976.

The tower's first platform is always open to visitors, and the National Park Service has started opening the top platform during designated times in the summer. From the top, there are sweeping views of Echo Lake and Cadillac, Sargent and Acadia mountains to the east; Southwest Harbor, Northeast Harbor and the Cranberry Isles to the southeast; and Long Pond to the west.

South Ridge Loop begins on Valley Trail at the southern end of the parking lot. Start with an easy walk on a wide path before reaching Canada Cliffs Trail junction, where the trail becomes narrower as it enters a lush mixed forest, winding between moss-covered boulders with a towering rock face on the right.

After less than a mile, join Beech Mountain South Ridge Loop, ascending a continuous stretch of steep stone steps. At the top, head through an open forest with ridge views to the south and east. Just under two miles in is the summit and fire tower. Enjoy panoramic views of the ocean and outlying islands from the platform, then return to the spacious rock-ledge area at the summit, where you and your dog can rest and take in the scenery.

Continue past the fire tower and head left toward Beech Mountain parking area. The trail follows a long stretch of open ledge with breathtaking views of Long Pond and Mansell Mountain. This is a popular spot to watch the sunset if you plan your hike for late afternoon.

Beyond this point, some scrambling over larger rocks is required and you may need to assist smaller dogs. Medium to large dogs will navigate this area with ease, while small dogs can consider it an achievement. The last part of this hike is straightforward for hikers of all skill levels, with a gentle descent leading to the northwest corner of the parking lot.

TURN-BY-TURN DIRECTIONS

1. Locate the trailhead at the south end of the large parking lot on Beech Mountain Road.
2. At 0.3 miles, bear right at the junction with Canada Cliffs Trail, continuing on Valley Trail.
3. At 1 mile, take a right to connect with Beech Mountain South Ridge Trail and ascend stone steps.
4. At 1.2 miles, continue right, following the blue blazes painted on rocks.
5. At 1.7 miles, reach Beech Mountain summit and fire tower.
6. At 1.8 miles, just beyond the fire tower, take a left at the fork and follow blue blazes toward Beech Mountain parking area.
7. At 1.9 miles, ignore West Ridge Trail on the left and continue straight on Beech Mountain Trail.
8. At 2 miles, enjoy open views of Long Pond, then continue following the blue blazes back to the parking lot.

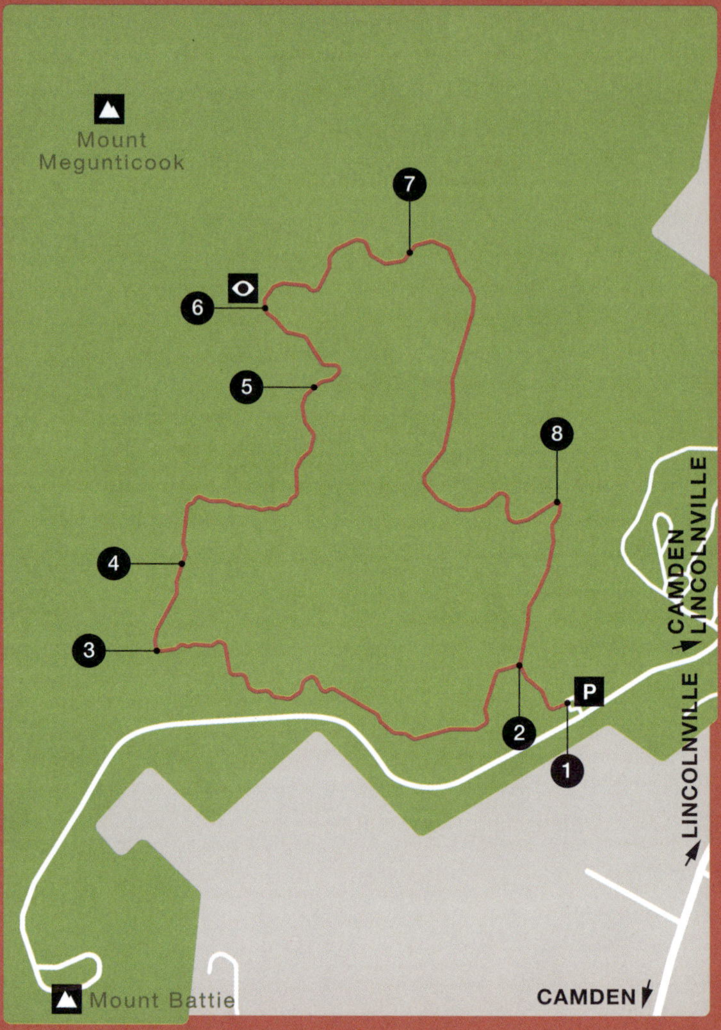

Mount Megunticook
7
6
5
8
4
3
2
P
1
CAMDEN
LINCOLNVILLE
LINCOLNVILLE
Mount Battie
CAMDEN

P Parking | Mountain | Viewpoint

ft
2500
2000
1500
1000
500
0
0.0
0.5
1.0
1.5
2.0
2.5
3.0 mi

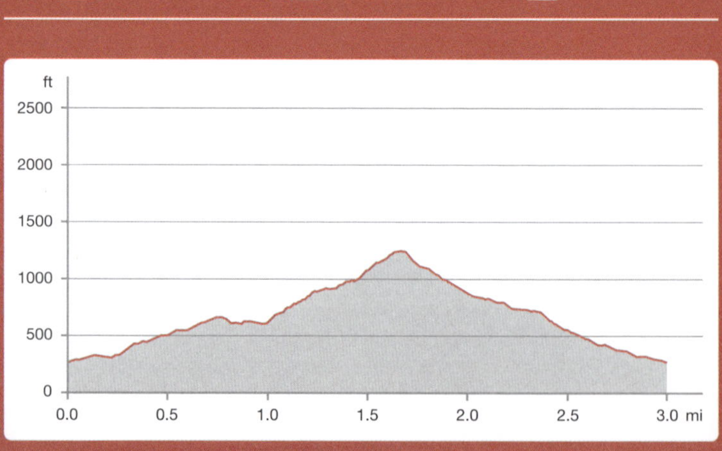

OCEAN LOOKOUT AT CAMDEN HILLS STATE PARK

PENOBSCOT BAY VIEWS ON SCENIC MIDCOAST

CAMDEN, ME

4

LENGTH

3 miles (loop)

TIME & MONEY

1 hour 30 minutes; park entrance fee

ELEVATION GAIN

997 feet

DIFFICULTY

Moderate

CONDITIONS

Year-round; stone stairs, streams

HIGHLIGHTS

Views of Mount Battie and Camden's waterfront

ESSENTIALS

- **Find the trailhead:** From downtown Camden, follow US Route 1 north. After 2 miles, take a left into Camden Hills State Park, then follow the road to the main gate and ranger's station, ignoring the road to the left leading to a small parking lot. Pay the small entrance fee, then bear left onto Mount Battie Road and follow it for 0.7 miles to the trailhead parking on the right.
- **Land manager:** Maine Bureau of Parks and Lands, 280 Belfast Road, Camden, ME 04843; (207) 236-3109
  maine.gov/dacs

WHY YOU'LL LOVE IT

- Minutes from the picturesque seaport town of Camden
- Easy parking and well-marked trails
- Options for a longer hike

Just outside downtown Camden, Midcoast Maine, this state park features mossy trails, intriguing landmarks and ocean views. The expansive trail network includes a range of options—from easy drives up carriage roads, to rocky climbs with clifftop overlooks.

Camden has been called "The Jewel of the Maine Coast," due to its scenic waterfront, historic downtown and New England charm. Tucked between the Atlantic Coast and the hills of Mount Megunticook, this area offers recreation, restaurants, shops, and hotels.

Many of these are dog-friendly, including the trails, campground and Megunticook Cabin at Camden Hills State Park. Originally a ski shelter, this wood-stove-heated cabin is now available to rent for one to six nights. Nothing says adventure like hiking 2.5 miles to accommodation with no electricity or cell phone service!

There are endless routes to explore at Camden Hills, but this is the best introductory hike leading to a stunning ocean view. For those seeking a full-day hike, two equally interesting options are also included.

From the trailhead at the northwest corner of the parking lot, begin your hike by crossing a marsh on a quarter-mile-long elevated boardwalk. Shortly after the boardwalk ends, go left at the junction onto Nature Trail, towards Mount Battie. The path becomes increasingly rocky with sections of ledge, but the steepest parts include stone steps, allowing for an easier ascent.

After around three-quarters of a mile, head right to connect with Tablelands Trail, following it all the way to the cliffs at Ocean Lookout. The views of Penobscot Bay, Mount Battie and the town of Camden are spectacular.

Enjoy the scenery at the overlook while your dog rests, then bear right on Mount Megunticook Trail towards Mount Battie Road. At two miles, there's a cascading stream on the trail's left, providing the perfect place for your dog to have a drink and cool off. At just over two and a half miles, bear right towards Hiker's Parking Lot. Shortly after, go left and cross the boardwalk back to the trailhead.

TURN-BY-TURN DIRECTIONS

1. From the trailhead, cross the 0.25-mile-long boardwalk marked by blue blazes.
2. At 0.1 miles, go left on Nature Trail towards Mount Battie. The trail begins to climb, with a large section of ledge at 0.8 miles.
3. At 0.8 miles, at the junction with Tablelands Trail, go right towards Ocean Lookout (to explore Mount Battie, you would go left here).
4. At 1 mile, stay right on Tablelands Trail, ignoring Bubba's Trail to the left. The trail is now marked by blue and red blazes.
5. At 1.4 miles, at the junction with Jack Williams Trail, stay straight on Tablelands Trail towards Ocean Lookout. After 0.1 miles, ignore Adams Lookout Trail to the right and continue on Tablelands Trail, which bears slightly left.
6. At 1.6 miles, arrive at Ocean Overlook, then bear right towards Mount Battie Road on Megunticook Trail, marked by blue blazes.
7. At 2 miles, arrive at a stream where your dog can have a drink. Then continue straight, ignoring Adams Lookout Trail to the right.
8. At 2.6 miles, bear right at the junction towards Hiker's Parking Lot, then take a left onto the boardwalk, returning the way you came.

To lengthen this hike and add more views and monuments, the following two pages show two additional routes that branch off from Ocean Lookout Loop.

Option 1

Mount Battie summit (an extra 2 miles to create a 5-mile hike in total): Hike one mile (in and out) to the summit of Mount Battie to an impressive 26-foot stone tower. Climb its internal staircase to the roof for panoramic views of Camden's waterfront and Penobscot Bay.

Mount Battie Tower was once the location of Summit House Hotel, built in 1898 by Columbus Bushwell. The hotel was purchased by the Mount Battie Association in 1899 and turned into a clubhouse and social center for wealthy summer residents (which included the daughter of Theodore Roosevelt). In 1918 a forest fire devastated the area.

Although Summit House was undamaged, it was torn down two years later due to a decline in use. In 1921, the stone tower honoring Camden's soldiers who served in World War I was built on the exact location where Summit House once stood.

To access this route, start on Nature Trail, then take a left onto Tablelands Trail at 0.8 miles. Follow it for one mile to the summit of Mount Battie. Return the way you came and continue following Ocean Lookout Loop clockwise.

There is also the option to drive up Mount Battie Road and park near the tower.

Option 2

Maiden Cliff (an extra 4.9 miles to create a 7.9-mile hike in total): For the longest hike made for the fittest dogs, traverse to the far west of the park to Maiden Cliff, marked by a large white cross, overlooking Lake Megunticook. This monument was erected in honor of Elenora French, who fell from the cliff in 1864. The cross has been replaced several times and continues to be cared for by the community to honor the young girl's memory.

To access this route, reach Ocean Lookout at 1.6 miles, then follow Ridge Trail northwest to the summit of Mount Megunticook, marked by a large stone cairn.

Although this summit does not offer views, the scenic path leading to it is filled with an abundance of lime-green moss. Continue along Ridge Trail for another 2 miles to the 0.5-mile Scenic Trail leading down to Maiden Cliff. Return via Ridge Trail or take the parallel Jack Williams Trail.

Maiden Cliff can also be done as a separate, shorter hike from the trailhead off ME Route 52.

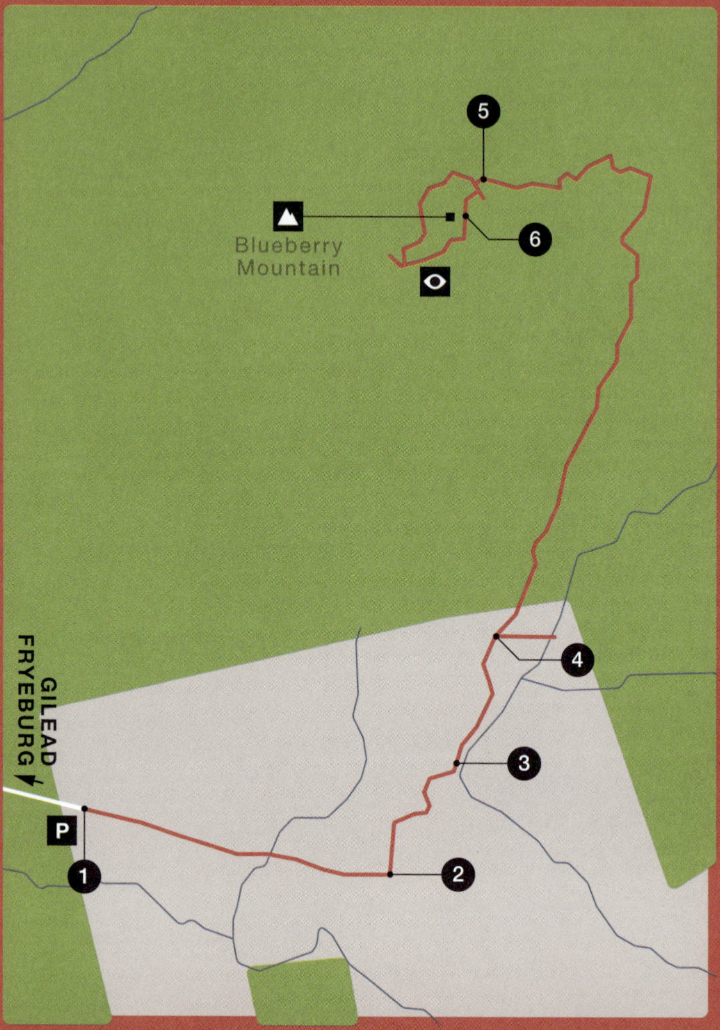

5

Blueberry Mountain

6

GILEAD
FRYEBURG

P

1

2

3

4

P Parking

Viewpoint

Mountain

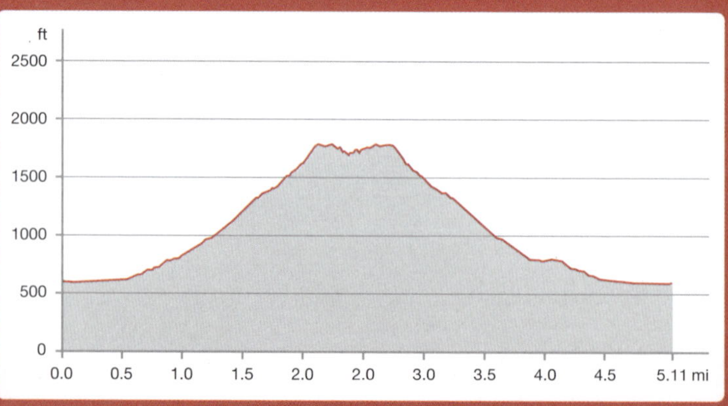

BLUEBERRY MOUNTAIN VIA STONE HOUSE TRAIL

SWEEPING VIEWS AND AQUAMARINE SWIM HOLE

STOW, ME

5

LENGTH
5.11 miles

TIME & MONEY
2.5 hours; free

ELEVATION GAIN
1257 feet

DIFFICULTY
Moderate

CONDITIONS
Year-round

HIGHLIGHTS
Rattlesnake Pool, open views, gorge

ESSENTIALS

- **Find the trailhead:** From Main Street in Bridgton, head southwest for 0.2 miles, then take a slight right onto ME-93 N. Follow ME-93 for 11 miles, then turn left onto ME-5 S. After 0.7 miles, turn right onto Shave Hill Road, then in 0.9 miles take a slight left onto Harbor Road. After 1.6 miles, turn right onto Union Hill Road. After 2 miles, turn left onto New Road. After 1.1 miles, continue onto Stow Road. Follow Stow Road and Main Road for 7.1 miles, then turn right onto Stone House Road, which turns right and becomes Shell Pond Road. After 1.1 miles, park on the shoulder of the road, just before the green gate.

- **Land manager:** White Mountain National Forest, 71 White Mountain Drive, Campton, NH 03223; (603) 536-6100
fs.usda.gov/recarea/whitemountain/recarea/?recid=74943

WHY YOU'LL LOVE IT

- Swimming holes
- Spectacular views
- Lowbush blueberries at summit

Enjoy breathtaking views of Evan's Notch while fueling up on lowbush blueberries, then take a refreshing plunge in an aquamarine swimming hole.

Evan's Notch is located in western Maine, about one mile east of the New Hampshire border. Blueberry Mountain is just one of the many spectacular hikes in this area, which includes Speckled Mountain and the Baldface-Royce mountain range. The summit offers sweeping views of Evan's Notch and a beautiful swimming hole, fed by a small waterfall, called Rattlesnake Pool.

The trail starts just beyond the green gate on the flat and wide Shell Pond Road. The first part of this hike passes through private land with open fields and distant views of Baldface Mountain. Less than half a mile after following Stone House Trail into the woods, there's a spur on the right leading to an impressive gorge with 25-foot rock walls rising up from Rattlesnake Flume. Walk the bridge across the gorge and marvel at the impressive view.

After returning to the main trail, you soon arrive at another spur leading to Rattlesnake Pool, tucked within a shady forest of hemlock, beech and birch. Watch your footing as you descend the steep, rocky slope leading to this deep pool that's part of a series of cascades. Many brave the frigid water for an exhilarating dip in the warmer months.

Although climbing in and out of a pool surrounded by rock ledge is manageable for a human, it's no easy task for a dog. Your four-legged friend will prefer wading in the shallow cascades below the swimming hole. In cooler temperatures, you may choose to just sit near the pool, absorbing its magnificence. If you do choose to swim in the pristine mountain water, I recommend saving the experience for a reward at the end of your hike. After two-plus hours of hiking and a cold plunge, you'll be fully relaxed and ready to head home.

Carefully climb the slope leading from the pool and return to the main trail. Continue your ascent for another mile before reaching the 0.7-mile Lookout Loop, marked by turquoise blazes. This path circles the summit of Blueberry Mountain, offering viewing spots from rocky ledges and wild blueberries in mid-July through late August. If you're hiking during this time, blueberries provide a natural snack for your dog after a challenging climb. Low in calories and high in vitamins, minerals and antioxidants, these tasty treats are safe for dogs in moderation.

Follow the loop clockwise to reach the most impressive view overlooking Shell Pond and Baldface Mountain on the south side. Enjoy several more cliff-edge views, then follow the rock cairns back to the intersection with Blueberry Ridge Trail, taking a right to follow Stone House Trail back to the start.

TURN-BY-TURN DIRECTIONS

1. From the trailhead parking, walk past the closed gate and continue on Shell Pond Road. Continue past the sign for White Cairn Trail on the left, then bear left at the sign for Rattlesnake Pool.
2. At 0.5 miles, take a left onto Stone House Trail, marked by Chatham Trail Association (CTA) signs and yellow blazes.
3. At 0.77 miles, head right at the fork and take the 30-yard spur to the bridge over a gorge. Return to Stone House Trail and continue uphill toward Rattlesnake Pool.
4. At 0.98 miles, cross a small footbridge over a stream, then take the spur on the right leading to Rattlesnake Pool. Explore the pool, then continue your ascent on Stone House Trail.
5. At 2.2 miles, bear right past the rock cairn, then go left at the junction between Stone House and Blueberry Ridge trails, then left again at the sign for Lookout Loop.
6. At 2.4 miles, arrive at the summit, then follow the loop clockwise for more views, keeping a close eye on the rock cairns marking the trail. Complete Lookout Loop, then take a right onto Stone House Trail, returning the way you came.

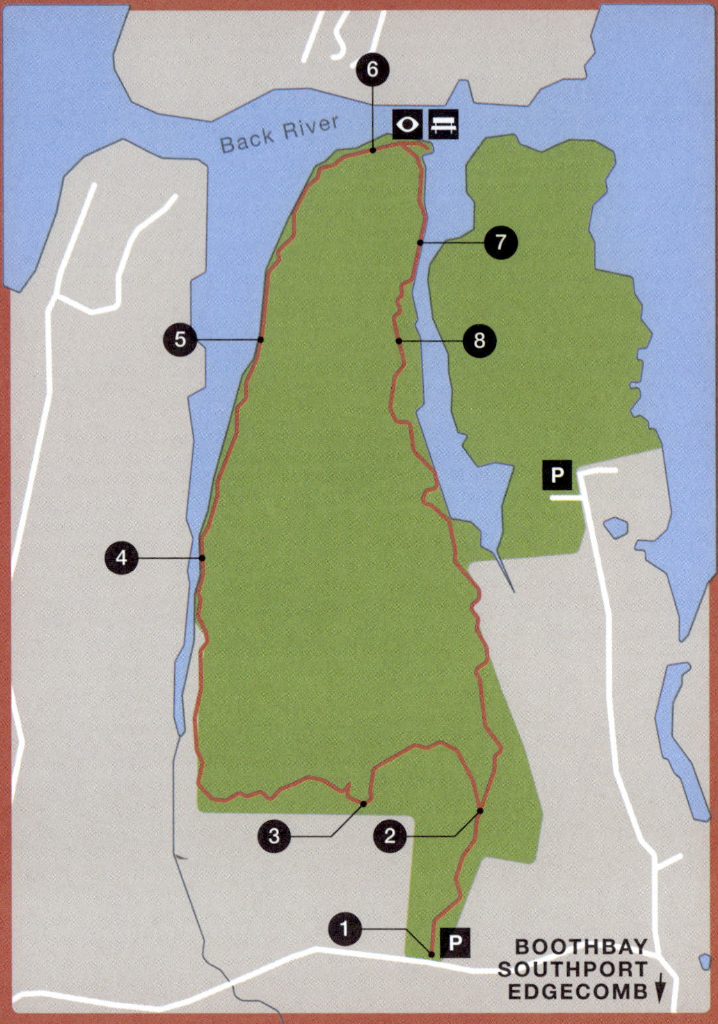

Back River
6
7
5
8
4
3
2
1
BOOTHBAY
SOUTHPORT
EDGECOMB

P Parking   Viewpoint   Bench

ft
2500
2000
1500
1000
500
0
0.0
0.5
1.0
1.5
2.0
2.5 mi

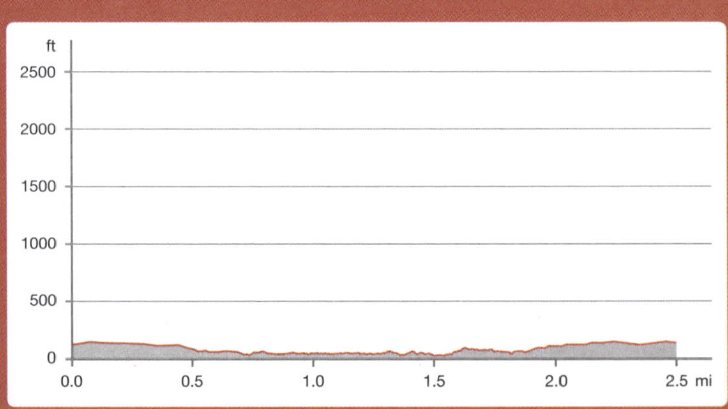

OVENS MOUTH WEST LOOP

PENINSULA WITH SCENIC SHORELINE

BOOTHBAY, ME

6

LENGTH

2.5 miles (loop)

TIME & MONEY

1 hour 15 minutes; free

ELEVATION GAIN

233 feet

DIFFICULTY

Moderate

CONDITIONS

Year-round; shady, hilly

HIGHLIGHTS

93-foot footbridge, water vistas

ESSENTIALS

- **Find the trailhead:** From the center of Boothbay, travel north on Route 27 for 1.6 miles. Take a left onto Adam's Pond Road. After 0.2 miles, turn right onto Dover Road. Continue 1.9 miles, then bear left onto Dover Cross Road. The small, dirt parking lot is 0.2 miles on the right. It's marked by the Ovens Mouth Preserve sign at the entrance.
- **Land manager:** Boothbay Region Land Trust, 60 Samoset Road, PO Box 183, Boothbay Harbor, ME 04538; (207) 633-4818; brlt@bbrlt.org bbrlt.org

WHY YOU'LL LOVE IT

- Water access points for your dog to cool off
- Plenty of shade with water vistas
- Options for a longer hike

Wander through lush, shady forests leading to shoreline views, blue-green waters and tidal salt marshes. Hilly sections of trail climb to sweeping ocean lookouts, then descend to water access points where your dog can take a refreshing break.

Ovens Mouth is a narrow ocean-water passage from the Sheepscot and Back rivers to a tidal basin. This area has been a hub for maritime activities since the mid-1700s and was one of the region's earliest shipyards. During the Revolution, British and American vessels hid in its protected coves. In 1880, the western cove was dammed to form a freshwater pond and icehouse. Ice from what is now known as "Ice House Cove" was shipped by schooner to Boston and New York. The dam is no longer here, but you'll see remnants from the footbridge at low tide.

Ovens Mouth Preserve is an extensive 5.3-mile trail network covering two peninsulas. Ovens Mouth East includes 1.6 miles of hiking trails and Ovens Mouth West includes 3.7 miles of trails. They're connected by a footbridge that spans the tidal salt marsh. The intersecting trails here provide a variety of hiking options. Here, you'll hike the 2.5-mile Ovens Mouth West Loop.

The route begins from a small parking lot on Dover Cross Road. From the kiosk, a dirt trail with a gentle incline leads you to the start of West Loop Trail, marked by white blazes. Continue straight to follow the loop clockwise. You'll wind through dense forest for about a mile before reaching the water. Eagles, osprey, otters, and deer live here, so be on the lookout for signs of wildlife.

The trail follows the water to the outer edge of the peninsula, where you'll find a short spur leading to expansive water views along a rocky shoreline. This is one of several water access points that offer your dog a chance to cool off. After a rest on the viewing bench, return to West Loop Trail and take a left. You'll soon arrive at the bridge—perfect for another swim for your dog while you enjoy the views. Continue straight to the end of the loop. At the T-junction, take a left to return to the parking lot.

TURN-BY-TURN DIRECTIONS

1. From the trailhead kiosk, follow a dirt trail marked with white and blue blazes.
2. At 0.2 miles, continue straight at the white loop sign. Do not turn right. At the next trail junction, marked by a white loop sign on the left and blue trail sign on the right, turn left to stay on the white loop trail.
3. At 0.3 miles, bear right to stay on the trail as indicated by the BRLT sign and white blaze.
4. At 0.8 miles, stay left, ignoring the BRLT sign on the tree pointing right.
5. At 1.1 miles, keep left at the unmarked fork to continue on the white loop as it winds toward the water's edge.
6. At 1.5 miles, bear right at the fork to stay on the white loop as indicated by the white blaze. At the next junction marked by white blazes on both routes, stay left, following the trail toward the water. Continue left onto Shore Loop Trail, marked by a Vista sign on the left and Shore Loop sign on the right. Continue left at the unmarked fork. This leads down to a viewpoint and bench at the water's edge. Retrace your steps to the Vista sign, then take a left to continue on the white loop trail.
7. At 1.7 miles, bear right at the fork marked by a BRLT sign and right again at the next BRLT sign. Then bear left on the white loop trail marked by white blazes.
8. At 1.8 miles, stay left at the kiosk sign. At 2.3 miles, return to the T-junction marking the start of the loop. Take a left and follow the trail to the parking lot.

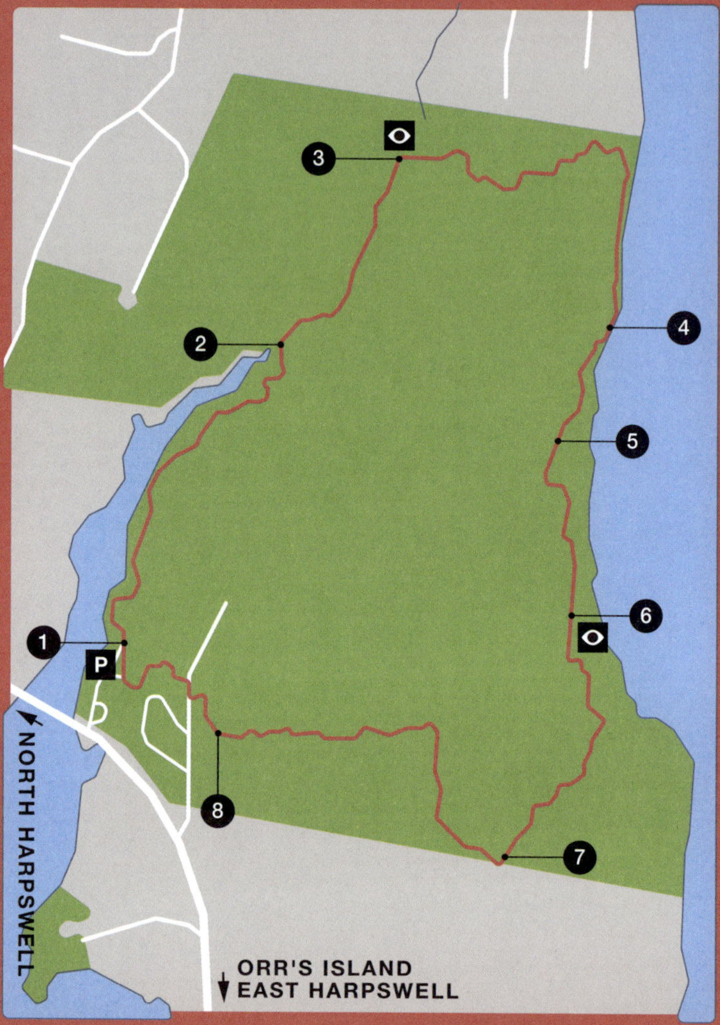

1
2
3
4
5
6
7
8
P
NORTH HARPSWELL
ORR'S ISLAND
EAST HARPSWELL

P Parking

Viewpoint

ft
2500
2000
1500
1000
500
0
0.0
0.5
1.0
1.5
2.0
2.3 mi

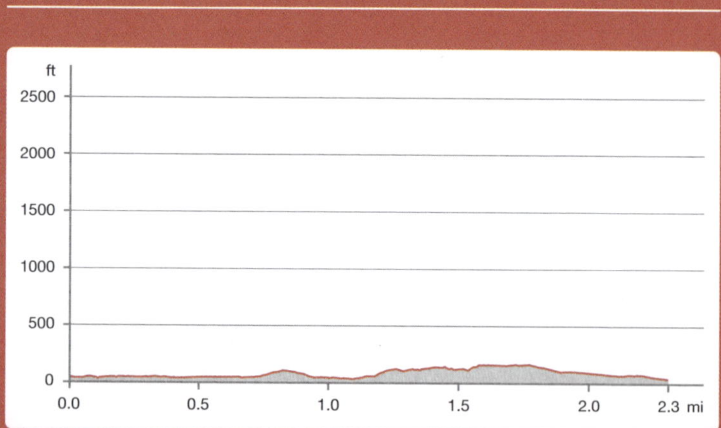

CLIFF TRAIL

VIEWS OF SHORELINE FROM 150-FOOT CLIFFS

HARPSWELL, ME

7

LENGTH
2.3 miles (loop)

TIME & MONEY
1 hour; free

ELEVATION GAIN
272 feet

DIFFICULTY
Moderate

CONDITIONS
Year-round; leash required 10 a.m. to 4 p.m.

HIGHLIGHTS
Cliffs, water vistas, cave

ESSENTIALS

- **Find the trailhead:** From Maine Street in Brunswick, turn left onto Bath Road. After 0.2 miles, turn right onto Sills Drive (ME-123 S). After 6.4 miles, turn left onto Mountain Road. After 1.3 miles, arrive at the parking lot behind Harpswell Town Office at 263 Mountain Road.
- **Land manager:** Town of Harpswell, PO Box 39, 263 Mountain Road, Harpswell, ME 04079; (207) 833-5771 x108;
harpswell@town.harpswell.me.us
harpswell.maine.gov

WHY YOU'LL LOVE IT

- Plenty of shade with shoreline views
- Ability to adjust the hike to be longer or shorter
- Close to Merrymeeting Dog Park in dog-friendly Brunswick

This rugged trail includes 150-foot cliffs overlooking Long Reach Preserve, a walk along tidal Strawberry Creek, and a cliffside cave that can be explored at low tide.

Cliff Trail is a 2.3-mile loop that winds along shady trails with shoreline views and a forest filled with a bird symphony. There is ample parking in a large, paved lot behind Harpswell Town Office on Mountain Road and a porta-potty at the trailhead. White blazes mark the route, which begins on a flat stretch of trail accessible for people with limited mobility. This easy section includes a viewing platform for Strawberry Creek and a short spur leading to a picnic area and cascade overlook. Beyond the picnic area, Cliff Trail bears right, away from the water and into the woods.

Just past Henry Creek Overlook, the trail begins to climb, becoming narrower, with more exposed roots. Shade provided by a canopy of white pine, red oak and hemlock keeps your dog cool, but you might also encounter those pesky Maine mosquitoes here, so don't forget your bug spray. The hilly trail eventually descends towards the water's edge; at just over a mile, take a short, unmarked spur down to the water. Look towards the shoreline on the right to discover a dome-shaped cave carved into the ledge, which you can explore at low tide.

Return to the Cliff Trail loop and continue on steeper terrain until you reach the warning sign for the 150-foot drop-off at Clifftop Overlook. If outside leash hours, you'll want to leash your dog here. Once you've arrived at the overlook, enjoy a large section of rock for resting while enjoying the view of Long Reach Preserve and its unnamed island. This 95-acre preserve offers one of the longest hiking trails in Harpswell and is dog-friendly, so you may want to explore this one next time. As you continue past the overlook, you'll arrive at two more viewing spots along the cliffs. If outside leash hours, keep your dog leashed until you safely return to the woods. The trail descends until Recycling Center Road. After crossing this road, reconnect with the trail and return to the parking lot.

After the hike, reward your dog with some play time at Merrymeeting Dog Park, located on Water Street in Brunswick, off of the Androscoggin River Bike Path. Or visit one of the many dog-friendly restaurants and coffee shops in downtown Brunswick, an easy 15-minute drive from Cliff Trail.

TURN-BY-TURN DIRECTIONS

1. From the trailhead, follow the flat, gravel Cliff Trail marked by white blazes. Pass Strawberry Creek viewing platform on the left, followed by Fairy House Building Zone on the right.
2. At 0.4 miles, ignore Old Road Trail Cut-Off on the right and continue straight over a short footbridge, then take a right to follow Cliff Trail, marked by a white sign. Before taking this right, explore the short spur on the left leading to the cascade overlook and picnic area. If you prefer a shorter hike, Cut-Off Trail leads directly to Clifftop Overlook.
3. At 0.6 miles, arrive at a blue sign for Henry Creek Lookout. Explore the lookout or continue on Cliff Trail, bearing right and following the white blazes. This is where the trail becomes more rugged with roots and hills, then starts descending.
4. At 1.08 miles, arrive at an unmarked fork and take the short spur on the left down to the water. Look towards the right along the water's edge to find a cave carved into the ledge. Return to the fork, then head left to continue on Cliff Trail.
5. At the junction of Cliff and Cut-Off trails, at 1.17 miles, stay straight on Cliff Trail, marked by a blue sign.
6. At 1.4 miles, reach Clifftop Overlook and enjoy the view of Long Reach Preserve and its unnamed island. Continue along Cliff Trail and enjoy more viewing spots along the way.
7. At 1.67 miles, bear left following the white blazes, ignoring Old Road Crossing on the right.
8. At 2.1 miles, arrive at Recycling Center Road, then head right and cross the road to reconnect with the trail leading back to the parking lot.

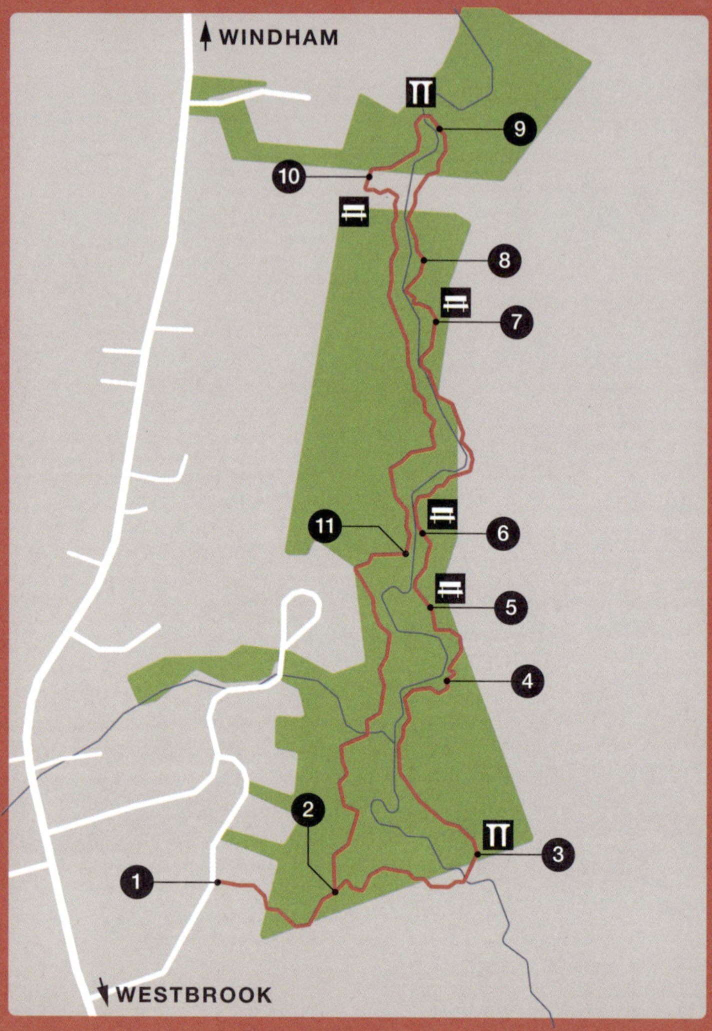

WINDHAM

WESTBROOK

Bench

Bridge

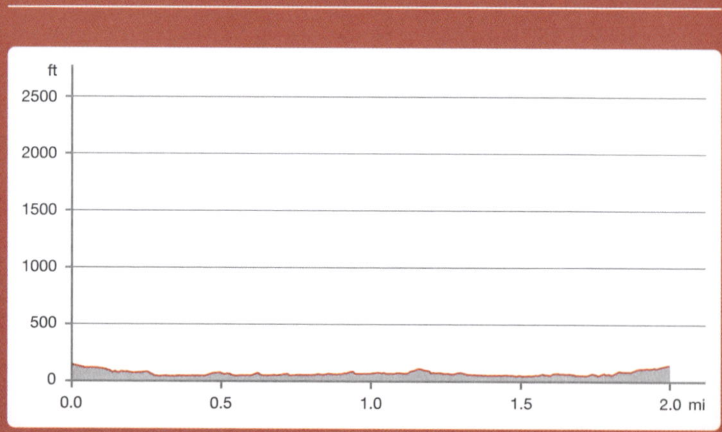

MILL BROOK PRESERVE

QUIET TRAIL BY A BABBLING BROOK

WESTBROOK, ME

8

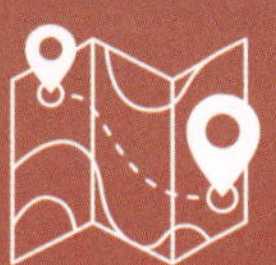

LENGTH
2 miles (loop)

TIME & MONEY
1 hour; free

ELEVATION GAIN
144 feet

DIFFICULTY
Moderate

CONDITIONS
Year-round; hilly, shaded

HIGHLIGHTS
Goldilocks Falls

ESSENTIALS

- **Find the trailhead:** From the intersection of Woodford Street and Forest Avenue in Portland, head north on Forest Avenue (Route 302). After 3.3 miles, turn left onto E. Bridge Street. After 1.9 miles, turn right onto Methodist Road. After 1.1 miles, turn right onto Perry Court. After 0.1 miles, park along the right side of the road in front of 55 Perry Court.
- **Land manager:** Presumpscot Regional Land Trust, PO Box 33, Gorham, ME 04038; (207) 536-8623; info@prlt.org prlt.org

WHY YOU'LL LOVE IT

- Running water for your dog along the entire loop
- Peaceful trail with few people
- Viewing pool for the alewife fish run in May and June

Explore a two-mile loop around a pristine brook flowing through dense forest. This peaceful preserve is located just outside of Portland, Maine's largest and most vibrant city.

Mill Brook Preserve features a six-mile trail network on 130 acres of forested land along a crystal-clear brook. Located just 15 minutes from Portland's urban center, these secluded woods offer a respite from the city's hustle and bustle. The hilly forest valley, part of the lands of the Wabanaki people for over 10,000 years, is perfect for those seeking tranquility.

Mill Brook is notable for hosting the largest annual migration of alewife fish to Highland Lake. If you walk this trail in late May and early June, you can witness the remarkable alewife run, which is best observed from Southern Fish Viewing Pool at the base of Goldilocks Falls.

Alewives are a species of river herring that are anadromous, living as adults in the ocean and migrating up freshwater rivers to spawn. They serve as a primary food source for many larger fish off the Maine coast, along with numerous seabirds, marine mammals, and land-based animals such as raccoons. Because they inhabit both fresh and saltwater, alewives link Maine's oceans, rivers and lakes, playing a vital role in the ecosystems of our watersheds. Dams, pollution and overfishing caused a significant decline in alewife populations over the past 200 years, but restoration efforts, including fishways and fish ladders, mean the alewife population is recovering.

We explore the two-mile southern loop of the preserve, starting in a quiet residential area. The trailhead kiosk is easily visible on the right as you drive down Perry Court from Methodist Road. Parking is permitted along this public road, and there is usually room near the kiosk. The trail begins between two private homes before entering the forest. As you make your way to the first trail sign, experience a sense of tranquility as the city's hustle fades away, leaving only the sounds of nature. After descending a short set of stone stairs, reach the start of the loop, marked by a trail map. Head right to follow the loop counterclockwise, ascending more stairs and then following an s-shaped curve over a small hill. As you descend, come to a large bridge crossing the water. From here, continue following the blue blazes as the trail runs along the water's edge.

In just under a mile, arrive at Goldilocks Falls and Southern Fish Viewing Pool. Take a break on the bench here, and if you're visiting during the alewife migration season, you'll surely see hundreds of fish circling the pool below. Please keep your dog out of the water to protect the migrating fish.

Continuing past the falls, reach the loop's outer edge, marked by a bridge over the brook. Enjoy a new view of Mill Brook as you return on the opposite side. The sounds of the babbling brook accompany you until the final climb into the woods, leading back to the loop's starting point.

TURN-BY-TURN DIRECTIONS

1. From the trailhead on Perry Court, walk between two private homes before entering the woods.
2. At 0.1 miles, reach a map and junction. Go right to follow the blue blazes.
3. At 0.3 miles, cross the Cornelia Warren Community Association bridge over Mill Brook.
4. At 0.5 miles, switchbacks will aid you on a steep descent.
5. At 0.6 miles, arrive at a bench with water access for your dog.
6. At 0.7 miles, there is another bench and resting area.
7. At 0.9 miles, arrive at Goldilocks Falls and Southern Fish Viewing Pool. There is another resting bench at this spot.
8. At 1 mile, reach a fork and bear left towards the water, then continue to stay left, following the yellow arrows on trees.
9. At 1.2 miles, go left at the junction with MAGAN and Northern trails. Continue left toward Methodist Road and Perry Court trailheads before crossing a bridge over Mill Brook. From here, head south, following the left side of the loop on your return trip.
10. At 1.3 miles, ignore Methodist Road trailhead on the right and continue straight toward Perry Court. Soon after, there's another bench for resting.
11. At 1.7 miles, the trail departs from the water's edge and leads into the woods. Climb a steep hill before reconnecting with the start of the loop and returning the way you came.

NEW HAMPSHIRE

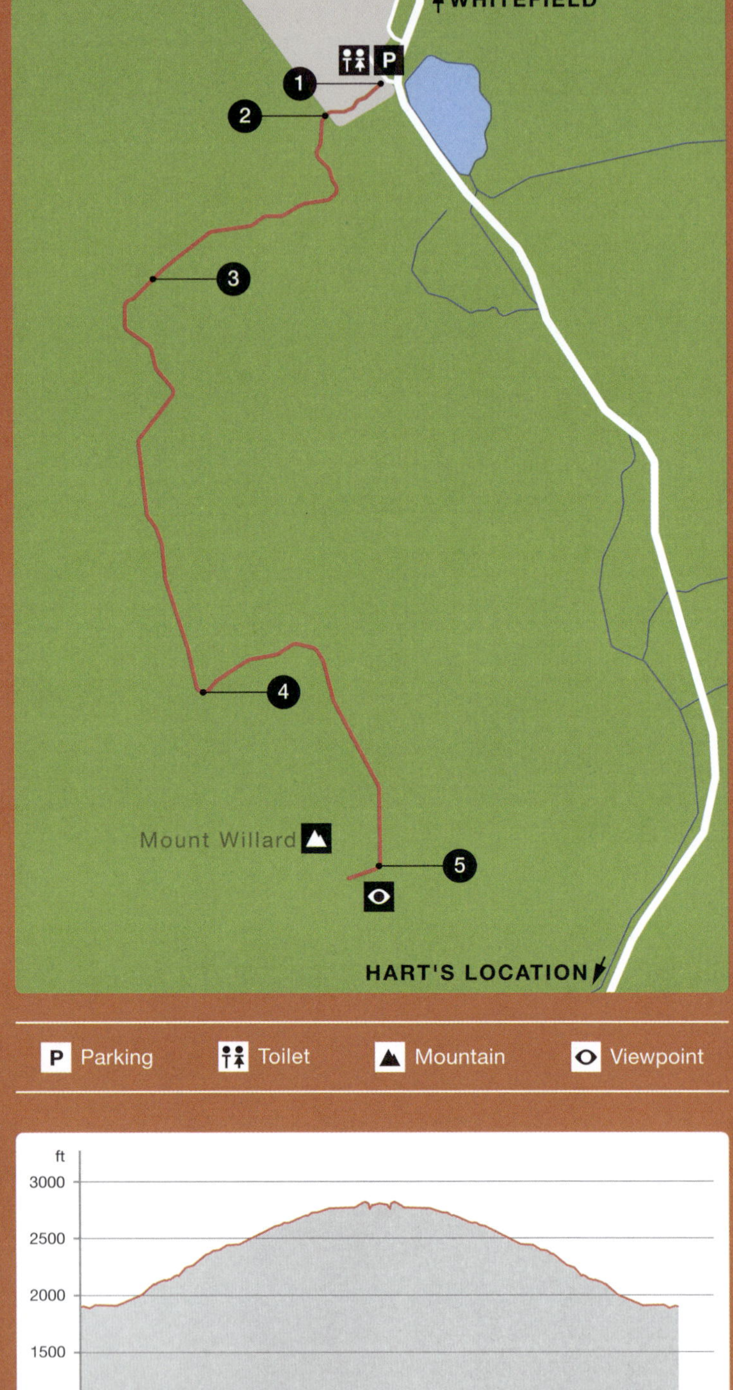
WHITEFIELD
1
2
3
4
5
Mount Willard
HART'S LOCATION
Parking
Toilet
Mountain
Viewpoint
ft
3000
2500
2000
1500
1000
500
0.0
0.5
1.0
1.5
2.0
2.5
3.0
3.3 mi

MOUNT WILLARD

CLIFFTOP VIEWS THROUGH CRAWFORD NOTCH

CARROLL, NH

9

LENGTH
3.3 miles
(out and back)

TIME & MONEY
1 hour 45 minutes;
free

ELEVATION GAIN
912 feet

DIFFICULTY
Moderate

CONDITIONS
Year-round;
rocky terrain,
stream crossings

HIGHLIGHTS
Panoramic views,
Centennial Pool

ESSENTIALS

- **Find the trailhead:** From North Conway, head northwest on US-302 W and follow it for 26 miles to Crawford Depot. Parking is on your left.
- **Land manager:** Appalachian Mountain Club, PO Box 298, 361 Route 16, Gorham, NH 03581; (603) 466-2721; AMCinformation@outdoors.org
  outdoors.org

WHY YOU'LL LOVE IT

- Dramatic views of Crawford Notch
- Easy navigation with a direct route to the summit
- Stream crossings and a pool where your dog can drink

Follow a direct path to the breathtaking peak of Mount Willard, which provides wide-ranging views of Crawford Notch and the surrounding mountain range. This clifftop position offers an unparalleled perspective directly through the southern part of the notch.

Mount Willard is situated in Crawford Notch State Park, offering almost 6000 acres of hiking trails, waterfalls and wildlife. If you plan to spend more than a day here, the dog-friendly Dry River Campground is centrally located in the heart of the park and is just an eight-minute drive from Mount Willard trailhead.

Crawford Notch is a major pass through the White Mountains, traversed by US Route 302. This U-shaped valley, carved by glaciers, reaches its highest point at the "Gateway of the Notch" in Carroll, near Crawford Depot. Here, you'll find the trailhead for Mount Willard.

The depot, constructed in 1891 as part of the old Maine Central Line, was one of the most elaborate railway stations built in the Queen Anne style. It now serves as a visitor's center with shops and restrooms, managed by the Appalachian Mountain Club. The railroad tracks are currently used by Conway Scenic Railroad, which operates seasonally. Just north of Crawford Depot is the AMC Highland Center Lodge and Conference Center, built on the site of the 19th-century Crawford House Hotel, which burned down in 1972. The center offers meals, overnight accommodation and a store with hiking supplies.

The rich history of Crawford Notch is marked by numerous avalanches and landslides. The most notable event took place in August 1826 at Willey House, off Route 302. After a severe rainstorm, a massive landslide forced the Willey family, who managed the Willey House Inn and Tavern, to flee their home in search of safety. Tragically, the family of five did not survive: Their bodies were later found beneath the avalanche debris. Remarkably, their house remained untouched due to its position near a rock ledge that split the major rockslide into two streams around the house. You'll pass Willey House, on the left, just a few miles before arriving at Mount Willard trailhead.

Mount Willard summit provides a stunning payoff for a fairly short hike. While no section of this trail is particularly challenging, the 900-foot elevation gain over less than two miles maintains a steady ascent to the summit. The trail is quite wide and straightforward, so if you struggle with navigation in the woods, this hike is for you!

Your hike starts at Crawford Depot opposite Saco Lake. Parking is available along Route 302, but these spots fill up fast. If you don't arrive early at this popular spot, there's additional parking along the roadside shoulder.

To find the trailhead, cross the train tracks behind the depot and search for a tall granite trail marker. After walking through a narrow section of trail, reach a kiosk, then veer left onto Mount Willard Trail. There are two stream crossings early in the hike, which your dog will enjoy, but you might prefer waterproof footwear.

About half a mile in, reach Centennial Pool on the right. This small flume with a mini waterfall is an ideal spot to listen to the soothing sounds of a brook while your dog enjoys a drink. The rest and hydration will energize you both for the remaining one-mile, steady ascent to the summit. At the top, take in endless views along a large open ledge before making your return trip.

TURN-BY-TURN DIRECTIONS

1. From the trailhead, follow Avalon and Mount Willard Trail to the kiosk and junction.
2. At 0.1 miles, go left at the kiosk to follow Mount Willard Trail, marked by blue blazes.
3. At 0.5 miles, reach Centennial Pool on the right.
4. At 1.1 miles, the trail takes a sharp left, heading east for 0.2 miles before returning south and straight to the summit.
5. At 1.9 miles, reach the summit of Mount Willard. Head right and follow it along the open ledge for more views, then return back the way you came.

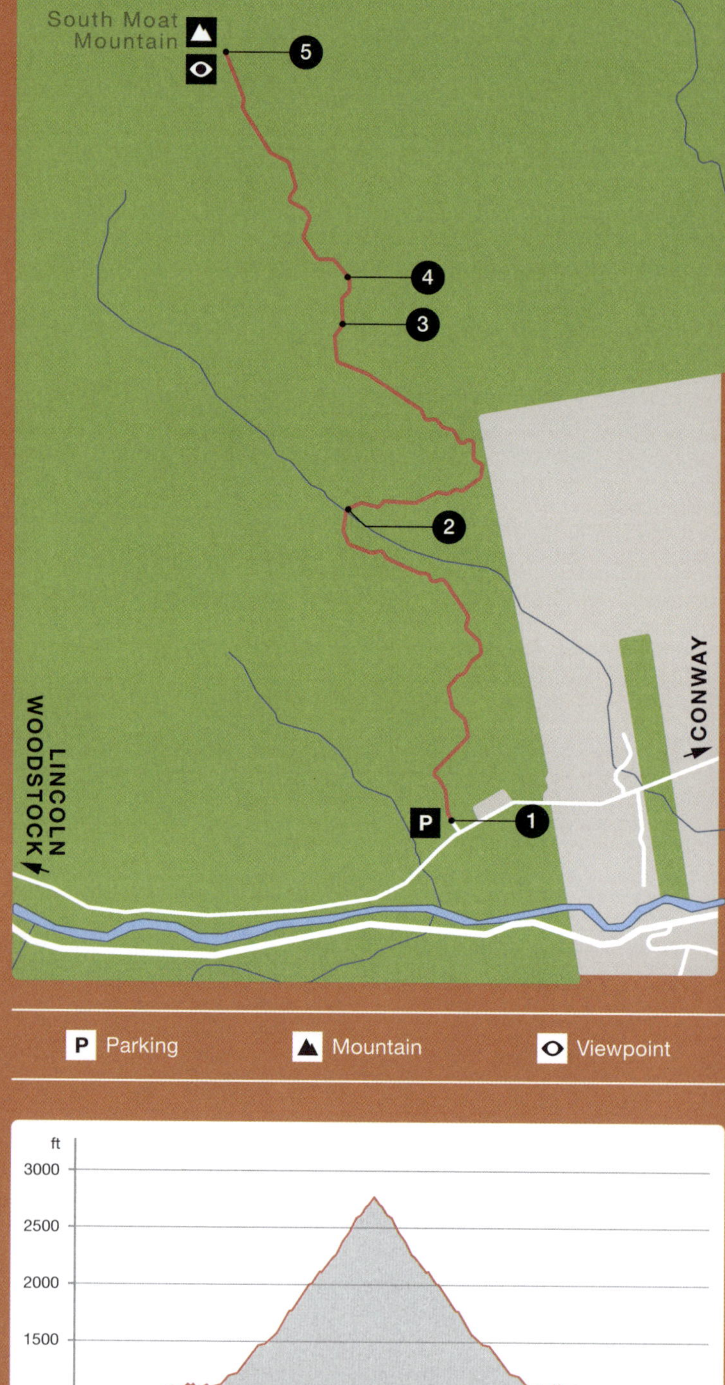
South Moat Mountain
5
4
3
2
1
P
CONWAY
LINCOLN
WOODSTOCK
P Parking
Mountain
Viewpoint
ft
3000
2500
2000
1500
1000
500
0.0 0.5 1.0 1.5 2.0 2.5 3.0 3.5 4.0 4.5 5.0 5.5 5.7 mi

SOUTH MOAT MOUNTAIN

360-DEGREE VIEWS OF THE WHITE MOUNTAINS

CONWAY, NH

10

LENGTH
5.7 miles
(round trip)

TIME & MONEY
3 hours 30 minutes;
free

ELEVATION GAIN
2123 feet

DIFFICULTY
Strenuous

CONDITIONS
Year-round;
rock scramble,
streams

HIGHLIGHTS
Clear view
of Mount
Washington

ESSENTIALS

- **Find the trailhead:** From North Conway, head southeast on NH-16 S/US-302 E toward Reporter Court. After 5.4 miles, turn right onto NH-113 W/NH-16 S. After 482 feet, turn right onto Washington Street. After 0.2 miles, bear left onto Washington Street/West Side Road. After 0.7 miles, turn left onto Passaconaway Road (which becomes Dugway Road). After 3.2 miles, turn right into the trailhead parking. Important note: Your GPS may direct you to the western end of Passaconaway via NH-112, but this side of Passaconaway is closed from November to May. To avoid the road closure, use the directions listed here to the eastern end.

- **Land manager:** US Forest Service, 71 White Mountain Drive, Campton, NH 03223; (603) 536-6100
fs.usda.gov

WHY YOU'LL LOVE IT

- Close to popular North Conway village
- Stunning panoramic views of the White Mountains
- Streams along the hike where your dog can refresh

Just 15 minutes from North Conway's shopping, dining and lodging area, this hike offers the best summit views in the region. Follow a babbling brook, then climb to granite ledges overlooking Mount Washington Valley.

Moat Mountain is a ridge extending from north to south with three main peaks: North, Middle and South Moat Mountain. Each offers panoramic views from exposed summits and all three can be hiked via the Moat Mountain Trail. Here, we focus on South Moat Mountain, the easiest to access due to its shorter length.

This mountain is located to the west of dog-friendly North Conway—a popular destination in Mount Washington Valley offering a downtown shopping area, restaurants, accommodation, and Conway Scenic Railroad, which allows dogs under 20 pounds. Stay at one of the many pet-friendly hotels, explore endless trails with waterfalls or bring your dog on a wild adventure tubing the Saco River.

The trail begins with a gentle ascent on a wide path. You cross several small streams and wet sections along this hike, so waterproof footwear will be helpful. After about half a mile, you hear the soothing sounds of a large stream at the base of a steep slope to the right of the trail. Cross a bridge over a babbling brook at one mile, where your dog can have a drink before the climb becomes more intense.

Just before the two-mile mark, there's a steep section of rock scrambles. We encountered many medium-sized dogs on this hike who seemed to have no difficulty with the terrain. That said, smaller dogs may need to be carried here, though this is something you might want to discuss with your dog's ego beforehand!

After completing the rock scrambles, you're rewarded with an open ledge and overlook with views of Mount Chocorua. The remaining half mile of the climb to the summit involves more open rock with sections winding in and out of the forest. Keep your eye on the yellow blazes on the ledges and trees marking the path, as this part of the hike can be more difficult to follow.

At the summit, delight in sweeping views of New Hampshire's most spectacular mountain ranges, including a clear view of Mount Washington to the northeast. Middle and North Moat Mountains are visible to the north. The exposed summit of South Moat offers no shade, so pack plenty of water for your dog when hiking during the warmer months.

For a longer adventure, continue another half mile to reach the summit of Middle Moat, and then two more miles to the summit of North Moat. This full traverse covers 9.9 miles, round trip, which is suitable for only the most athletic pups. My large dog was perfectly content with the shorter hike to South Moat, which provided ample challenges.

TURN-BY-TURN DIRECTIONS

1. From the trailhead beyond the kiosk, follow a gradual path marked by yellow blazes. There is a small stream crossing at 0.3 miles. At 0.7 miles, there's a steep slope to the right with a river at the base of it running parallel to the trail.
2. At 1 mile, cross a bridge over a babbling brook. The trail ascends quickly from here, climbing a dry, rocky stream bed.
3. At 2 miles, reach a steep section of rocky scrambles. Small dogs will need assistance on this difficult section.
4. At 2.2 miles, arrive at an overlook on a wide section of rock slab. Enjoy a view of Mount Chocorua to the southwest.
5. At 2.8 miles, reach the open summit. Explore panoramic views of the White Mountains, then return back the way you came.

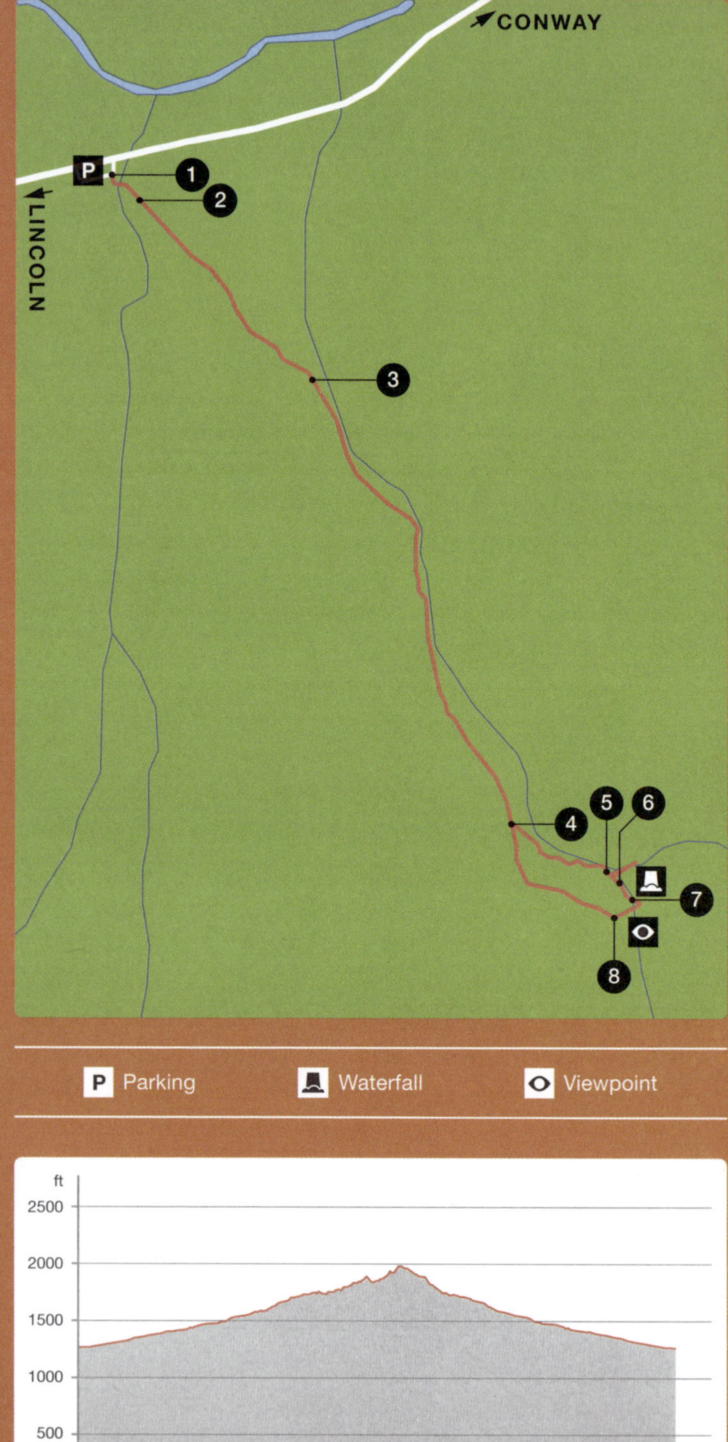
CONWAY
LINCOLN
P
1
2
3
4
5
6
7
8
P Parking
Waterfall
Viewpoint
ft
2500
2000
1500
1000
500
0
0.0
0.5
1.0
1.5
2.0
2.5
3.0
3.5 mi

CHAMPNEY FALLS TRAIL

TWO WATERFALLS AND 70 FEET OF CASCADES

ALBANY, NH

11

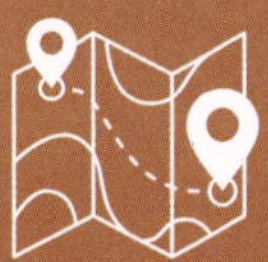

LENGTH

3.5 miles (lollipop loop)

TIME & MONEY

2 hours 30 minutes; parking fee (cash only)

ELEVATION GAIN

702 feet

DIFFICULTY

Moderate

CONDITIONS

Year-round; stone stairs, steep sections

HIGHLIGHTS

Waterfalls, cascades, vista

ESSENTIALS

- **Find the trailhead:** From North Conway, head southeast on NH-16 S/US-302 E toward Reporter Court. After 5.4 miles, turn right onto NH-113 W/NH-16 S. After 0.8 miles, turn right onto NH-112 W (Kancamagus Highway). After 10.6 miles, the parking lot is on your left.
- **Land manager:** US Forest Service, 71 White Mountain Drive, Campton, NH 03223; (603) 536-6100
fs.usda.gov

WHY YOU'LL LOVE IT

- Cascades provide plenty of water for your dog
- Mountain views from the top of the loop
- Breathtaking waterfalls

Hike alongside a series of 70-foot cascades that lead to two stunning waterfalls and a mountain vista.

The large parking lot for this trail is located off the Kancamagus Highway, which is designated an American Scenic Byway for its rich history and natural beauty. Renowned as one of the premier spots for observing fall foliage in the United States, this 34.5-mile stretch through Northern New Hampshire and the White Mountains meanders past rivers, waterfalls, gorges, and forests. There are six campgrounds along "The Kanc," but you won't find any gas stations or businesses in this untouched area.

The trailhead is located just past the main kiosk near the outhouses. At the start of the hike, cross a stream, then gradually climb on an old logging road. After just over half a mile, there's a swimming hole and waterfall, then a large climbing boulder. Another mile ahead, at the junction with a sign for Champney Falls, continuing straight here would lead you to the open summit of Mount Chocorua, a challenging seven-mile trek suitable only for the most agile and energetic dogs. Instead, take a left to follow the loop to the waterfalls. The left side of this loop is much steeper than the right, so go clockwise for an easier descent.

At just over a mile and a half, take a spur on the left towards Pitcher Falls, where Champney Brook cascades over a rock ledge in a sheet of white water. These falls are most impressive during the spring melt or after rainfall but can be quite sparse during dry periods. Follow this spur a short distance further to a passage between towering rock walls that rise vertically like a street flanked by skyscrapers. The right side of this gorge features water cascading from its top, a spot favored by ice climbers in winter.

After rejoining the main loop, begin a steep ascent on stone steps before reaching another detour leading to a cascade and small pool—an ideal watering spot for your dog. Just beyond, arrive at Champney Falls—a series of smaller waterfalls. Continue climbing to reach an incredible viewpoint at the loop's summit, offering views of the mountains to the north. From here, follow the loop west until the junction. Turn right to complete the loop, then retrace your steps to return.

TURN-BY-TURN DIRECTIONS

1. Find the trailhead in the parking lot's southeast corner, then follow Champney Brook Trail as it crosses Twin Brook.
2. At 0.1 miles, continue straight, ignoring Bolles Trail, which branches off to the right.
3. At 0.5 miles, arrive at a stream crossing, followed by another stream crossing at 0.7 miles.
4. At 1.4 miles, reach the junction of Champney Falls and Mount Chocorua, marked by a wooden sign and trail map. Take a left onto Champney Falls Trail. Do not go straight towards Mount Chocorua.
5. At 1.6 miles, take the spur on the left towards Pitcher Falls. Reach the first cascade, then continue for another 0.1 miles to the tall, narrow gorge. Pitcher Falls flows over the top of the right rock face. Return to Champney Falls Trail.
6. At 1.8 miles, take a spur on the left from the steep climb up the stone stairs. This short detour leads to cascades and a pool for your dog to have a drink or cool off.
7. At 1.9 miles, arrive at Champney Falls. Just beyond this point, reach the top of the loop and enjoy a vista with mountain views.
8. At 1.96 miles, reconnect with Champney Brook Trail, marked by two wooden signs on a post. Take a right toward Kancamagus Highway and return the way you came back to the parking lot.

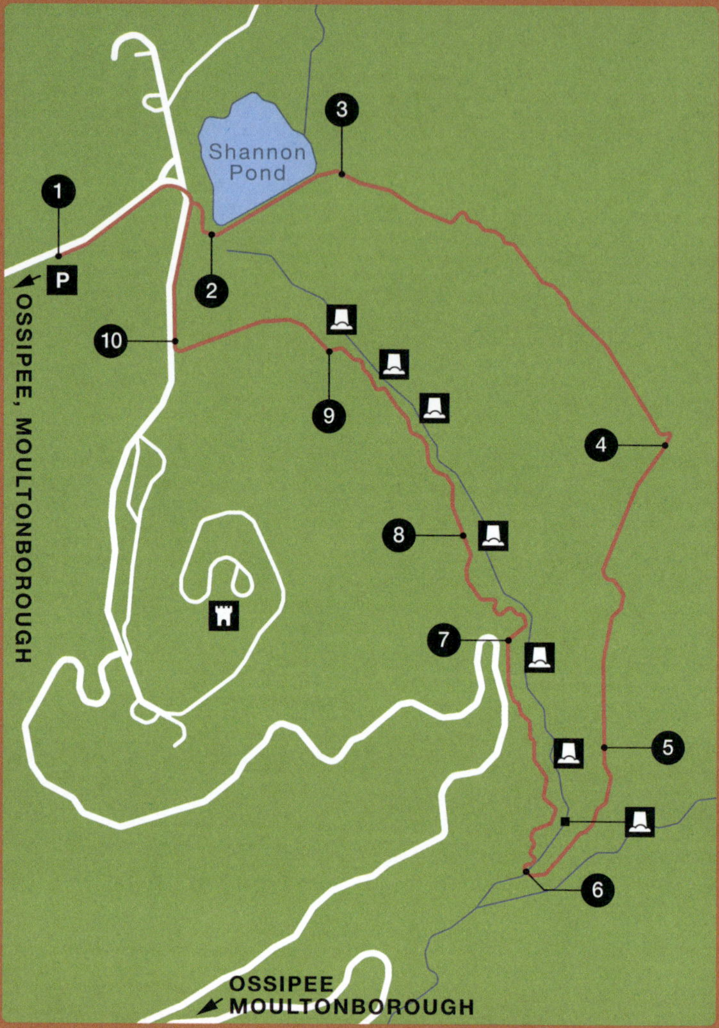

Shannon Pond
1
2
3
4
5
6
7
8
9
10
P
OSSIPEE, MOULTONBOROUGH
OSSIPEE
MOULTONBOROUGH

P Parking — Lucknow Mansion — Waterfall

ft
2500
2000
1500
1000
500
0
0.0
0.5
1.0
1.5
1.9 mi

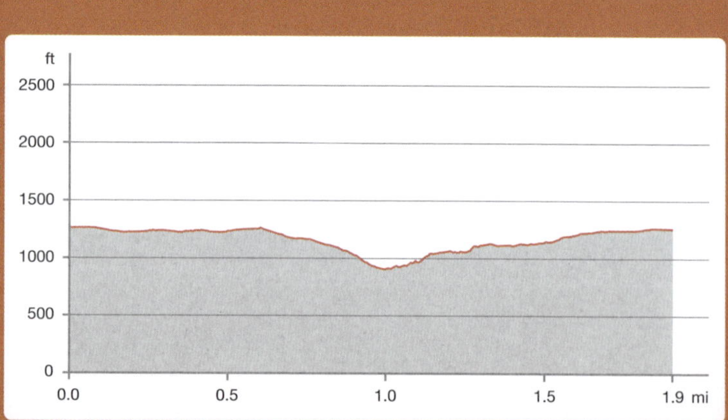

BROOK WALK AT CASTLE IN THE CLOUDS

A LOOP WITH FIVE SPECTACULAR WATERFALLS

MOULTONBOROUGH, NH

12

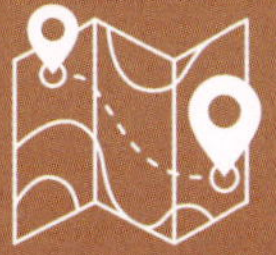

LENGTH
1.9 miles
(loop)

TIME & MONEY
1 hour; free

ELEVATION GAIN
371 feet

DIFFICULTY
Moderate

CONDITIONS
Year-round;
stone stairs, hilly

HIGHLIGHTS
Five waterfalls,
historic grounds

ESSENTIALS

- **Find the trailhead:** From Center Harbor in New Hampshire, take NH-25 E/New Meredith Road. Follow for 5.4 miles, then turn right onto NH-109 S. After 0.2 miles, turn right onto Sills Drive (ME-123 S). After 2.2 miles, continue straight onto NH-171 E. After 0.4 miles, turn left onto Ossipee Park Road. After 1.3 miles, arrive at the small parking area for hikers on the right.

- **Land manager:** Lakes Region Conservation Trust, PO Box 766, 156 Dane Road, Center Harbor, NH 03226; (603) 253-3301 lrct.org/property/castle-in-the-clouds

WHY YOU'LL LOVE IT

- Plenty of water access points near waterfalls
- Ability to increase length of hike, adding additional waterfalls
- Historic grounds and ruins to explore

Explore five spectacular waterfalls along this loop trail, including the 40-foot Falls of Song. This hike is part of a large trail network at the Castle in the Clouds Conservation Area, home to the historic Lucknow Mansion.

Castle in the Clouds Conservation Area encompasses 5500 pristine acres in Moultonborough, NH. Located on the property is Lucknow Mansion, a mountaintop castle with stunning views of Lake Winnipesaukee and the Ossipee Mountains, constructed by shoe tycoon Thomas Plant for his wife, Olive, in the early 1900s. Presently under the ownership of Lakes Region Conservation Trust, the property features a 28-mile trail system that is dog-friendly and open to the general public.

Upon entering the conservation area, you'll first see a charming stone house on your left, followed by the designated parking area for hikers on the right. Take in the beauty of the manicured gardens along Pond Trail before venturing into the forest to join Turtleback Mountain Trail. In less than half a mile, make sure to explore the remains of a historic pine lodge on your left.

Shortly after passing the Brook Walk sign, proceed with caution as the trail descends steeply towards the footbridge, where you'll catch your first glimpse of the 40-foot Falls of Song—the most impressive of the five waterfalls.

Take a break on the bench here before ascending the stone steps to Bridal Veil Falls, which cascade over the cliffs and rocks below. Follow the water's edge past three more waterfalls until you reach Ossipee Park Road, where you'll turn right to return to the parking lot.

Between late April and early October, treat yourself to an ice cream at Cafe in the Clouds, located conveniently between the two trailheads of this loop.

TURN-BY-TURN DIRECTIONS

1. From the parking area, continue northeast on Ossipee Park Road, then bear right towards Shannon Pond.
2. At 0.2 miles, take a left onto Pond Trail.
3. At 0.3 miles, arrive at the kiosk and continue straight on the yellow-blazed Turtleback Mountain Trail.
4. At 0.6 miles, take a right onto Shannon Brook Trail.
5. At 0.8 miles, bear right at the fork following signs for Brook Walk and Waterfalls, marked by white blazes.
6. At 1.0 mile, cross the bridge and take a right to follow the boardwalk to the Falls of Song. Return in the direction you came, then go right through an opening in the boardwalk fence. Follow the trail up stone steps to Bridal Veil Falls.
7. At 1.2 miles, bear right as the trail follows the water's edge to Emerald Pool Falls.
8. At 1.3 miles, take a right at an unmarked T-junction. Continue to follow white blazes as you reach The Cascades, then Whittier Falls.
9. At 1.5 miles, go right at the T-junction.
10. At 1.7 miles, the trail reconnects with Ossipee Park Road. Return to the parking lot the way you came.

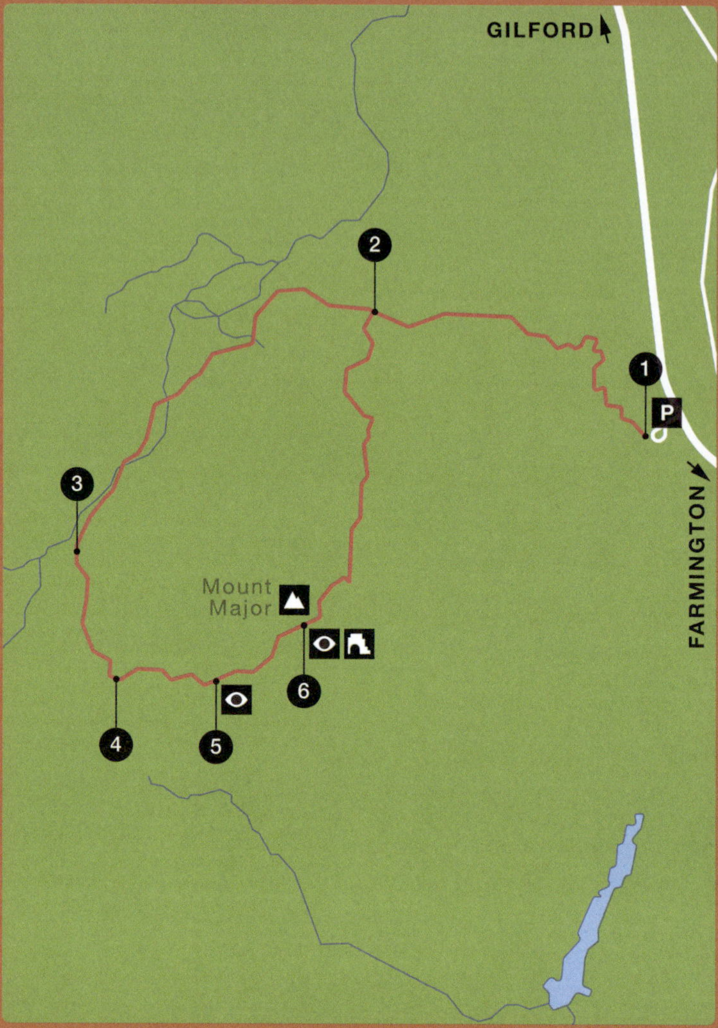

GILFORD
FARMINGTON
Mount Major
1
2
3
4
5
6
P

P Parking
Ruins
Mountain
Viewpoint

ft
2500
2000
1500
1000
500
0
0.0
0.5
1.0
1.5
2.0
2.5
3.0
3.5
4.0
4.3 mi

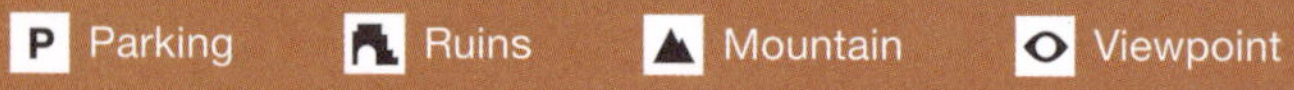

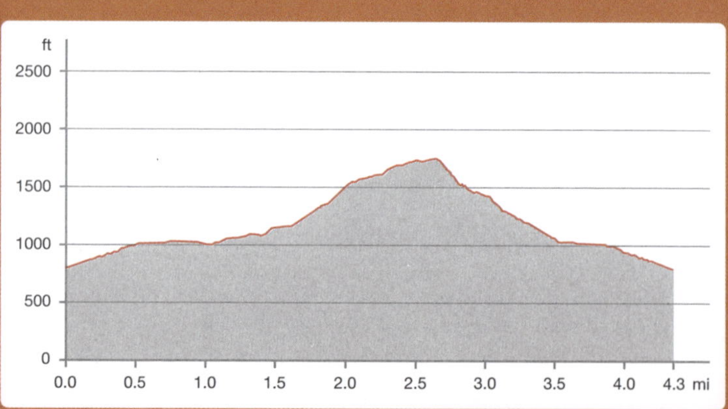

MOUNT MAJOR

SWEEPING VIEWS OF NH'S LAKES REGION

ALTON BAY, NH

13

LENGTH
4.3 miles
(loop)

TIME & MONEY
2 hours 30 minutes

ELEVATION GAIN
1158 feet

DIFFICULTY
Moderate

CONDITIONS
Year-round;
some rocky
sections, shaded

HIGHLIGHTS
Views, stone hut
ruins

ESSENTIALS

- **Find the trailhead:** From Wolfeboro, head southeast on S Main Street. After 2.4 miles, turn right onto NH-28 S. After 7.5 miles, turn right onto Bay Hill Road. After 0.4 miles, turn right onto NH-11 W. After 4.2 miles, turn left into the parking lot.
- **Land manager:** Society for the Protection of New Hampshire Forests, 54 Portsmouth Street, Concord, NH 03301; (603) 224-9945; info@forestsociety.org
forestsociety.org

WHY YOU'LL LOVE IT

- Well-marked trails
- Entirely forested and shady until the summit
- Large, open area at summit to enjoy lake views

Enjoy a shady, forested hike to an open summit with panoramic views over Lake Winnipesaukee.

Mount Major is the easternmost peak of Belknap Range, located in the Lakes Region of New Hampshire, just south of the White Mountains in the central-eastern part of the state. This region is named for the great many lakes found here, the largest of which are Lake Winnipesaukee, Lake Winnisquam, Squam Lake, and Newfound Lake. This summit offers the best views of Lake Winnipesaukee, in addition to ruins from Mr. Phippen's Hut—a stone shelter built as a refuge for hikers in 1925.

George Phippen, who purchased this mountain summit in 1914 for a whopping $125, offered the hut as a place to warm up beside a wood stove or spend the night for a spectacular sunrise. In 1926, fierce winds blew the roof off the hut, and the roof was replaced the following summer with a sturdier one. That, too, was blown off in the winter winds of 1927 and never replaced. The old roof remains on the mountainside just yards from the stone foundation, which hasn't had a roof in almost a century.

The large parking area for this hike fills up quickly on weekends, so it's best to visit during the week to avoid the crowds. Shortly after beginning Mount Major Main Trail, you'll see a large glacial erratic on the left, then continue along a logging road with a gentle slope. As you join Brook Trail, the path stays easy until a steeper climb through a hardwood forest at about 1.5 miles in. Expect muddy conditions in the spring and some loose rocks on eroded sections due to several brook crossings on this trail.

After another mile, there's a spur on the left leading to a lovely vista, which is just a preview of better views ahead. As you leave the forested area, the trail opens up, and you'll cross exposed ledges with wide-ranging views of Lake Winnipesaukee to the east and north. Rest and snack at one of the many viewing spots at the summit, or take shelter in Mr. Phippen's Hut, just beyond the summit, on a windy day.

As you descend on Main Trail, take it slow due to some steep rock scrambles near the top. To bypass these sections, watch for several alternate routes offering detours around the steepest parts. After your hike, stroll along the dog-friendly Weirs Beach Boardwalk or relax on one of their benches, enjoying a closer view of Lake Winnipesaukee.

TURN-BY-TURN DIRECTIONS

1. Locate the trailhead in the northwest corner of the parking lot and follow the blue-blazed Mount Major Main Trail along a wide dirt path.
2. At 0.8 miles, bear right at the junction, following the yellow-blazed Brook Trail.
3. At 1.8 miles, stay left at an unmarked fork and continue along Brook Trail.
4. At 2.1 miles, stay left toward the Mount Major Main Trail.
5. At 2.4 miles, take a short spur to a vista on the right, then return to Main Trail.
6. At 2.6 miles, arrive at the summit. Explore Mr. Phippen's Hut and enjoy the view. Continue on the Mount Major Main Trail as it descends a steep section of rock scrambles before leveling out. Return to the start of the loop, then take a right to return to the trailhead.

BRATTLEBORO
KEENE
HINSDALE
Daniel's Mountain
1
2
3
4
5
6
7
8
9
P
P Parking
Ruins
Mountain
Viewpoint
ft
2500
2000
1500
1000
500
0
0.0
0.5
1.0
1.5
2.0
2.5
3.0
3.5
4.0
4.4 mi

MADAME SHERRI FOREST

TWO WOODED LOOPS WITH VIEWS AND POND

CHESTERFIELD, NH

14

LENGTH
4.4 miles (loop)

TIME & MONEY
2 hours; free

ELEVATION GAIN
899 feet

DIFFICULTY
Moderate

CONDITIONS
Year-round; sections of narrow trail

HIGHLIGHTS
Castle ruins, expansive views, spooky forest

ESSENTIALS

- **Find the trailhead:** From Maine Street in Keene, head south to the traffic circle, then take the first exit onto Winchester Street. After one mile, merge onto NH-10 N/NH-12 N. Continue onto NH-9 W and follow for 9 miles, then turn left onto NH-63 S. Continue onto NH-63 S, then in 1.6 miles turn right onto Stage Road. After 0.2 miles, take a slight left onto Castle Hill Road. After 1 mile, merge onto Gulf Road and follow it for 1.6 miles, then take a left into the parking lot.

- **Land manager:** Society for the Protection of New Hampshire Forests, 54 Portsmouth Street, Concord, NH 03301; (603) 224-9945; info@forestsociety.org
forestsociety.org

WHY YOU'LL LOVE IT

- Pond with easy water access for dogs
- Ability to shorten the hike by doing just one of the two loops
- Castle ruins near the trailhead

Explore connecting loop trails with several viewpoints, a pond, and castle ruins with a grand stone staircase once attached to the home of Madame Sherri.

Madame Sherri Forest encompasses 513 acres of serene woodland with scenic views in Chesterfield, NH. The property is adjacent to the 847-acre Wantastiquet State Forest to the west and connects with the 50-mile Wantastiquet-Monadnock Hiking Trail.

It's home to castle ruins from the former summer home of Paris-born Madame Antoinette Sherri, who designed costumes for royalty and produced shows for the vaudeville circuit. She built what was known as "The Castle" in the woods and was renowned for throwing wild parties for New York City friends during the Roaring Twenties. Due to financial trouble the castle fell into neglect before burning to the ground in 1963.

Following Madame Sherri's passing in 1965, the property was acquired by Ann Stokes, who later gifted complete ownership to the Society for the Protection of New Hampshire Forests. Today, the castle ruins continue to be a destination for weddings, photographers, ghost hunters, and dog walkers.

At the trailhead, there's a kiosk with a timeline of Madame Sherri's life. After reading about her extravagant lifestyle, cross a short bridge over a marsh. Just beyond the bridge, bear right at the fork and follow a side trail 100 feet uphill to the castle ruins.

The first thing you see is the remarkable Roman-arch staircase. Although the top section of the staircase collapsed in 2021 and is roped off for safety, you can still explore the stone foundations and old fireplace by following a trail around the back of the ruins.

According to legend, Madame Sherri's spirit is said to haunt the castle, and her ghost has allegedly been seen slowly descending the grand staircase. These woods have an eerie atmosphere, and my dog stayed unusually close to me during our hike. It's believed that dogs can sense spirits, so it's wise to keep them on a leash in case the tales of the haunted forest are true.

After exploring the castle, return to the main trail and continue on to the east branch of Ann Stokes Loop before taking a left to connect with Daniel's Mountain Loop. Less than half a mile beyond the viewless summit of Daniel's Mountain, arrive at Moon Ledge, a rocky outcrop with expansive views of Massachusetts and Vermont from the south side of the mountain.

Just past the three-mile mark, enjoy another scenic vista by taking a short spur to the right. The hike culminates at Indian Pond, where you'll reward yourself with tranquil water views while your dog can take a refreshing swim.

TURN-BY-TURN DIRECTIONS

1. From the trailhead, cross a foot bridge, then take the spur on the right leading to the castle ruins. Return to the trail and continue straight past a marsh and pond.
2. At 0.24 miles, arrive at Ann Stokes Loop and go left towards Daniel's Mountain.
3. At 0.8 miles, take a left onto Daniel's Mountain Loop, marked by a blue diamond. Shortly beyond this point, the trail takes a sharp right. Continue to follow blue diamonds as the trail climbs toward a series of rock ledges.
4. At 0.9 miles, stay left at an unmarked fork. The trail becomes narrow here as it weaves through mountain laurel.

5. At 1.4 miles, reach Daniel's Mountain summit, then go right, continuing on Daniel's Mountain Loop.
6. At 1.8 miles, arrive at the junction with Bear Mountain/Pisgah Trail. A short spur here leads to Moon Ledge. Enjoy the view, then return to the trail and go left.
7. At 2.6 miles, complete Daniel's Mountain Loop and take a left on Ann Stokes Loop, marked by white diamonds. Just past this junction, stay left at an unmarked fork.
8. At 3.2 miles, enjoy a short spur on the right leading to a scenic vista.
9. At 3.5 miles, arrive at a junction and go left, following Wantastiquet Mountain Trail the short distance to Indian Pond. After your dog has had a swim, return to Ann Stokes Loop and, after completing it, go left to return to the trailhead.

VERMONT

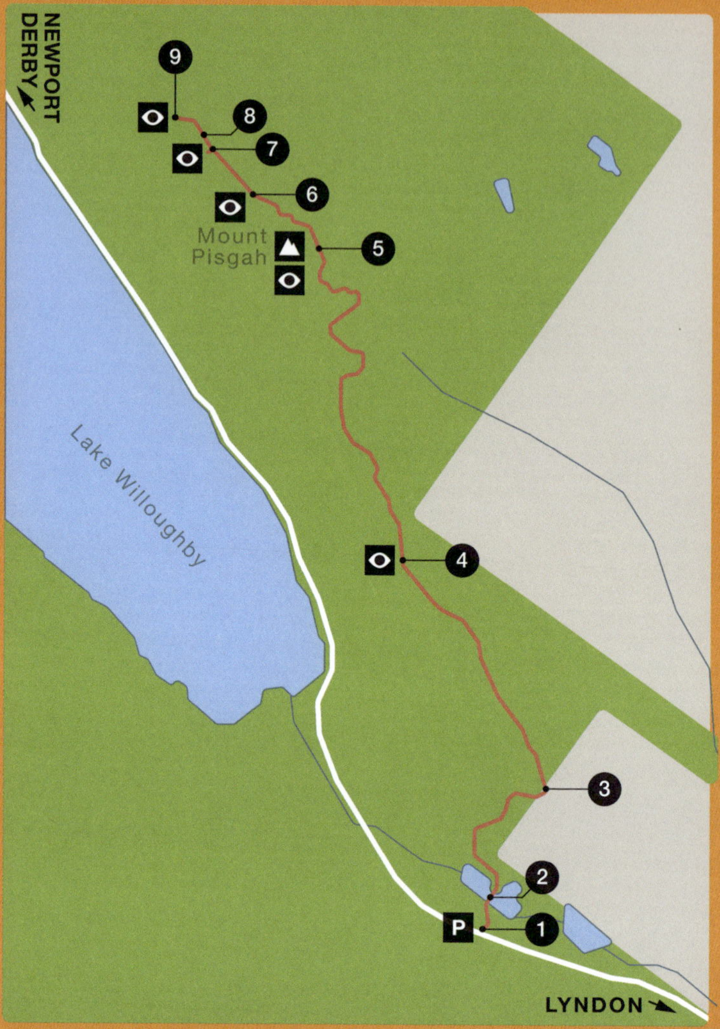

NEWPORT
DERBY

9
8
7
6
Mount
Pisgah
5
Lake Willoughby
4
3
2
P
1
LYNDON

P Parking
Mountain
Viewpoint

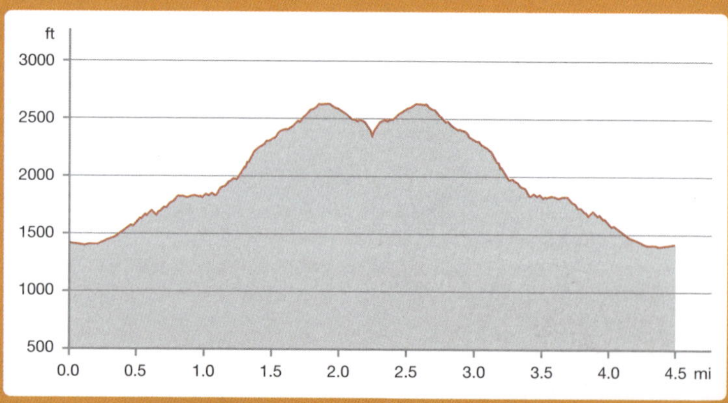

MOUNT PISGAH

BIRD'S-EYE VIEW OF SCENIC LAKE WILLOUGHBY

WESTMORE, VT

15

LENGTH
4.5 miles
(out and back)

TIME & MONEY
2 hours; free

ELEVATION GAIN
1759 feet

DIFFICULTY
Strenuous

CONDITIONS
Year-round;
stone stairs,
switchbacks

HIGHLIGHTS
Several clifftop
viewpoints

ESSENTIALS

- **Find the trailhead:** From Burke, head northeast on Bugbee Crossing Road toward Burke Hollow Road. After 0.1 miles, turn left onto Burke Hollow Road. After 2.1 miles, take a slight left to stay on Burke Hollow Road. After 131 feet, turn left to stay on Burke Hollow Road. After 154 feet, turn right onto VT-5A N. After 5.6 miles, the parking is on your right.

- **Land manager:** North Woods Stewardship Center, 154 Leadership Drive/PO Box 220, East Charleston, VT 05833; (802) 723-6551; info@northwoodscenter.org
northwoodscenter.org

WHY YOU'LL LOVE IT

- Multiple overlooks of Lake Willoughby and surrounding mountains
- Early viewpoints—perfect for dogs that prefer a shorter hike
- Easy navigation to the summit

Enjoy a steady ascent to stunning views of the Northeast Kingdom and Lake Willoughby, Vermont's deepest lake.

Formed by glaciers over 12,000 years ago, Lake Willoughby is nestled between the dramatic cliffs of Mount Pisgah to the east and Mount Hor to the west. The breathtaking landscape of this elongated, pristine lake with towering mountains on both sides will make you feel as though you've been whisked away to a Norwegian fjord.

Reaching a maximum depth of 308 feet, Lake Willoughby is one of the deepest lakes in the northeastern United States. This breathtaking attraction draws summer visitors who come to swim, paddle and boat on the five-mile-long lake. There are two public sandy beaches on Lake Willoughby. Dogs are not allowed at North Beach but are welcome at South Beach. This beach is the closest to the trailhead, providing a convenient spot for your dog to cool off after the hike. However, be aware that this is also a clothing-optional beach.

Just a half hour from the Canadian border, the summit of Mount Pisgah offers views of the Green and White Mountains and Canadian mountains; and you may encounter French-speaking hikers along the trail. We met a small pup in a stylish puffy coat, named Schopi after the German philosopher Schopenhauer. Schopi enjoyed a strong start to his hiking adventure, but after tiring his little legs, his owners carried him to the summit. Moose and Milo, two medium-sized dogs we met along the way, had no difficulty reaching the top.

Parking is located off VT-5A on the southern side of the lake. As this is a popular trail, the lot can fill quickly, so it's best to arrive early if you can. There are three routes to the summit of Mount Pisgah. The most dog-friendly is South Trail, which is the shortest and most gradual route. This path hugs the mountain's western cliffs, offering views along the way. Be cautious of steep drop-offs while enjoying the views at each overlook, and be sure to keep your dog on a leash.

From the trailhead parking, enter the forest and cross a long boardwalk before reaching a second boardwalk between two ponds. About half a mile into the hike, the trail becomes steeper, featuring stone stairs and switchbacks. At just under a mile, reach the first bird's-eye view of Lake Willoughby from Pulpit Rock. Continuing the steady climb, reach South Overlook just before the 2751-foot summit, which is nearly two miles in.

Beyond the summit, there are three more stunning overlooks. The final viewpoint provides expansive views of Quebec to the north and Mount Hor to the south. There's also a large rock where you can sit, enjoy a snack and give your dog some water. Return the way you came, relishing the incredible overlooks once more during your descent.

TURN-BY-TURN DIRECTIONS

1. From the trailhead, follow South Trail.
2. At 0.1 miles, cross a boardwalk between two small ponds.
3. At 0.5 miles, arrive at stone stairs and a switchback.
4. At 1 mile, reach the first overlook of Lake Willoughby from Pulpit Rock.
5. At 1.8 miles, reach South Overlook just before arriving at Mount Pisgah summit. Beyond the summit, South Trail connects with North Trail, continuing towards West Overlook.
6. At 2 miles, reach West Overlook, then continue climbing.
7. At 2.1 miles, explore a short spur leading to North Overlook on the left, then continue straight until reaching a junction.
8. At 2.2 miles, bear left at the fork, following the trail to the west.
9. At 2.3 miles, reach the final overlook offering expansive views of Quebec to the north and Mount Hor to the south. Return back the way you came.

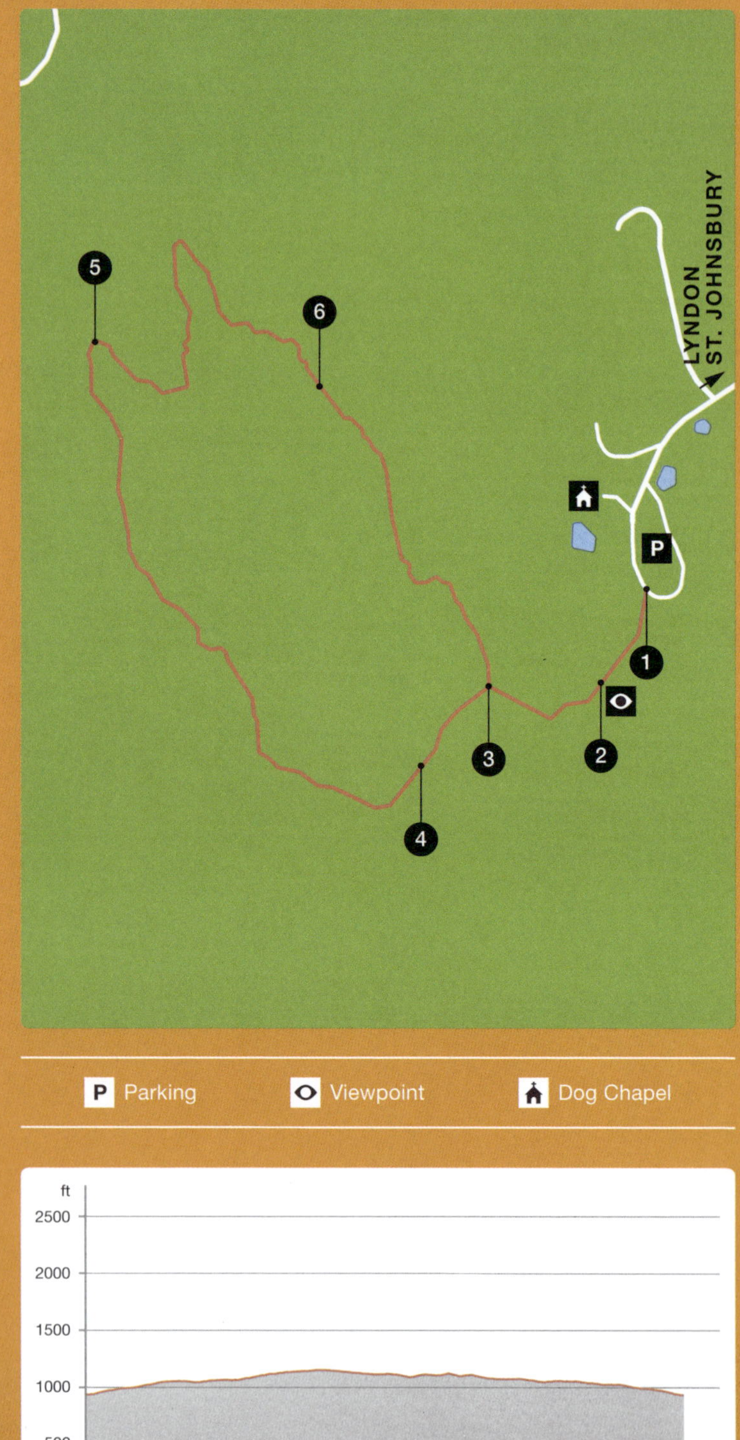
LYNDON
ST. JOHNSBURY
1
2
3
4
5
6
P
Parking
Viewpoint
Dog Chapel
ft
2500
2000
1500
1000
500
0
0.0
0.5
1.0
1.5 mi

DOG MOUNTAIN

OFF-LEASH MOUNTAINTOP DOG UTOPIA

ST. JOHNSBURY, VT

16

LENGTH
1.5 miles (loop)

TIME & MONEY
45 minutes; free

ELEVATION GAIN
256 feet

DIFFICULTY
Easy

CONDITIONS
Year-round; grassy fields, hilly section in woods

HIGHLIGHTS
Dog chapel, views

ESSENTIALS

- **Find the trailhead:** From St. Johnsbury's center, head east on Breezy Hill Road toward Sanger Circle. After 0.4 miles, turn left onto Lackey Hill Road. After 0.6 miles, take a slight right onto Spaulding Road. After 2.5 miles, turn right onto Parks Road. After 0.1 miles, turn right into the parking lot at 143 Parks Road.
- **Land manager:** Friends of Dog Mountain, 143 Parks Road, St. Johnsbury, VT 05819 dogmt.com

WHY YOU'LL LOVE IT

- Off-leash on the entire property
- Dog trails, ponds, obstacle courses, and open fields
- The Dog Chapel

Dogs are cherished at this off-leash mountaintop property that offers hiking trails, dog ponds, a dog chapel, an art gallery, and a gift shop ... all devoted to dogs!

Set on 150 acres of mountaintop in Vermont's Northeast Kingdom, Dog Mountain features hiking trails and open meadows filled with wildflowers. The grounds are open to the public and dogs are welcome to run off-leash. Throughout the year, Dog Mountain hosts free outdoor concerts and dog parties, attracting hundreds of people and their furry friends.

This dog utopia was created by the late Stephen Huneck, a woodcarver, artist and author of a *New York Times* best-selling children's book series inspired by his black lab, Sally. Experience Stephen's artwork by wandering through his gallery and shop, housed in a renovated farmhouse on the property, and admire the original wood-cut prints, furniture and gifts displaying whimsical depictions of dogs.

Apart from the hiking, the other main drawcard here is the Dog Chapel, which Huneck was inspired to build after recovering from a serious illness. Modeled after an 1820s Vermont church, the chapel celebrates departed dogs. It's an incredibly moving experience. You feel the joy that dogs bring into our lives and the inevitable sadness of losing a cherished pet. Every space on the walls is covered with photos and messages.

Walking past the thousands of images and love letters, it's hard not to get emotional. It truly is a special place, and I can see myself leaving my own photos here someday, hopefully many, many years from now.

The venue has two main hiking loops, blue and yellow, that join in the middle. We're going to walk the yellow trail, which connects with the west side of the blue trail as you make your return trip to the trailhead. For a longer walk and additional loop, go left where the yellow and blue trails merge to follow the blue trail. These loops begin and end at the same place, so it's difficult to get lost here. There is an agility course, plus a dog pond near the end of the blue trail—a bonus you'll want to explore if you have a social dog.

If your dog is less social, like ours, you'll appreciate the less-crowded trails leading through quiet woods. Soon after climbing the steep, dirt road at the start of this hike, you arrive at a spur leading to Angel Dog Overlook. This breathtaking vista is the highlight of this trail, so take some time to stop and enjoy the grassy play area with sweeping views of the mountains. There's also a tall sculpture displaying a dog with wings, a feature Huneck gave to several dog sculptures located around the property.

Once you return to the trail and connect with the start of the yellow trail, you enter the woods. Although there are no more views along this loop, you and your buddy will experience the peace and tranquility of a wooded walk with a gentle incline. Shortly after the yellow trail joins the blue trail and heads south towards the start of the loop, there's a steep descent with a rope handrail; your dog's four legs give them stability here, so they should have no problem, but you'll need to keep your wits about you.

Just before completing the blue trail and reconnecting with the dirt road, a trail to the left leads down to the dog play area, "The Playpen," and pond. This is where your social dog will find the dog party. To opt out of play time, continue straight to return to the trailhead.

TURN-BY-TURN DIRECTIONS

1. From the main parking lot, walk down the drive, then take a right on Parks Road. Follow it past a barn on the left and trail kiosk on the right. Just beyond the kiosk, take a right onto a wide dirt road up a steep hill. This is the start of the trail loop.
2. At 0.1 miles, take the spur on the left leading to Angel Dog Overlook. Explore the view and grassy play area, then return to the main trail and take a left. From here, the trail bears right onto a grassy path.
3. At 0.2 miles, arrive at a trail map and go left at the fork to follow the yellow trail marked by a dog paw.
4. At 0.24 miles, at the junction with the short pink trail, continue straight to remain on the yellow trail.
5. At 0.7 miles, bear right at the fork. If you were to continue straight here, it would lead you on a longer, outer yellow loop that eventually leads back to the main loop.
6. At 1 mile, the yellow trail joins the blue trail. Continue straight on the blue trail and follow it to the end of the loop. Then take a left to return to the start of the trail.

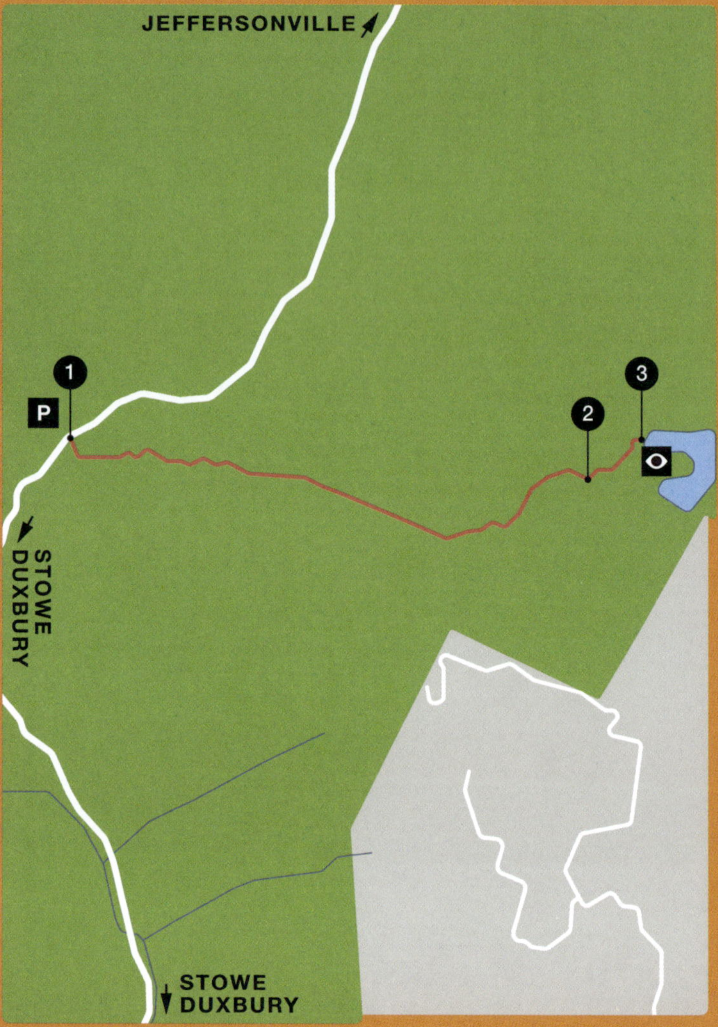

JEFFERSONVILLE
1
2
3
P
STOWE
DUXBURY
STOWE
DUXBURY

P Parking

Viewpoint

ft
3500
3000
2500
2000
1500
1000
0.0
0.5
1.0
1.5
2.0 mi

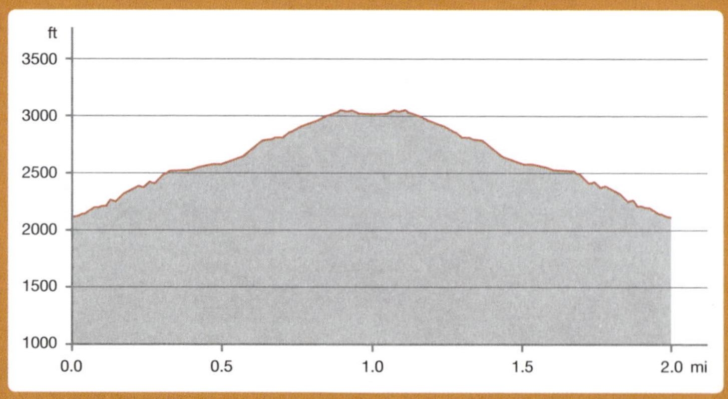

STERLING POND TRAIL

VERMONT'S HIGHEST TROUT POND

STOWE, VT

17

LENGTH
2 miles
(in and out)

TIME & MONEY
1 hour 30 minutes;
free

ELEVATION GAIN
938 feet

DIFFICULTY
Moderate

CONDITIONS
Late May to
mid-October;
stone stairs,
stream crossings

HIGHLIGHTS
Mountain pond,
smuggler's cave

ESSENTIALS

- **Find the trailhead:** From the intersection of Vermont Route 100 and VT-108 N/Mountain Road in Stowe, head north on VT-108 N/Mountain Road. After 9.7 miles, the trailhead parking is on the right.

- **Land manager:** VT Department of Forests, Parks & Recreation, 5 Perry Street, Suite 20, Barre, VT 05641; (802) 476-0182 fpr.vermont.gov

WHY YOU'LL LOVE IT

- Plenty of stream crossings for pups to hydrate
- Easy parking and well-marked trails
- Options for a longer hike or to visit a gorgeous waterfall nearby

Hike to a pristine mountain lake from historic Smuggler's Notch. Dogs are allowed to swim in the refreshing alpine water but should be leashed on trail to protect sensitive areas.

The drive to the trailhead in Smuggler's Notch is nearly as stunning as the hike itself. This narrow pass through 1000-foot cliffs in the Green Mountains includes a steep and winding road lined with massive boulders that balance in remarkable ways.

Across from the trailhead is Smuggler's Cave, which was used to hide contraband during the early 1800s when trade with Canada was prohibited. Smugglers would cross The Notch with donkeys and horses carrying supplies, hiding themselves within the large caverns of the towering boulders. Transporting illegal goods through The Notch continued into the 1920s, during the height of Prohibition, when an improved road allowed access for automobiles.

The road through Smuggler's Notch is closed in the winter, so this hike is best done between Memorial Day and mid-October. To avoid crowds on this popular trail, start early and plan for a weekday. There are two parking lots for Sterling Pond Trail. The first is just south of the trailhead on the right and the second is just beyond it on the left, near the Smuggler's Notch Visitor Center and bathrooms.

Locate the trailhead across the road from the visitor center, then prepare for a cardio workout as you ascend a long section of stone steps. The blue-blazed trail continues to steadily climb, following a path with dirt, rock steps and stream crossings. During the rainy months of spring, little waterfalls appear alongside the path—your dog will appreciate access to small pools for drinking and cooling off. Consider trekking poles and supportive footwear to assist with these slippery surfaces.

At just under a mile, at the junction with Long Trail, leash your dog to protect sensitive areas near the pond. Go left as the trail descends along a section of rock ledge before arriving at the mountaintop pond, at 3000 feet in elevation. Our hike was socked in with fog, but on a clear day, Sterling Pond features stunning views across the water to Madonna Peak. The pond is stocked with trout, and we encountered two eager boys with fishing poles on our descent, along with many cheerful dogs and hikers.

To lengthen this hike, continue further along Long Trail North, bearing left for mountain views at the top of Smuggler's Notch Resort, or go right to follow the trail around the pond. Or after you've returned to your car, stop off on the way home at the nearby 1.3-mile (in and out) Mill Trail to Bingham Falls, a spectacular hike past a series of cascades leading to a 40-foot waterfall.

TURN-BY-TURN DIRECTIONS

1. Start from the trailhead across the road from Smuggler's Notch Visitor Center.
2. At 0.9 miles, at the intersection with Long Trail, take a left and follow it to the pond.
3. At 1 mile, arrive at Sterling Pond. Enjoy the views and a cold swim, then return the way you came. Or opt to lengthen your hike, as mentioned before, or do the extra hike to Bingham Falls.

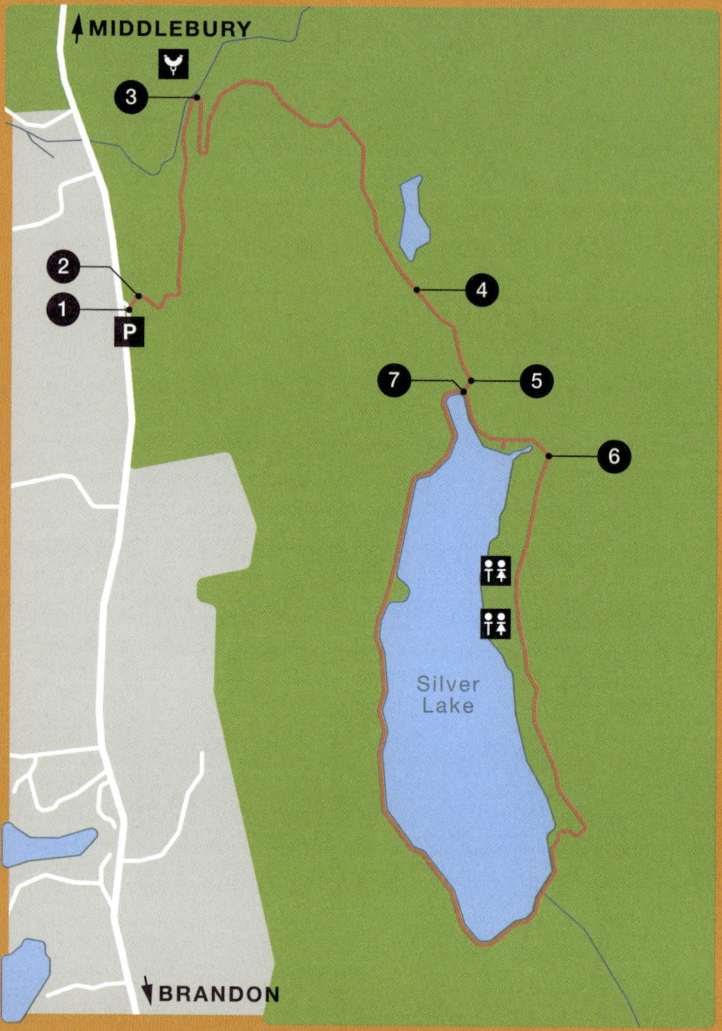

MIDDLEBURY
3
2
1
P
4
7
5
6
Silver Lake
BRANDON

P Parking | Toilet | Picnic area

ft
2500
2000
1500
1000
500
0
0.0
0.5
1.0
1.5
2.0
2.5
3.0
3.5
4.0
4.5
5.0
5.4 mi

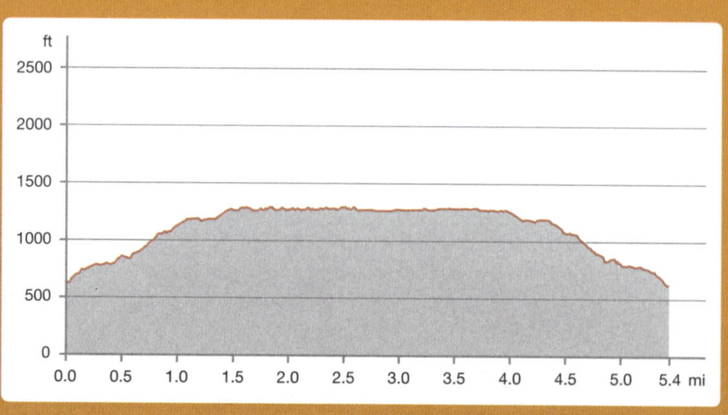

SILVER LAKE TRAIL

ENDLESS WATER ACCESS ON MID-SIZE LAKE

SALISBURY, VT

18

LENGTH
5.4 miles (loop)

TIME & MONEY
2 hours; free

ELEVATION GAIN
722 feet

DIFFICULTY
Moderate

CONDITIONS
Year-round; rocky sections near lake, shady

HIGHLIGHTS
Lake views, picnic area, cascading falls

ESSENTIALS

- **Find the trailhead:** From Middlebury, head south on North Pleasant Street toward Seymour Street. After 482 feet, turn left onto Court Square. After 233 feet, turn right onto US-7 S/Court Street. After 6.8 miles, turn left onto State Route 53/Lake Dunmore Road. After 4 miles, turn left into the parking lot.
- **Land manager:** Green Mountain National Forest, 231 North Main Street, Rutland, VT 05701; (802) 747-6700 fs.usda.gov/r09/gmfl

WHY YOU'LL LOVE IT

- Peaceful, quiet lakeside trail
- Perfect place to keep cool and hydrated on hot days
- Bathrooms located halfway around the lake

Begin on a carriage trail along the cascading waterfalls of Sucker Brook, then climb to a tranquil loop around pristine Silver Lake. This route includes the Falls of Lana, Silver Lake Dam and a picnic area at Silver Lake Campground.

Silver Lake is within Moosalamoo National Recreation Area, situated in the northern part of Green Mountain National Forest. Silver Lake State Park is located on the northeastern shore of the lake and features a campground and sandy swimming area. While pets aren't allowed on the sandy beach, they're welcome elsewhere throughout the park. The lake is popular for paddling, fishing and quiet recreation.

The hike begins with a climb up stone steps before joining an old carriage road that continues uphill. You'll soon pass underneath a penstock, a huge pipe that feeds water from Silver Lake to a local hydroelectric power station on Route 53. The station, constructed in the early 1900s to supply power to iron mines in Mineville, NY, now provides electricity to over 800 homes in the Moosalamoo area.

After just under half a mile, the path reaches the cascading falls of Sucker Brook, offering an ideal spot for your dog to cool off and have a drink. The trail runs alongside the brook for a short stretch before diverging near the Falls of Lana Picnic Area. The wide dirt-and-gravel path takes a long, wide switchback before reaching a grassy area on the lake's northern side. Follow signs for Rocky Point Interpretive Trail, which will guide you over a dam, then veer left to navigate the narrow and rocky path around the lake's perimeter.

Most of this hike hugs the lake shore, leading to a healthy bug population. Bug spray is an essential item to include in your pack.

As you approach the end of the lake loop, the trail meanders through the campground, providing an opportunity for a bathroom break if needed. Dogs are allowed on-leash in the picnic area near the sandy beach, which you'll pass through before completing the lake loop. Stop here for some lunch or save your picnic for the Falls of Lana Picnic Area towards the end of your hike.

TURN-BY-TURN DIRECTIONS

1. Find the trailhead on the northeast end of the parking lot, then ascend stone steps.
2. At 0.4 miles, bear right toward Falls of Lana and Silver Lake. The wide dirt-and-gravel path passes a series of cascades on the left.
3. At 0.5 miles, go right toward Silver Lake. Continuing straight here would lead to the Falls of Lana Picnic Area, a stop you may consider for later on.
4. At 1.3 miles, continue straight, ignoring Lenny's Lookout to the right.
5. At 1.5 miles, at the sign saying pets must be leashed beyond this point, take a right toward Rocky Point Interpretive Trail. Cross a narrow metal bridge over a dam, then bear left as the trail follows the lake edge.
6. At 3.6 miles, take a left on a narrow trail leading towards the water, marked by a Picnic Area sign.
7. At 3.9 miles, complete the lake loop, then take a left to return the way you came.

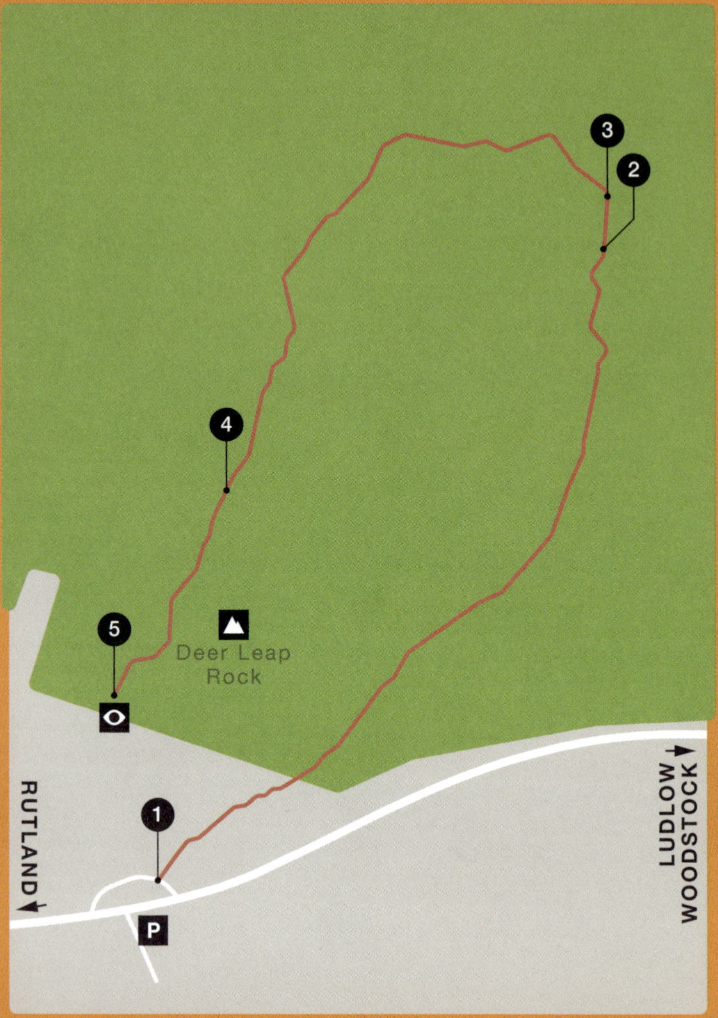

3
2
4
5
Deer Leap
Rock
1
P
RUTLAND
LUDLOW
WOODSTOCK

P Parking
Mountain
Viewpoint

ft
2500
2000
1500
1000
500
0
0.0
0.5
1.0
1.5
2.0 mi

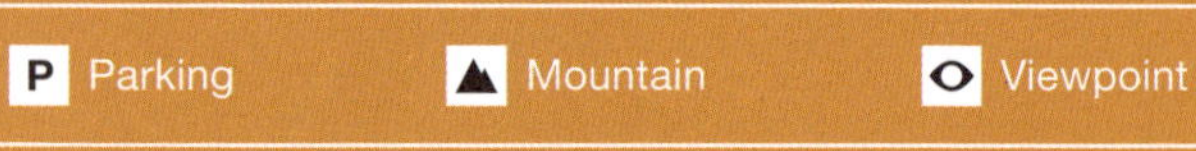

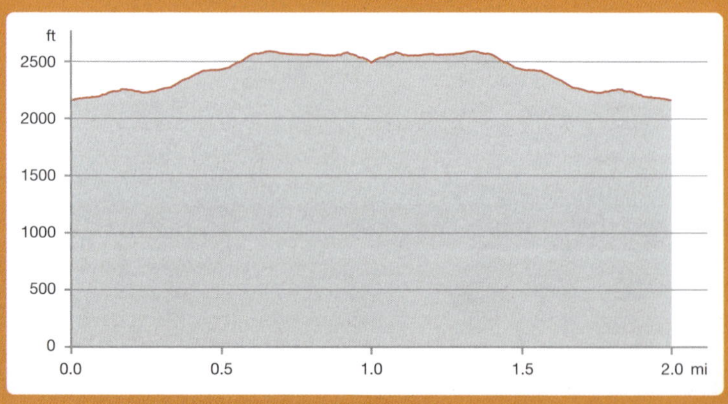

DEER LEAP OVERLOOK

VIEWS OF SHERBURNE PASS

KILLINGTON, VT

19

LENGTH

2 miles
(in and out)

TIME & MONEY

1 hour; free

ELEVATION GAIN

502 feet

DIFFICULTY

Moderate

CONDITIONS

Year-round;
wet trails, shady

HIGHLIGHTS

Dramatic views,
birch forest

ESSENTIALS

- **Find the trailhead:** From Killington Village, head south on River Road Fork toward Quimby Mountain Road. After 1.4 miles, take a slight right to stay on River Road Fork. After 194 feet, turn right onto US-4 W. After 3.5 miles, turn right into the small lot for the Inn at Long Trail and park at the far east end near the trailhead. (There is additional parking on the south side of US-4, but you have to cross the busy road.)

- **Land manager:** Green Mountain National Forest, 231 North Main Street, Rutland, VT 05701; (802) 747-6700 fs.usda.gov/r09/gmfl

WHY YOU'LL LOVE IT

- Quick hike to expansive views
- Mossy forest with plenty of shade
- Ability to lengthen hike

This mossy trail bordered by birch trees offers a stellar reward for a short climb. The hike begins on Sherburne Pass Trail, the former route of the historic Long Trail, then leads to a large rock outcrop with expansive views of Sherburne Pass, Pico Peak and the north face of Killington.

Begin your hike from the Inn at Long Trail's parking area, located on the north side of US-4. Built in 1938, it was the first lodge constructed for Vermont's ski community. Although dogs can't stay at the inn, the staff provides many services for Appalachian Trail and Long Trail thru-hikers.

The first section of this hike takes you along Sherburne Pass Trail, once the official route of Vermont's Long Trail. Although the Long Trail has been rerouted to the west, Sherburne Pass Trail still links up with the Appalachian Trail before merging back with the Long Trail. Built between 1910 and 1930, the Long Trail is the oldest continuous footpath in the US. It spans 272 miles and has 70 backcountry campsites and 166 miles of side trails.

Large rocks and some road noise dominate the first 0.3 miles of Sherburne Pass Trail, but you soon leave all that behind for a tranquil, shaded path. After walking just under half a mile, pass the junction with the Appalachian Trail before taking a left onto Deer Leap Trail. From this point, the trail bears west through a birch forest carpeted with moss, then south towards Deer Leap Rock.

Before arriving at the rock outcropping, cross a short boardwalk and descend some wooden steps. The leash requirement for this hike becomes quite clear after stepping onto the large rock outcrop, which has steep drop-offs on many sides. Take in the spectacular views of Sherburne Pass, Coolidge Range and New York's Adirondacks to the west.

For a longer hike to Deer Leap Overlook, start at Gifford Woods State Park, located off Route 100 in Killington. From this trailhead, it's a 3.7-mile round trip. Adding Deer Leap Mountain Loop, too, extends that hike an additional 1.3 miles for a 5-mile round trip.

While in the area, you might also like to check out the breathtaking Thundering Brook Falls, where dogs are allowed to swim.

TURN-BY-TURN DIRECTIONS

1. Find the trailhead in the northeast corner of the small parking lot, then ascend the rocky Sherburne Pass Trail marked by blue blazes.
2. At 0.4 miles, reach a junction with the Appalachian Trail, then go left towards Maine Junction and Deer Leap Trail.
3. At 0.5 miles, go left on Deer Leap Trail, also marked by blue blazes.
4. At 0.8 miles, stay left on Deer Leap Trail, ignoring the sign for Willard Gap to the right. Continue on Deer Leap Trail as it bears right, joining a spur trail marked by a wooden Deer Leap Overlook sign.
5. At 1 mile, arrive at Deer Leap Rock and enjoy the view, then return the way you came.

BARNARD
1
2
3
4
5
6
P
The Pogue
WEST WOODSTOCK

P Parking

ft
2500
2000
1500
1000
500
0
0.0
0.5
1.0
1.5
2.0
2.5
2.8 mi

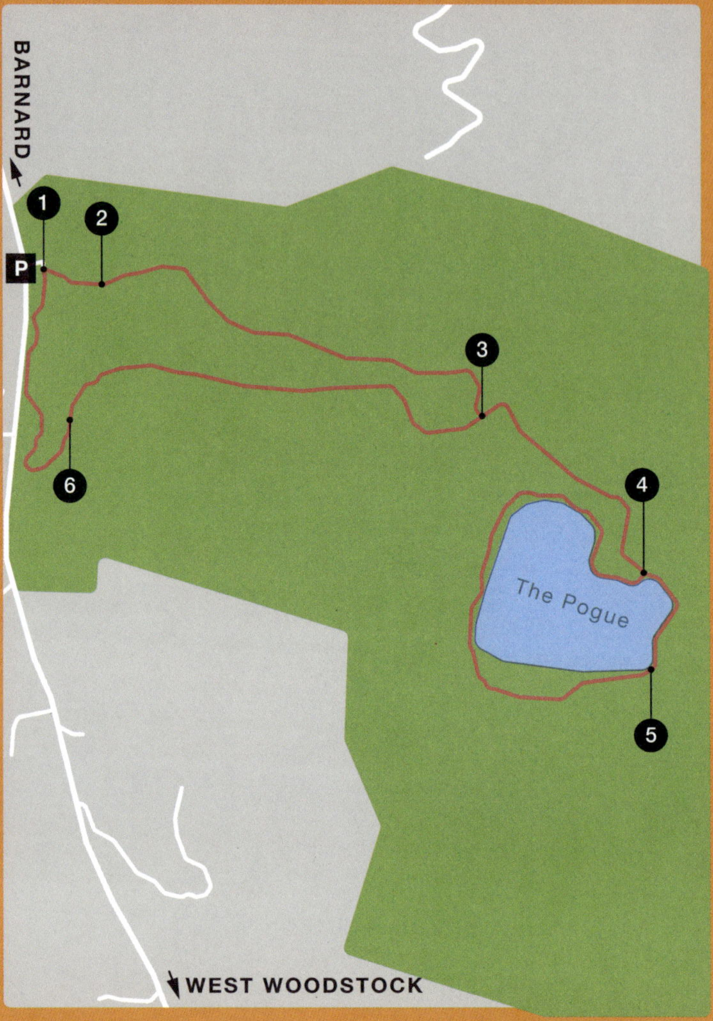

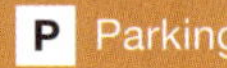

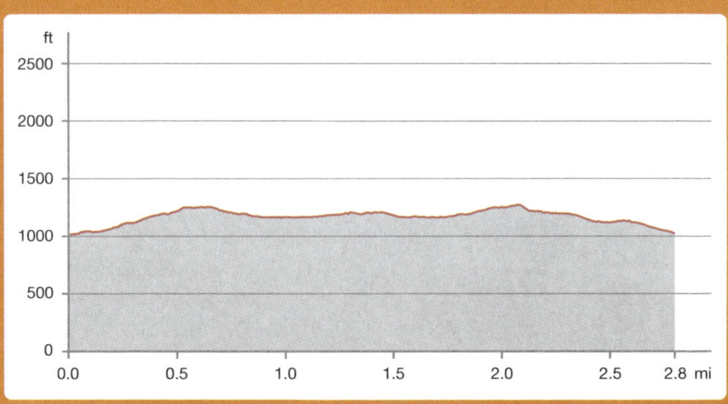

THE POGUE LOOP FROM PROSPER ROAD

CARRIAGE TRAIL LEADING TO A POND

WOODSTOCK, VT

20

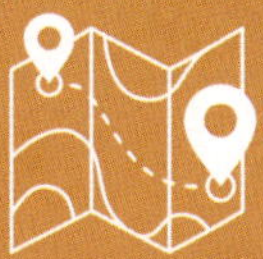

LENGTH
2.8 miles (loop)

TIME & MONEY
1 hour 30 minutes; free

ELEVATION GAIN
358 feet

DIFFICULTY
Moderate

CONDITIONS
Year-round; wide paths

HIGHLIGHTS
14-acre pond, historic park

ESSENTIALS

- **Find the trailhead:** From Central Street in Woodstock, head southwest towards Mechanic Street. After 246 feet, continue on N Park Street for 0.2 miles, where it turns slightly right, becoming Church Street. After 0.3 miles, Church Street turns left and becomes US-4 W/River Street/W Woodstock Road. Continue for 0.9 miles, then turn right onto Prosper Road. Follow it for 1.5 miles, then take a right into the parking lot.
- **Land manager:** National Park Service, 54 Elm Street, Woodstock, VT 05091; (802) 457-3368 nps.gov/mabi/planyourvisit/hiking-trails.htm

WHY YOU'LL LOVE IT

- Wide, gently sloping trails
- National Historic Park
- Shade and a pond

A historic carriage trail loop leads to a smaller loop around The Pogue: a 14-acre pond tucked within the hills of Mount Tom at Vermont's National Historic Park.

Located in charming Woodstock, the Marsh-Billings-Rockefeller National Historic Park shares the story of generations of families working toward conservation near the Green Mountains. George Perkins Marsh grew up on this family farm in the early 1800s. Observations made during his travels, combined with his love of the outdoors, led him to write *Man and Nature*, which became a founding text of the environmental movement.

The farm was later bought by Frederick Billings and his family, who continued managing it with the same commitment to conservation. When Billing's granddaughter Mary and her husband Laurance S. Rockefeller donated the property to the state in 1992, it was turned into a National Historic Park. Visitors can explore the mansion, gardens, working dairy farm, Billings Museum, and 20 miles of carriage trails that crisscross Mount Tom on this pristine property.

Parking for this hike can be found in a large dirt lot on Prosper Road, a six-minute drive from the mansion and visitors center. The trail starts with a gentle ascent on a narrow path before merging with the broader North Ridge Loop after a little over half a mile. From there, it's a relatively level carriage trail to the pond. Turn left to walk clockwise around the water's edge. While dogs (and humans) are not allowed to swim here, you can break the news to them gently during the initial part of your hike.

At slightly over a mile, there's a lovely birch fence followed by a patch of wildflowers. Shortly beyond this point, pass open fields on the left and then meander through a mixed hardwood forest filled with ferns and wildflowers.

After completing the smaller pond loop, return to Prosper Trail and follow the south side of this loop back to the trailhead.

TURN-BY-TURN DIRECTIONS

1. Locate the trailhead on the east side of Prosper Road parking lot.
2. At 0.1 miles, stay left at the unmarked fork. Continue straight on Prosper Trail, ignoring both North Slope Trail, then Middle Pass Trail, on the left.
3. At 0.5 miles, take a left at the unmarked T-junction. As the trail connects with a short section of North Ridge Loop, go right toward The Pogue, then right again as you leave North Ridge Loop, continuing on to the pond.

4. At 0.9 miles, arrive at the pond and go left to follow the lakeside loop clockwise.
5. At 1.1 miles, stay right at the fork near the birch fence. Follow the trail as it circles the pond. Return to the start of the loop, then start the walk back to the trailhead. When reconnecting with Prosper Trail, follow it straight to return on the south side of the main loop towards McKenzie Road.
6. At 2.5 miles, reach the junction with McKenzie Road and take a right towards Prosper Road trailhead. Take a left at the next fork to return to the parking lot.

MASSACHUSETTS

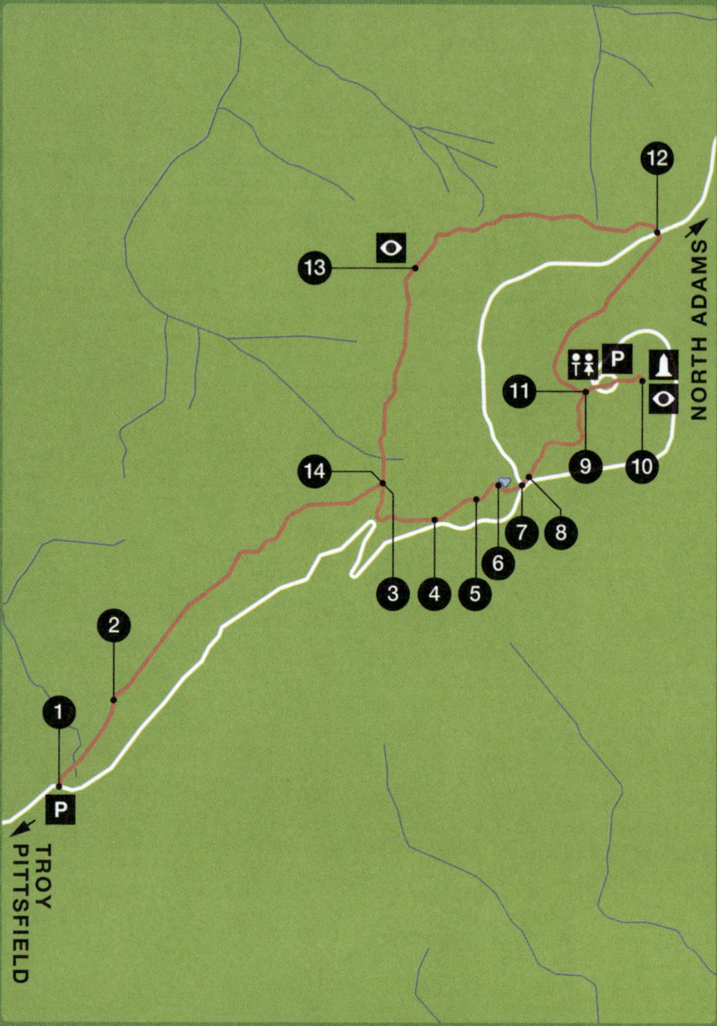

NORTH ADAMS

TROY
PITTSFIELD

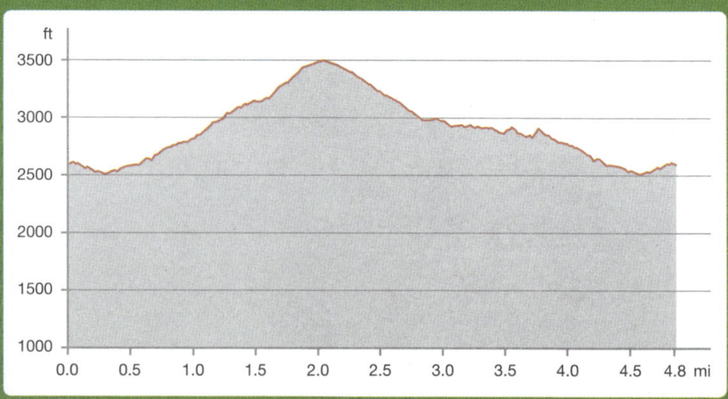

MOUNT GREYLOCK VIA HOPPER TRAIL

CLIMB MASSACHUSETTS'S TALLEST MOUNTAIN

LANESBOROUGH, MA

21

LENGTH

4.8 miles (loop)

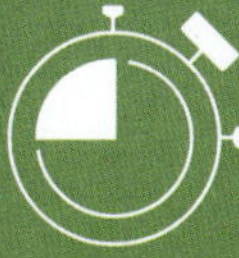

TIME & MONEY

2 hours 15 minutes; free

ELEVATION GAIN

1106 feet

DIFFICULTY

Moderate

CONDITIONS

Road open mid-May to end of October

HIGHLIGHTS

360-degree views, swim spot, shaded trail

ESSENTIALS

- **Find the trailhead:** From Mount Greylock State Reservation Visitor Center, continue heading north on Rockwell Road. The sign for CCC Dynamite Parking, with several spaces, is on your right.
- **Land manager:** Massachusetts Government, 30 Rockwell Road, Lanesborough, MA 01237; (413) 499-4262; mount.greylock@state.ma.us mass.gov/locations/mount-greylock-state-reservation

WHY YOU'LL LOVE IT

- Varied, mostly wide paths
- Rockwell Pond
- Wide-open summit with room to spread out and enjoy the view

Summit Mount Greylock and earn sweeping views into five states and bragging rights for climbing Massachusetts's tallest mountain.

Adams, MA—a charming little New England town in Berkshire County—was settled in 1762 and named after Samuel Adams, one of the Founding Fathers. The town's history is deeply rooted in the American textile industry, which thrived in this area in the 19th century. Just a bit to the west is Mount Greylock—Massachusetts's highest peak at 3491 feet.

Renowned for its unobstructed vistas, the mountain has inspired famous literary giants like Herman Melville, who wrote much of *Moby-Dick* while gazing at its lofty peak. The Veterans War Memorial Tower atop Greylock, built in 1933, stands as a tribute to the state's fallen soldiers and offers panoramic views on clear days.

Starting at CCC Dynamite Trailhead parking area, the path begins across the street along the gravel path of Sperry Road. Entering the woods, Sperry Road soon connects to Hopper Trail, where you begin a gradual ascent. Your pups will love the variety of terrain here, from soft forest floors to rocky outcrops, as well as the cool shade provided by dense trees.

After one mile, Hopper Trail intersects with Overlook Trail, which is where the loop portion begins. The turn-by-turn directions take you counterclockwise to the summit, on a shorter but steeper route.

Once at the top, you'll find the summit area open and spacious, allowing for a relaxing break while you and your pups roam around and take in the scenery. Be sure to stop in Bascom Lodge for a hot chocolate or bakery treat if you're visiting when it's open (Wednesday to Sunday).

We also recommend climbing the 89 steps up the tower (open seasonally). Dogs can't go up the tower, unfortunately, so hike with a friend and take turns checking out the tower and its 360-degree views!

TURN-BY-TURN DIRECTIONS

1. From the parking lot on Rockwell Road, walk across the street to the gravel path with the Sperry Road trail sign to begin the hike.
2. At 0.3 miles, bear right to leave Sperry Road and join Hopper Trail, marked by blue blazes.
3. At 1 mile, at the start of the loop portion of the trail, turn right onto Overlook Trail to begin the counterclockwise hike.
4. At 1.28 miles, bear left at the Summit to AT sign.
5. At 1.38 miles, bear left, away from the road, and walk along the wooden planks.
6. At 1.45 miles, arrive at Rockwell Pond, where the dogs can go for a swim.
7. At 1.5 miles, the trail pops out onto Rockwell Road. Cross the road and walk to the left and enter back into the woods at an Appalachian Trail and Greylock Summit sign.
8. At 1.55 miles, cross Summit Road and enter back into the woods at the Appalachian Trail N and Summit Bascom Lodge sign.
9. At 1.9 miles, cross a paved driveway and start heading toward Veterans War Memorial Tower.
10. At 2 miles, arrive at the tower and Bascom Lodge. After taking in the views, exit back down the way you came in, walking back into the woods.
11. At 2.18 miles, turn right at the Overlook Trail sign and begin your clockwise descent.
12. At 2.63 miles, walk across Notch Road and enter back into the woods, following the Overlook Trail sign.
13. At 3.24 miles, a sign points to the right for an optional vista that's less than 100 feet off the main trail.
14. At 3.73 miles, the loop portion ends at the junction with Hopper Trail (that you took on the way in). Turn right onto Hopper Trail and follow the Sperry Road signs for 1.1 miles back to your car.

ASHFIELD

CONWAY

WILLIAMSBURG
NORTHAMPTON

P Parking | Viewpoint | Waterfall | Bridge | Bench

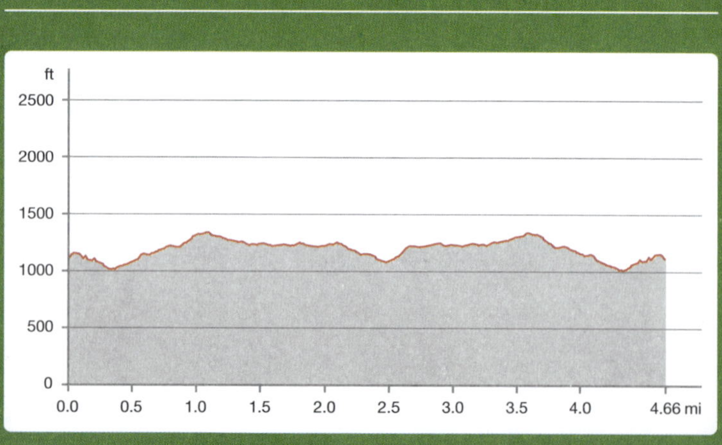

TWO BRIDGES AND CHAPEL FALLS TRAIL

CASCADING WATERFALL AND MEADOW VIEWS

SOUTH ASHFIELD, MA

22

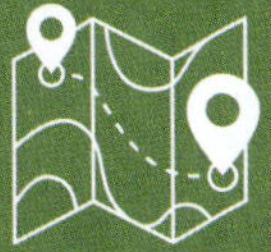

LENGTH
4.66 miles
(in and out)

TIME & MONEY
2 hours 45 minutes;
free

ELEVATION GAIN
761 feet

DIFFICULTY
Moderate

CONDITIONS
Year-round;
soft trail,
mostly shaded

HIGHLIGHTS
Chapel Falls
waterfall,
meadow views

ESSENTIALS

- **Find the trailhead:** From Belding Memorial Library in the center of Ashfield, head northeast on Williamsburg Road. After 2.3 miles, merge onto MA-116 N/Williamsburg Road. After 1.7 miles the trailhead is on your left. Parking is located on both sides of MA-116.

- **Land manager:** The Trustees, 200 High Street, Boston, MA 02110; (617) 542-7696; info@thetrustees.org
thetrustees.org

WHY YOU'LL LOVE IT

- Multiple falls and pools for the dogs
- Wide-open Bullitt Reservation meadow and views
- Streams, bridges and well-marked trails

This scenic trail connects the 173-acre Chapel Brook Reservation to the 265-acre Bullitt Reservation and includes the impressive Chapel Falls and expansive meadow views.

Just 25 minutes northwest of bustling downtown Northampton, the town of Ashfield awaits with several land trusts, state forests and plenty of hiking opportunities.

Two Bridges and Chapel Falls Trail is one of the best hikes for dogs in Ashfield because of its abundance of water, thanks to streams and cascading falls. It's also a gentle hike for the dogs—padded pine paths, wide trails and no big climbs or descents—with a lovely view.

The trail begins in Chapel Brook Reservation and makes a small loop at the end in Bullitt Reservation. Both properties are managed by the Trustees of Reservations in Massachusetts.

Several signs throughout this hike make it easy to follow. Beginning from one of the two parking areas on either side of MA-116/ Williamsburg Road, head over to the eastern side of the road and find the Chapel Brook trailhead and sign.

Start on the blue-blazed trail and head left down along the falls, which are reached after just 0.1 miles. If it's been a long ride in the car, the dogs will appreciate the early arrival at the falls where they can hydrate before the start of the hike. Chapel Falls is a three-tiered waterfall system that cascades a total of 45 feet, with steps guiding your way down.

Cross a wooden bridge over Chapel Brook and continue on the blue trail, following signs for Two Bridges Trail. After 2 miles, pick up the yellow-blazed Pebble Trail to make the small loop around Bullitt Reservation.

There is a bench at the top with great meadow views, where you and your dog can take in the scene and rest before continuing on with the remainder of the hike.

TURN-BY-TURN DIRECTIONS

1. Make your way to the eastern side of MA-116/Williamsburg Road to the large Chapel Brook trailhead and sign.
2. At 0.1 miles, bear left on the blue-blazed trail down to Chapel Falls. The falls will shortly be on your left, with plenty of photo opportunities along the way and water for the dogs.
3. At 0.31 miles, follow the Two Bridges Trail sign and bear left on the blue-blazed trail, crossing a wooden bridge over Chapel Brook.
4. At 0.91 miles, the trail curves around to the left.
5. At 2 miles, follow the Pebble Trail sign and take a left on the yellow-blazed trail.
6. At 2.2 miles, arrive at Bullitt Reservation. Take a rest on the bench at the top of the meadow with a view facing northeast. After taking in the view, continue walking north on Pebble Trail (walk down the meadow) to begin a loop around the meadow.
7. At 2.4 miles, turn right onto the signposted, yellow-blazed Pebble Trail.
8. At 2.7 miles, turn left to get back onto Two Bridges Trail. Follow this blue-blazed trail all the way out, returning to the car the same way you came in.

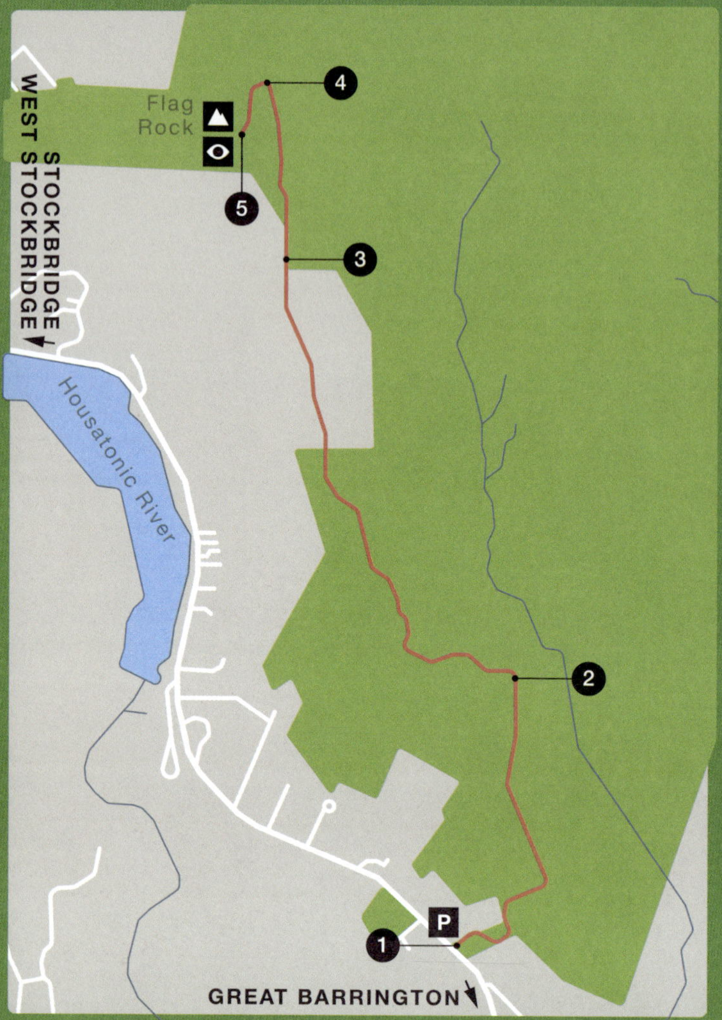

Flag Rock
WEST STOCKBRIDGE
STOCKBRIDGE
Housatonic River
GREAT BARRINGTON
P
1
2
3
4
5

P Parking — Viewpoint — Mountain

ft
2500
2000
1500
1000
500
0
0.0
0.5
1.0
1.5
2.0
2.5
3.0
3.5
3.83 mi

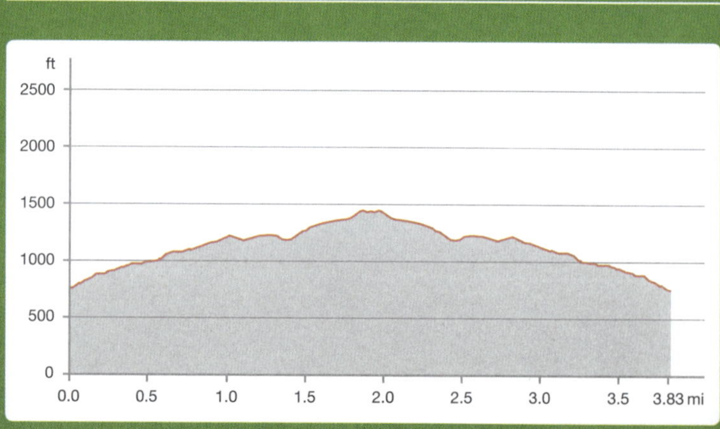

WILLOW'S TRAIL TO FLAG ROCK

IN-AND-OUT PATH WITH DIVERSE ECOSYSTEMS

GREAT BARRINGTON, MA

23

LENGTH
3.83 miles

TIME & MONEY
1 hour 45 minutes; free

ELEVATION GAIN
797 feet

DIFFICULTY
Moderate

CONDITIONS
Year-round; broad trail, evergreen forest

HIGHLIGHTS
West-facing views over Housatonic River Valley

ESSENTIALS

- **Find the trailhead:** From Mason Library at 231 Main Street in Great Barrington, turn right (head north) on Main Street (Route 7). After 0.4 miles, turn right onto State Road (US-7). After 1.9 miles, turn left onto Old Stockbridge Road (Route 183). After 0.5 miles, stay straight as it becomes Park Street N (Route 183). After 1 mile, there's a small pull-off on the right, with room for a few cars, and the trailhead sign.
- **Land manager:** The Trustees, 200 High Street, Boston, MA 02110; (617) 542-7696; info@thetrustees.org thetrustees.org

WHY YOU'LL LOVE IT

- Wide, forested trail with gradual incline
- Rocky outcrops and wide-open views
- Easy to follow trails and signs

Hike the western side of the popular 555-acre Monument Mountain Reservation and enjoy views from Flag Rock across Housatonic River Valley.

Great Barrington, Massachusetts, is a quaint New England town in the heart of the Berkshires with a rich history in manufacturing and culture. Founded in 1761 and known as the birthplace of renowned civil rights leader W.E.B. Du Bois, it has long been a hub for progressive thought and action. Great Barrington has become a popular destination for artists and nature enthusiasts with its museums, historical buildings and lots of nearby hiking. Be sure to check out the numerous cafes and restaurants after your hike!

Flag Rock is located within Monument Mountain Reservation, which is managed by The Trustees of Massachusetts: the nation's first and Massachusetts's largest preservation and conservation nonprofit. Monument Mountain is a very popular hiking spot outside of downtown Great Barrington, but Flag Rock and the trail to get here are lesser known. This allows you to enjoy the area's beauty without the crowds. We only saw a couple other people while hiking, who kindly informed us of a bear up ahead on trail, which we also spotted through the woods.

Starting from a small parking area on Route 183 (Park Street N) on the western side of Monument Mountain, pick up the orange-blazed Willow's Trail, which winds through diverse ecosystems. Hike through areas with evergreen spruce, pine forests, and deciduous trees like oak and maple, with a vibrant underbrush of mountain laurels, hobblebush and ferns.

Walk about 1.9 miles with a gradual incline along Willow's Trail, staying left the whole time and following orange blazes, until an impressive overlook with an American flag set atop a rocky outcrop. This highlight offers hikers and hounds breathtaking westerly and southerly views of Housatonic River Valley and the surrounding Berkshires. From here you will see the rolling Taconic Mountain range along the New York border and even the Catskill Mountains on a clear day.

TURN-BY-TURN DIRECTIONS

1. From the top left corner of the parking lot, find the trailhead with a map and several signs welcoming you to Monument Mountain. Start on the wide dirt path along the orange-blazed trail.
2. At 0.55 miles, turn left at the Willow's Trail sign to join Willow's Trail. Continue following the orange markers.
3. At 1.54 miles, explore the large rocky outcrop on the right.
4. At 1.76 miles, turn left to continue on the orange Willow's Trail.
5. At 1.9 miles, arrive at the top of Flag Rock. After taking in the views, return the way you came.

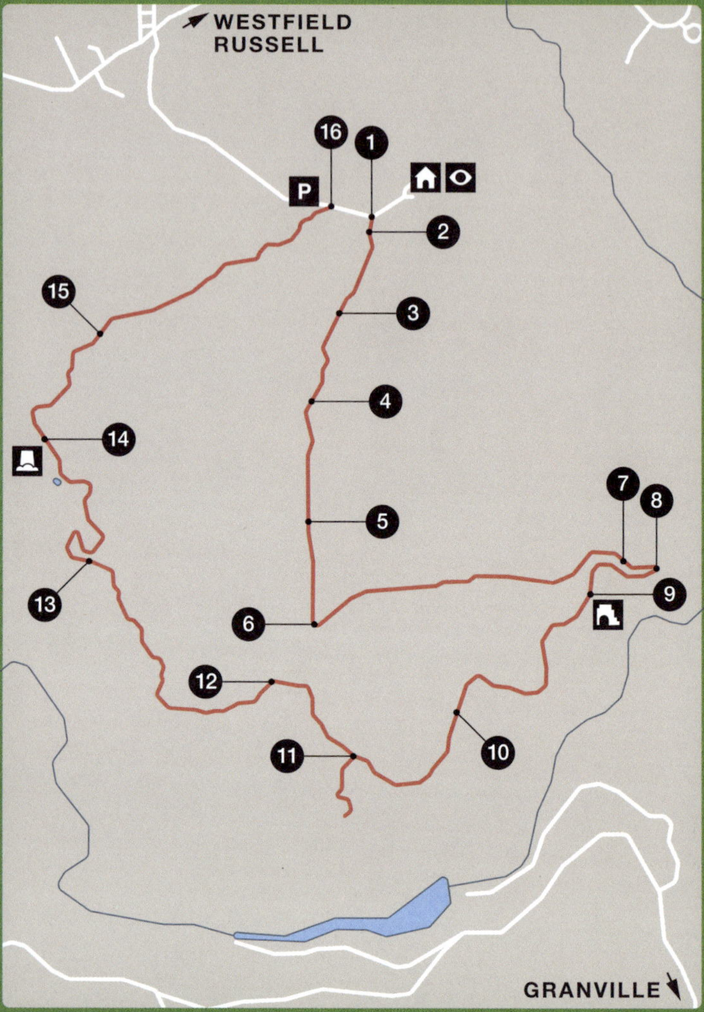

WESTFIELD RUSSELL

GRANVILLE

P Parking · Outdoor Center · Viewpoint · Ruins · Waterfall

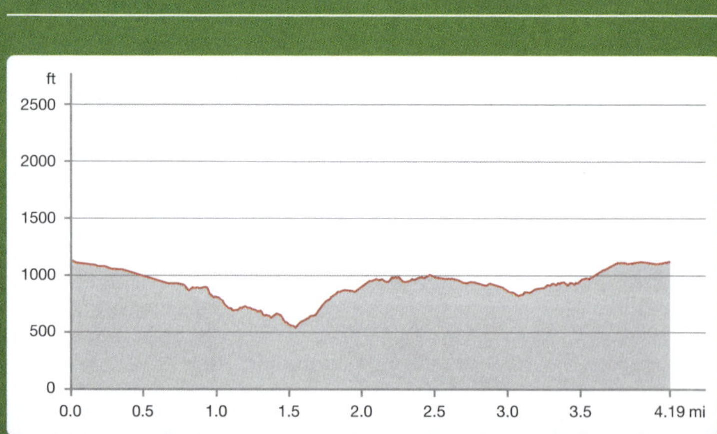

LAUREL LANE TO PITCHER BROOK LOOP

HIKE AT AN EXPANSIVE OUTDOOR CENTER

RUSSELL, MA

24

LENGTH
4.19 miles (loop)

TIME & MONEY
2 hours 15 minutes; free

ELEVATION GAIN
764 feet

DIFFICULTY
Moderate

CONDITIONS
Year-round; wide, forested trails

HIGHLIGHTS
View from AMC Outdoor Center, Pitcher Falls, serene trails

ESSENTIALS

- **Find the trailhead:** From Interstate 90, take exit 41 toward US-202/MA-10/Westfield/Northampton and merge onto MA-10 S/US-202 S/Southampton Road. Turn right on Franklin Street in Westfield and continue onto Russell Street (US-20). Turn left onto Lloyd's Hill Road. Turn right onto Western Avenue and continue onto General Knox Road. Turn left onto S Quarter Road. The parking lot is on your right after about 1.5 miles.

- **Land manager:** Appalachian Mountain Club, 10 City Square, Boston, MA 02129; (603) 466-2727; amclodging@outdoors.org outdoors.org

WHY YOU'LL LOVE IT

- Shaded trails wind under a canopy of trees
- Quieter woods loop
- Visit to the AMC Noble View Outdoor Center

Discover an Appalachian Mountain Club (AMC) Outdoor Center with waterfalls, streams, lodging, and views of Pioneer Valley.

Just 18 minutes (10 miles) west of downtown Westfield, or 24 miles west of Springfield, lies a hiking oasis with over 12 miles of woodland trails to explore. Even the drive to get here, all along the country roads of western MA, feels like an adventure in itself.

During the Great Depression in the 1930s, the AMC Berkshire Chapter wanted to provide members with an affordable way to enjoy the outdoors together. So, the land was purchased and the original buildings repaired. Today, in addition to the trails, there's also lodging, including fully updated cabins and dog-friendly campsites.

This hike within the 360-acre AMC Noble View Outdoor Center gives you a tour of the property's main highlights. While not a big summit, it's a perfect "woods walk" for the dogs, with abandoned farm fields, woodlands, streams, waterfalls, and more to enjoy along the way. The trail also features stone walls, cellar holes and diverse habitats.

At certain points along this quiet, tucked-away trail, I felt comfortable letting the dogs off-leash. We also came across a couple of locals, hiking with their own off-leash dogs, who mentioned they visit this spot often.

Perched about 1100 feet above the Connecticut Valley, AMC Noble View Outdoor Center boasts expansive views of the rolling countryside, nearby towns, and the cities of Westfield and Springfield in the distance. You can walk to the view before or after the hike, as it's located just a couple hundred feet up S Quarter Road beyond the parking lot.

TURN-BY-TURN DIRECTIONS

1. From the parking lot, walk back onto S Quarter Road and head right for about 150 feet until you see the large old barn. Laurel Lane Trail starts in the woods to the barn's right.
2. At 0.1 miles, bear left to start the loop (green blazes on the trees).
3. At 0.22 miles, bear left onto the blue-blazed Laurel Lane Trail.
4. At 0.4 miles, at a set of trail signs, stay straight on the wide path and continue on Laurel Lane Trail. Blue and orange blazes mark the trees here.
5. At 0.58 miles, continue straight, past the 26 sign, on Laurel Lane Trail.
6. At 0.76 miles, at another trail juncture marked by sign 27, take a left onto the white-blazed Country Road Trail to head towards Charcoal Kiln Trail.
7. At 1.42 miles, pass a large glacial erratic rock on the left.
8. At 1.44 miles, at the end of this straight section, take a sharp right at sign 32 to continue on the yellow-blazed Charcoal Kiln Trail.
9. At 1.68 miles, at sign 31, continue straight on Charcoal Kiln Trail; the old charcoal kiln will soon be on the right.
10. At 2.13 miles, at sign 30, continue straight on Charcoal Kiln Trail.
11. At 2.31 miles, at sign 29, continue straight. (There is a detour to the left here onto Lookout Trail, which we took, but unfortunately there was no lookout!)
12. At 2.5 miles, at the junction marked by sign 28, turn left onto the orange-blazed trail. Look out for the cellar hole on the right.
13. At 3.1 miles, at the Pitcher Brook sign, follow the red-blazed trail.
14. At 3.45 miles, Pitcher Brook Falls is on the left. Take the short trail down to the falls so the dogs can have a swim.
15. At 3.8 miles, at sign 17, continue straight, following the sign for the parking lot.
16. At 4.19 miles, arrive back at the parking lot.

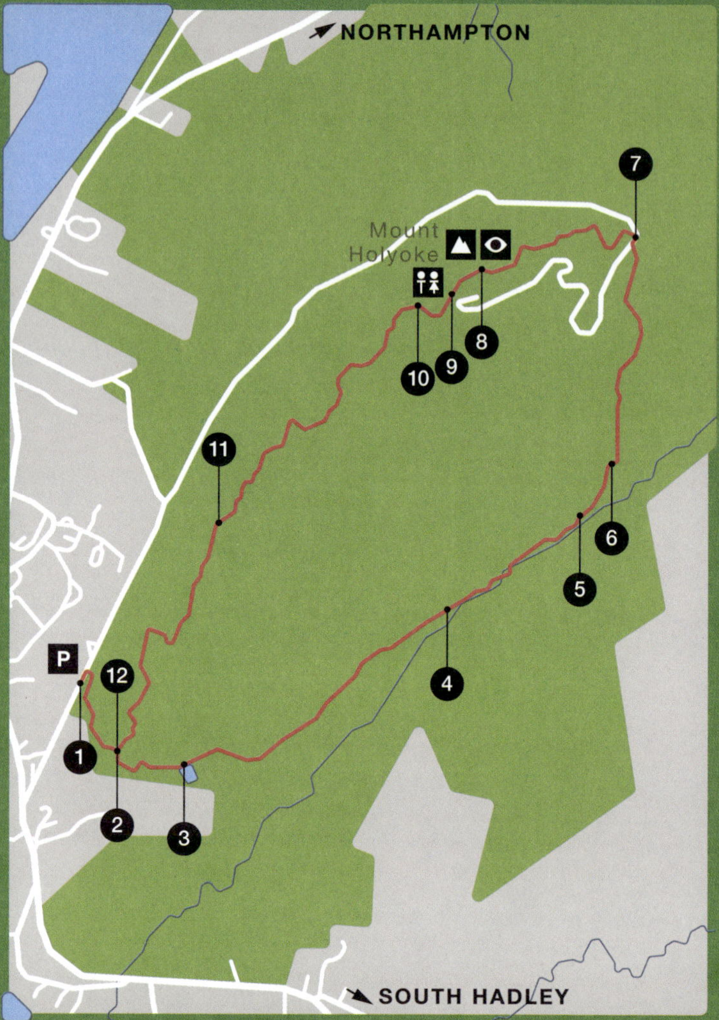

NORTHAMPTON
Mount Holyoke
7
8
9
10
11
6
5
4
P
12
1
2
3
SOUTH HADLEY

P Parking Toilet Mountain Viewpoint

ft
2500
2000
1500
1000
500
0
0.0
0.5
1.0
1.5
2.0
2.5
3.0
3.64 mi

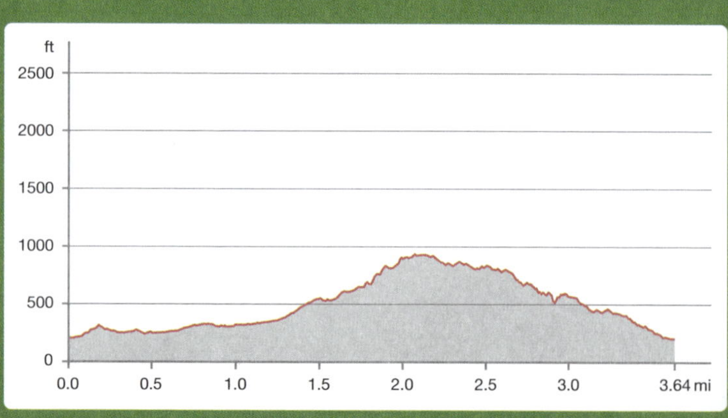

DRY BROOK TRAIL TO NEW ENGLAND TRAIL

SWEEPING VIEWS AND HISTORIC OLD HOTEL

SOUTH HADLEY, MA

25

LENGTH
3.64 miles (loop)

TIME & MONEY
1 hour 50 minutes; free

ELEVATION GAIN
797 feet

DIFFICULTY
Moderate

CONDITIONS
Year-round; wide-open summit

HIGHLIGHTS
Shaded wide path, rocky section near summit

ESSENTIALS

- **Find the trailhead:** From Mount Holyoke College, head north on College Street/Route 116. Turn left onto MA-47/Hadley Street. After 2.8 miles, turn right onto Old Mountain Road. After 0.3 miles, on the right, arrive at a small pull-off for the trailhead, across from residential houses.

- **Land manager:** Department of Conservation and Recreation, 10 Park Plaza, Suite 6620, Boston, MA 02116; (617) 626-1250; mass.parks@mass.gov
mass.gov/locations/skinner-state-park

WHY YOU'LL LOVE IT

- Historic Summit House (Prospect House)
- Streams for dogs
- Quieter than other trails at this popular state park

Hike a less-popular trail in Skinner State Park to the top of Mount Holyoke with picnic tables, room to enjoy the views, and Summit House, an old hotel from 1851.

Skinner State Park is located in the towns of South Hadley and Hadley in the Connecticut River Valley of Massachusetts. At over 800 acres, the park surrounds Mount Holyoke, the westernmost peak of Holyoke Mountain Range.

Summit House, also known as Prospect House, was an old hotel that opened in 1851 with 44 guest rooms and a 200-person dining room. Instead of guests hiking to the top with their luggage, they took a tram to the top. The hotel was so badly damaged by the Great Hurricane of 1938 that part-owner Joseph Skinner offered to donate the hotel and surrounding land to the Commonwealth of Massachusetts—as long as it became a state park bearing his name. Look for the plaque at the top that commemorates Skinner and reminds people that he wanted the park to be "a thing of beauty and a source of joy to the people of the Commonwealth."

This hike is a less popular and quieter loop to the top, but you should note that there's a road leading up too; so, don't be surprised if you're alone on the trail then joined by other guests at the peak. Since the views face west, we went for sunset and got to enjoy the summit and views from the deck of the old hotel all by ourselves; most people had cleared out by then.

With parking for several cars on Mountain Road, walk the loop counterclockwise, starting on Dry Brook Trail which, after half a mile in, starts to run right alongside Dry Brook. After 1.2 miles, the trail bends to the left where the incline leads you up to Skinner State Park Road. Walk directly across the road and pick up the white-blazed New England Trail to the summit of Mount Holyoke and Summit House.

At the top you'll find a spacious area, scattered with picnic tables, to relax and take in the stunning views of rolling hills and Connecticut River Valley below. Walking on the wrap-around deck of Summit House allows for another perspective: You see what attracted people to this hotel over a century ago.

Follow the New England Trail for the last 1.6 miles back down to the car, catching glimpses of the river valley below through the trees as you go. Some spots can be a little steep here, with larger rocks to step down or navigate around. We hiked in October, and the added layer of leaves made it difficult to find good footing on the way down. Sturdy boots are recommended, and hiking poles may be useful, but the dogs had no issue with the terrain.

TURN-BY-TURN DIRECTIONS

1. From the parking area on Mountain Road, go to the New England Scenic Trail Entrance sign and trail kiosk on the eastern side of Mountain Road.
2. After 0.2 miles, bear right to begin the loop counterclockwise, following the sign to Dry Brook Trail marked by red blazes on the trees.
3. At 0.33 miles, pass a large pond on the right and continue straight on Dry Brook Trail.
4. At 1 mile, the trail runs directly beside Dry Brook, where the dogs can get wet if the brook is running.
5. At 1.2 miles, take a left at the intersection with the yellow trail to continue on Dry Brook Trail.
6. At 1.35 miles, the incline begins.
7. At 1.72 miles, cross the paved Skinner State Park Road (cars use this road, so keep dogs and kids close as you approach) to take New England Trail, marked by a sign, with steps leading up into the woods.
8. At 1.97 miles, reach the top of Mount Holyoke, with 180-degree views, and 270-degree views atop Summit House, with views facing west from its wrap-around deck.
9. Walk along the deck of the house, then head west down the flight of stairs into the woods to begin your descent on the white-and-blue-blazed trail.
10. At 2.5 miles, the path splits (the blue, a mountain biking trail, branches off to the right). Bear left to stay on the white-blazed trail.
11. At 2.86 miles, the white-blazed trail curves around to the right.
12. At 3.42 miles, arrive at the intersection with Dry Brook Trail, where you started. Turn right here to head back to your car.

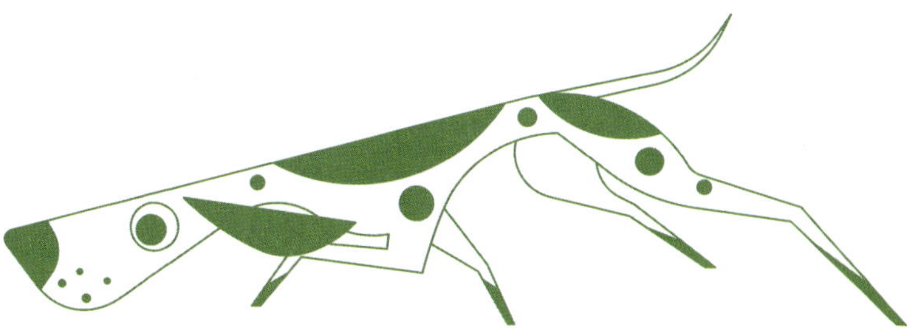

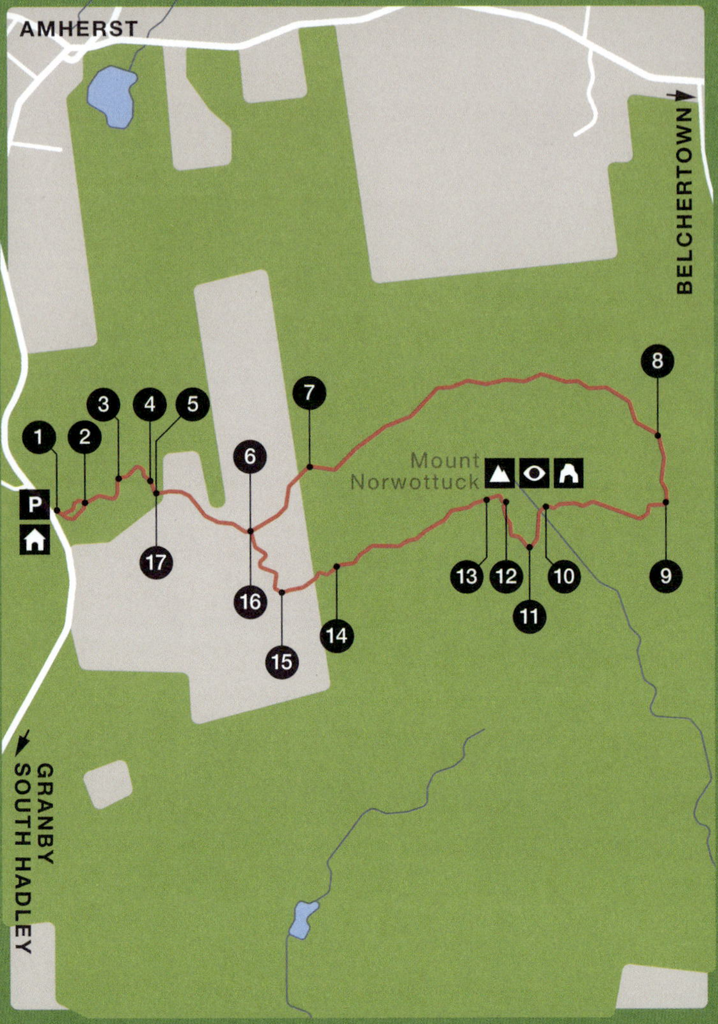

AMHERST
BELCHERTOWN
GRANBY
SOUTH HADLEY
Mount
Norwottuck
P
1
2
3
4
5
6
7
8
9
10
11
12
13
14
15
16
17

P Parking | Visitor Center | Mountain | Viewpoint | Caves

ft
2500
2000
1500
1000
500
0
0.0
0.5
1.0
1.5
2.0
2.5
3.0
3.5
3.88 mi

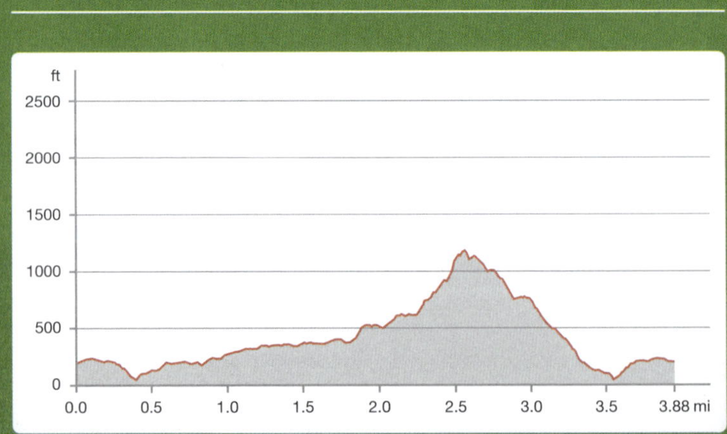

MOUNT NORWOTTUCK LOOP

CAVES AND CLIFF VIEWS

AMHERST, MA

26

LENGTH

3.88 miles (loop)

TIME & MONEY

2 hours; free

ELEVATION GAIN

830 feet

DIFFICULTY

Moderate to strenuous

CONDITIONS

Year-round; short, steep scramble section

HIGHLIGHTS

Many viewing points, caves to explore

ESSENTIALS

- **Find the trailhead:** From Amherst Center, head south on South Pleasant Street for 1.4 miles. Continue on West Street (Route 116) for 3.8 miles, passing through three roundabouts, and the large parking lot for Mount Norwottuck is on your left.
- **Land manager:** Department of Conservation and Recreation, 10 Park Plaza, Suite 6620, Boston, MA 02116; (617) 626-1250; mass.parks@mass.gov
mass.gov

WHY YOU'LL LOVE IT

- Wide-open views to the east and north
- Exploring Horse Caves
- Well-marked trails

Embark on a challenging loop leading to multiple sweeping views over Pioneer Valley and have fun exploring Horse Caves.

Just 10 minutes (five miles) south of Amherst Center and 15 minutes (nine miles) east of Northampton, Mount Norwottuck stands, at 1106 feet, as the highest peak in Holyoke Range. Mount Holyoke Range State Park encompasses 3000 acres and has a seven-mile mountain ridgeline and 30 miles of blazed trails. It's dream hiking land in the southern part of Pioneer Valley.

Mount Norwottuck's name honors the Norwottuck, a subgroup of the Pocomtuc people indigenous to this region. Norwottuck translates to "in the midst of the river," reflecting the people's deep connection to Connecticut River Valley, where this hike is located.

Despite the name Horse Caves, they aren't full caves—just overhanging rock ledges formed from sedimentary layers beneath the summit of Mount Norwottuck.

While this hike is worth it—with its multiple lookouts and the thrill of hiking around Horse Caves—it's important to note that there's a short but steep scramble at the two-mile mark. This rocky section is a few feet high (slanted, not vertical), and the dogs will either have to jump up or navigate around. My six-year-old lab mix, Captain, did it just fine, but our younger lab mix, Bruin, was spooked and needed to be walked around the scramble. If you, too, need to find a path around instead of over, walk to the right, in front of Horse Caves, for about 200 feet. At the end of the ledge, the trail heads up to the left.

From the large parking lot on West Street, head up the stairs, following the orange blazes, to The Notch Visitor Center (open late April through October, 9 a.m. to 4 p.m.), which has restrooms, drinking water, trail maps, and historical information.

Start the loop clockwise. After 2.5 miles, the trail opens up to sweeping views to the east; be careful as you explore along the rocks and ledges. And at 2.55 miles, reach the official summit of Mount Norwottuck, with views to the north.

After the hike, take a short drive over to Atkins Farms Country Market for their award-winning apple cider donuts, breakfast, lunch, or snacks!

TURN-BY-TURN DIRECTIONS

1. From the parking lot, follow the orange blazes that lead up the stairs. Pass the visitor center on the left and enter the forest. Keep following the orange-blazed Robert Frost Trail.
2. At 0.13 miles, bear left to continue along the orange trail.
3. At 0.18 miles, where a trail leads to the left toward power lines, stay on the main path to the right. A trio of blue, white and orange trail markers show the way.
4. At 0.3 miles, at a fork, continue on Robert Frost Trail, marked orange and white.
5. At 0.32 miles, turn left onto the wide gravel path/orange trail.
6. At 0.6 miles, bear left to begin the loop portion of this hike, going clockwise.
7. At 0.75 miles, bear right to stay on the orange-blazed trail and cross a wooden bridge.
8. At 1.65 miles, bear right to stay on the orange trail. This is where the incline begins.
9. At 1.8 miles, bear right to follow Mount Norwottuck and New England Trail on the white trail.
10. At 2.09 miles, arrive at Horse Caves and the short but steep scramble section.
11. At 2.4 miles, bear right on white. Follow the white blazes up to the summit.
12. At 2.5 miles, arrive at the first view with steep cliffs on your right. After taking in this view, get back on the white trail and continue uphill.
13. At 2.55 miles, arrive at the official summit of Mount Norwottuck. After taking in the view, return to the white-blazed trail and start heading downhill.
14. At 3 miles, bear right to continue on the white trail.
15. At 3.15 miles, continue straight on the white trail.
16. At 3.31 miles, at the start of the loop, turn left onto the orange trail to start exiting the way you came in.
17. At 3.55 miles, bear right to stay on the white-and-orange-blazed trail (the same trail you came in on). Stay straight to continue on the orange, white and blue trail, which leads you back to the parking area.

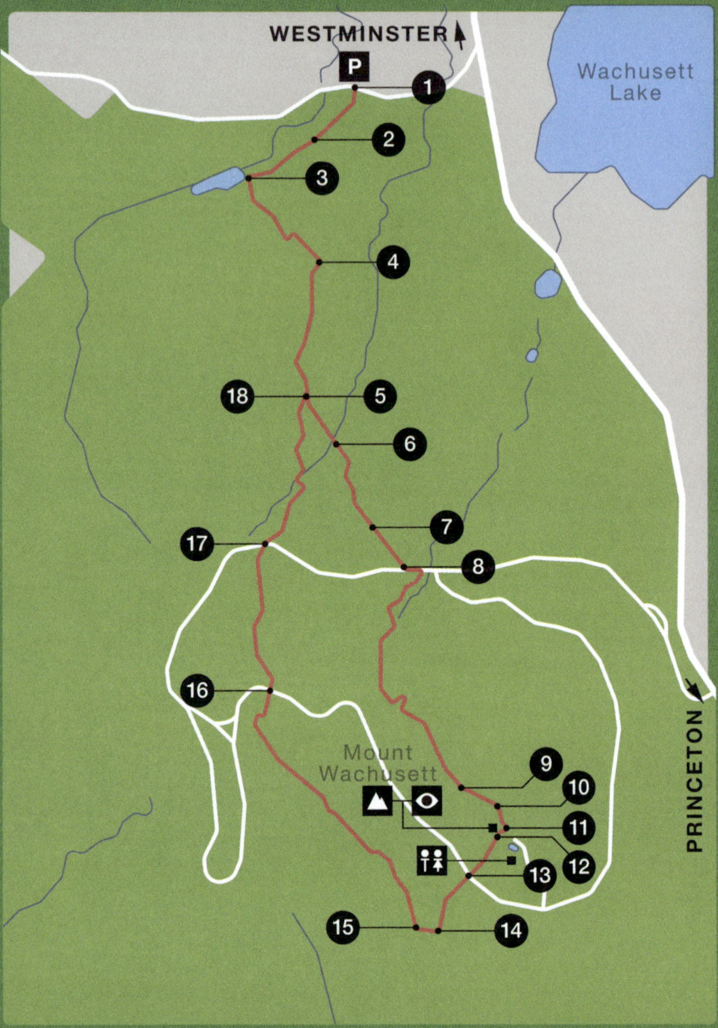

WESTMINSTER

Wachusett Lake

Mount Wachusett

PRINCETON

P Parking

Toilet

Mountain

Viewpoint

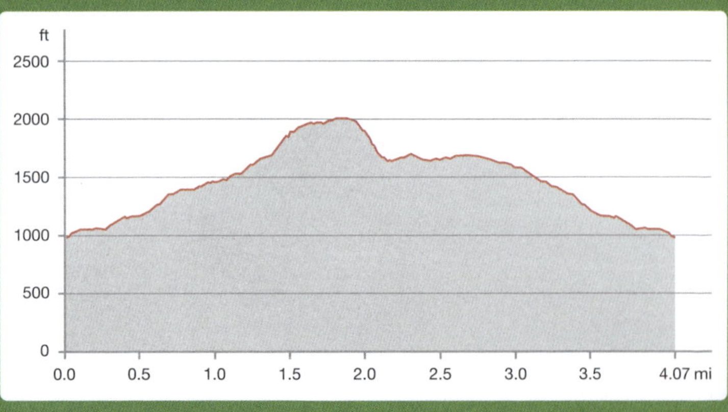

MOUNT WACHUSETT LOOP

MOUNTAIN VIEWS OUTSIDE BOSTON

WESTMINSTER, MA

27

LENGTH
4.07 miles (loop)

TIME & MONEY
2 hours 30 minutes; free

ELEVATION GAIN
1089 feet

DIFFICULTY
Moderate to strenuous

CONDITIONS
Year-round; pine paths, rocky scrambles

HIGHLIGHTS
Forests, Balance Rock, challenging hike

ESSENTIALS

- **Find the trailhead:** From Princeton Public Library, turn left onto Town Hall Drive and after 200 feet turn left onto Mountain Road. After 3.9 miles, Mountain Road becomes Mile Hill Road. After 0.5 miles on Mile Hill Road, turn sharp left onto Bolton Road. Parking is all along the right side of Bolton Road after a third of a mile.
- **Land manager:** Department of Conservation and Recreation, 10 Park Plaza, Suite 6620, Boston, MA 02116; (617) 626-1250; mass.parks@mass.gov
  mass.gov

WHY YOU'LL LOVE IT

- Forested trails with a true mountain feel
- Well-marked, easy-to-follow loop
- Steady incline to summit views

Hike to Massachusetts's tallest mountain east of the Connecticut River. A steady climb up well-marked trails and forested switchbacks leads to summit views, followed by a short scramble section on the way down—perfect for adventurous dogs.

If you're looking for a hike that feels like a real mountain adventure conveniently located in central MA, then this loop at Mount Wachusett delivers. This hike is for adventurous pups who enjoy the challenge of a few scrambles and a multi-hour adventure.

The 3000-acre Wachusett Mountain State Reservation is 20 miles north of Worcester and under 60 miles west of Boston. Even though the hike has over 1000 feet of elevation gain, it's mostly a steady climb with no big jumps for the dogs. But it's worth noting that on the way down there are a few scramble sections where we let go of the leashes to safely navigate with our hands and take our time.

At 2006 feet, the summit of Mount Wachusett is the highest point in Massachusetts east of the Connecticut River. It offers wide-open views of Mount Monadnock and Vermont to the north, Mount Greylock to the west and Boston to the east.

The hike begins from the parking area along the side of Bolton Road. Find the trailhead and Bolton Pond Trail sign on the south side of Bolton Road. After just a quarter of a mile, arrive at Bolton Pond, which provides water and splash time for the dogs before the incline begins.

Stay on Bolton Pond Trail until Balance Rock at 0.5 miles—a fun photo opportunity with the dogs. See if your dog will sit next to the pair of silently stacked boulders left behind by a glacier that moved across the region thousands of years ago. It's a reminder of the glacial activity here that shaped Wachusett and other mountains in New England.

After Balance Rock, bear right to pick up the yellow-blazed Old Indian Trail for the next 1.25 miles to the top. The trail crosses two ski runs, providing scenic views to the east on the way up.

While there may be solitary time with your dog in the woods early on in this hike, be prepared to share the views later, especially during the peak season from end of May to October, when road access brings visitors to just below the summit.

After taking in the views, head back down via the red-blazed Harrington/Mid-State Trail—look for the sign on the southwest side of the summit. This initial descent is fairly steep.

At around 2.16 miles, the red-blazed Harrington Trail meets Semuhenna Trail. From here, turn right onto the light-blue-blazed Semuhenna Trail and follow it until reaching the yellow-blazed Old Indian Trail. Then, turn left and continue on Old Indian Trail to complete this true mountain adventure for you and your pup!

TURN-BY-TURN DIRECTIONS

1. Find the trailhead kiosk on the south side of Bolton Road. Start the hike here on the blue-blazed Bolton Pond Trail.
2. At 0.14 miles, continue straight.
3. At 0.3 miles, arrive at Bolton Pond, where the dogs can swim.
4. At 0.55 miles, turn right on the yellow-blazed Old Indian Trail and arrive at Balance Rock.
5. At 0.8 miles, bear left on yellow, beginning the loop clockwise following Old Indian Trail.
6. At 0.9 miles, walk directly across the first of three consecutive ski fields, continuing to follow the yellow blazes.
7. At 1.07 miles, enter back into the woods. Walk across wooden planks, following the yellow trail.
8. At 1.18 miles, go left onto Up Summit Road. Continue to the Old Indian Trail sign, then turn right onto yellow to re-enter the woods.
9. At 1.74 miles, bear left to stay on the yellow-blazed trail.
10. At 1.8 miles, bear left to stay on yellow, passing a ski lift on the left.
11. At 1.85 miles, arrive at the summit of Mount Wachusett. After taking in the view, find the red-blazed Harrington Trail on the southwest side of the summit to begin the descent.
12. At 1.95 miles, cross Up Summit Road and follow the red-blazed Harrington Trail.
13. At 2.05 miles, cross Up Summit Road to continue on Harrington Trail.
14. At 2.17 miles, at the bottom of the steep section, turn right to stay on the red-blazed Harrington Trail. Look for the yellow Midstate Trail triangle on a tree.
15. At 2.21 miles, turn right onto the light-blue-blazed Semuhenna Trail, following the sign.
16. At 2.75 miles, cross Up Summit Road and continue on the blue-blazed Semuhenna Trail.
17. At 2.98 miles, cross Up Summit Road again and follow the blue-blazed Semuhenna Trail back into the woods.
18. At 3.29 miles, reach the loop's end. Turn left at the Old Indian Trail sign to finish the hike.

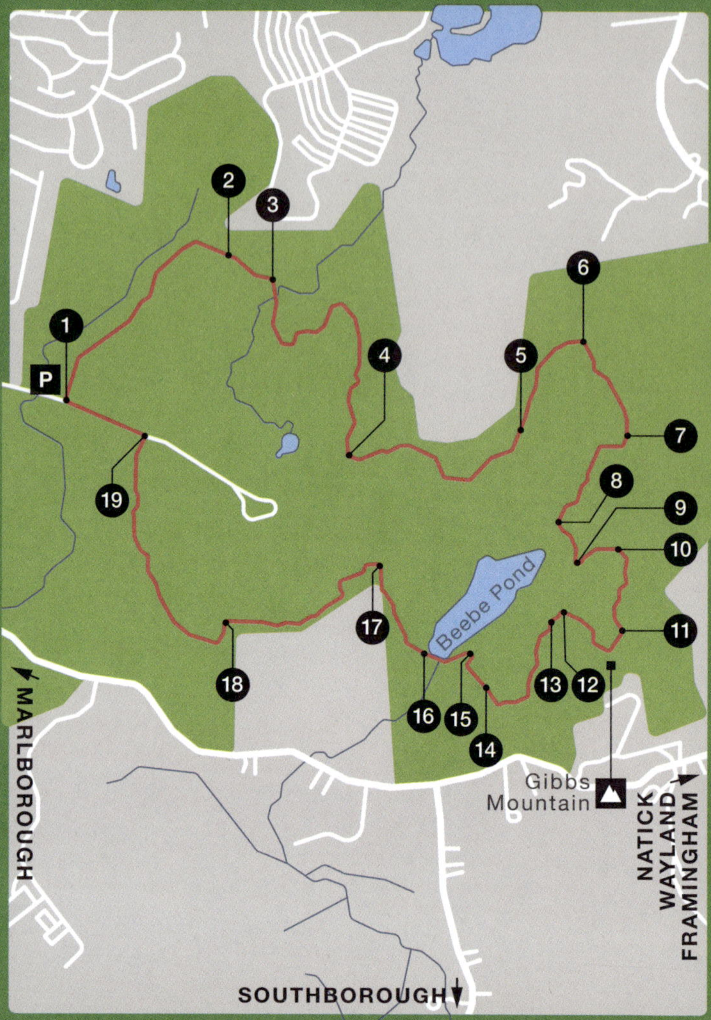

Beebe Pond
Gibbs Mountain
MARLBOROUGH
SOUTHBOROUGH
NATICK
WAYLAND
FRAMINGHAM
P
1
2
3
4
5
6
7
8
9
10
11
12
13
14
15
16
17
18
19

P Parking
Mountain

ft
2500
2000
1500
1000
500
0
0.0
0.5
1.0
1.5
2.0
2.5
3.0
3.5
3.88 mi

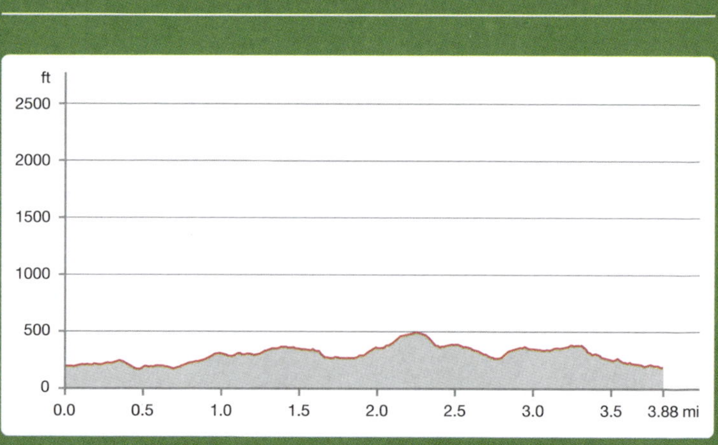

GIBBS MOUNTAIN LOOP

FERN-FILLED FOREST AND QUIET TRAILS

MARLBOROUGH, MA

28

LENGTH
3.88 miles (loop)

TIME & MONEY
1 hour 45 minutes; free

ELEVATION GAIN
446 feet

DIFFICULTY
Moderate

CONDITIONS
Year-round; wide pine paths

HIGHLIGHTS
Remote forest feel, pond for swimming

ESSENTIALS

- **Find the trailhead:** From Marlborough Public Library, turn left on W Main Street, then make a quick right on Granger Boulevard (US-20). After 0.9 miles, turn right onto E Main Street (US-20). After 1.8 miles, turn sharp right onto Farm Road. After 0.5 miles, turn left onto Broadmeadow Street, then after 0.8 miles parking is on the left at 466 Broadmeadow Road.

- **Land manager:** Department of Conservation and Recreation, 10 Park Plaza, Suite 6620, Boston, MA 02116; (617) 626-1250; mass.parks@mass.gov
mass.gov

WHY YOU'LL LOVE IT

- Peaceful pine woods with a soft, dog-friendly trail
- Sea of ferns and tall trees create a lush, calming vibe
- A quiet escape that feels far from the city

Soft pine trails, quiet forest groves and a feeling of escape make Gibbs Mountain Loop Trail in eastern Massachusetts a hidden gem for dogs and their people. Roam in the meadows, smell the pine forests and cool off in the pond!

Located just 30 minutes east of Worcester and 38 minutes west of Boston, within the beautiful 958-acre Callahan State Park, Gibbs Mountain Loop offers a tranquil multi-mile walk through dense pine forest, gently rolling terrain, open meadows, and fern-filled undergrowth.

Though you won't find sweeping summit views here, the peaceful woodland atmosphere and elevated feeling of walking along Gibbs Mountain create a sense of being far away from suburban life without having to drive too far. Dogs will enjoy the chance to swim at picturesque Beebe Pond, and the almost-four-mile loop provides enough challenge without any big inclines, making it a great option for dogs of all ages.

This hike is especially ideal for dogs thanks to its natural pine-needle carpet and wide, forgiving paths. Pine cones scatter the trail and tall trees provide shade as you wind your way up and around the top of Gibbs Mountain.

From the large parking lot off Broadmeadow Road, find the trail kiosk and follow signs for the blue-blazed Backpacker Trail to start the hike. This park is well-marked and well-maintained, but since there are mountain biking trails weaving through there are multiple turns and signs to follow, as noted in the turn-by-turn directions.

Continue following signs for the blue-blazed Backpacker Trail and Backpacker Trail S for about 2.15 miles, then pick up Gibbs Summit Trail. Around 2.45 miles, the trail follows a high path above an open meadow, giving the hike an airy, elevated feel.

At 2.85 miles, the dogs are rewarded with a well-deserved sip and swim at the expansive Beebe Pond. From here, Bear Paw Trail leads back to the parking lot, passing through old stone walls and more open meadows for the dogs to explore.

TURN-BY-TURN DIRECTIONS

1. From the trail kiosk, follow signs for the blue-blazed Backpacker Trail.
2. At 0.4 miles, continue straight following signs for Backpacker Trail.
3. At 0.46 miles, turn right to follow Backpacker Trail South.
4. At 1 mile, turn left to follow Backpacker Trail South.
5. At 1.35 miles, bear right to follow Northeast Loop Trail, leaving the open field and heading back into the woods.
6. At 1.56 miles, turn right into an open field. Walk along the yellow gas-pipeline markers. (If you see the Callahan SP Northeast Loop sign, you've gone too far!)
7. At 1.77 miles, at the bottom of the hill with the pipeline markers, turn right. There are Sudbury Valley Trustees markers on the trees. Follow a narrow trail between ferns.
8. At 1.96 miles, turn left on the blue-blazed trail to follow the Backpacker/Bay Circuits sign, walking along the left side of the pond.
9. At 2.05 miles, turn left at the top of the hill to follow Backpacker Trail South. After 150 feet, bear right to follow Backpacker Trail South.
10. At 2.15 miles, bear right and go uphill following the Gibbs Mountain sign.
11. At 2.28 miles, notice the cairns on the left and bear right.
12. At 2.45 miles, turn left at the bottom of the hill at the F29 Framingham Callahan State Park sign. Follow the Berne Pond via meadow sign.
13. At 2.48 miles, turn left and follow the Berne Meadow sign. After 100 feet, bear right to take the trail along the meadow.
14. At 2.63 miles, bear left on the narrow path at the fork at the bottom of the meadow.
15. At 2.75 miles, at the three-way intersection, turn left to head downhill toward the lake. Continue walking along the left side of the lake.
16. At 2.85 miles, stay straight to follow Bear Paw Trail, where you see an old chimney and leave the lake behind you.
17. At 3 miles, turn left at the Bear Paw Trail sign to walk between the stone walls at the top of the small hill. After 100 feet, continue staying left on the path along the open meadow.
18. At 3.32 miles, turn left following Bear Paw Trail. After 200 feet, keep right and begin heading downhill.
19. At 3.75 miles, turn left onto Broadmeadow Road, which goes back to the parking lot.

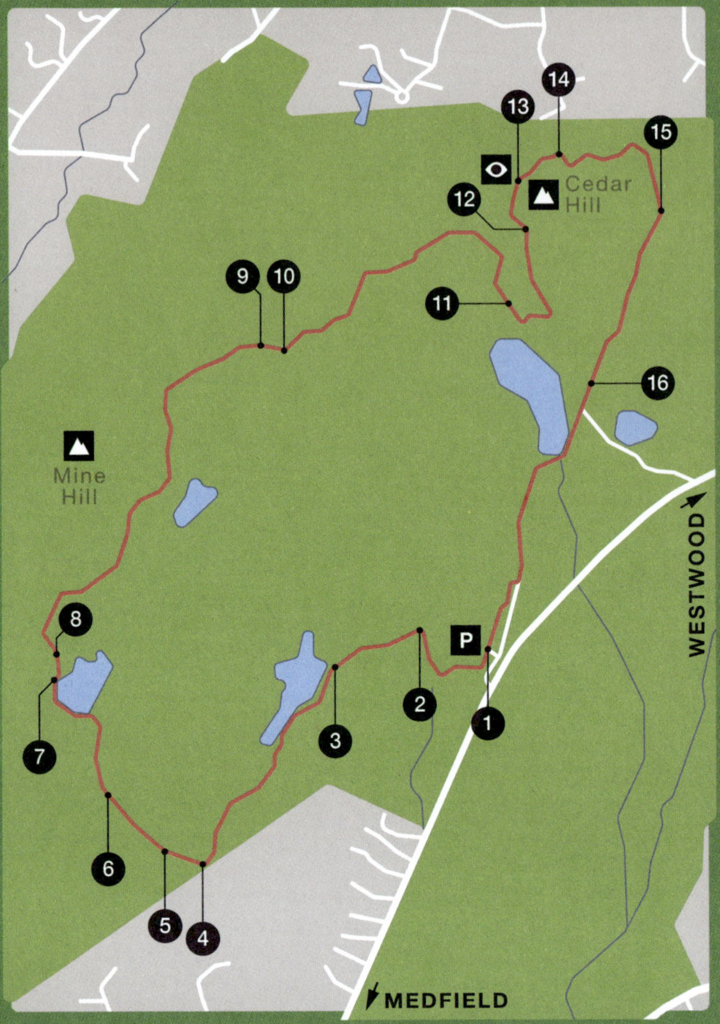

Cedar Hill

Mine Hill

WESTWOOD

MEDFIELD

P Parking

Mountain

Viewpoint

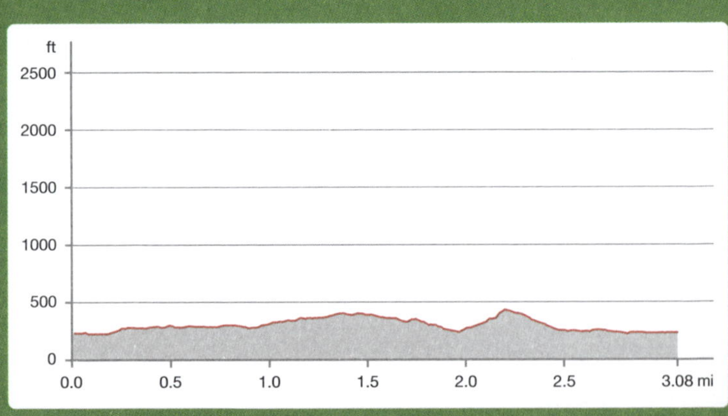

ROCKY WOODS RESERVATION RIDGE TRAIL

APPROVED OFF-LEASH AND LAKESIDE TRAILS

MEDFIELD, MA

29

LENGTH
3.08 miles (loop)

TIME & MONEY
1 hour 30 minutes; $6 parking fee for non-Trustees members

ELEVATION GAIN
384 feet

DIFFICULTY
Easy to moderate

CONDITIONS
Year-round; pine paths, lakeside trails

HIGHLIGHTS
Swimming for dogs, views, easy to navigate, shady

ESSENTIALS

- **Find the trailhead:** From I-95/Route 128, take exit 31B onto Route 109 West. After 5.7 miles, turn right onto Hartford Street. After 0.6 miles, parking (100 cars) is on the left. Or if you're coming from the Route 27 and 109 intersection in Medfield, take Route 109 East and bear left onto Hartford Street. After 0.6 miles, parking is on the left.
- **Land manager:** The Trustees, 200 High Street, Boston, MA 02110; (617) 542-7696; info@thetrustees.org
thetrustees.org

WHY YOU'LL LOVE IT

- Approved off-leash trails
- Diverse scenery: woods, water, and small overlook
- Well-marked, wide paths

This beautifully maintained Trustees property includes peaceful woods, lakefront paths with water access, and well-marked and off-leash trails. The dogs will be grateful for the freedom to roam, splash around and take in the views.

Tucked away in the quiet town of Medfield just 25 miles southwest of Boston, Rocky Woods Reservation is part of the Massachusetts Trustees of Reservations and offers a laid-back adventure for dogs and their humans.

There are over six miles of trails within the reservation's 491 acres, and this loop along the ridge trail shows you all this property has to offer. Many of the trails within this three-mile loop are off-leash, allowing pups to roam free—what a treat! That alone makes it a destination-worthy hike, but when you add in two lakes where the dogs can swim and the scenic view from Cedar Hill, it becomes a must-do.

Park in the large lot off Hartford Street and pay the $6 fee at the self-serve kiosk (credit cards accepted), unless you're a Trustees member, in which case parking is free. From there, the trail loops clockwise.

After 0.3 miles, at Echo Lake, the path is a bit rocky as it hugs the shoreline. If you had a long car ride, now's a great time for the dogs to enjoy the water and take a dip.

Rocky Woods sits at the intersection of two watersheds—the Charles and Neponset rivers—making it home to wetlands that support a thriving mix of wildlife, including frogs, turtles, beavers, and songbirds. Our dogs were very curious about the frogs and tadpoles on the shoreline.

The trail opens into wide, pine-covered paths, where shade is plentiful, as you make your way to Cedar Hill Overlook at 2.1 miles. There's one steep stretch here to get to the view, but it's not technical—just a wide path with a steep incline.

After taking in the view, enjoy the downhill stretch to Chickering Lake at 2.8 miles, where the dogs can have one last swim and sip before arriving back at the parking lot.

What makes this trail especially nice is how easygoing it is—a hike that offers interest and variety without being strenuous or technical. It's well-marked and well cared for. We saw only a few others with their dogs off-leash, yet under control and enjoying the trails.

TURN-BY-TURN DIRECTIONS

1. Start the trail to the left of the kiosk (south side of the parking lot). Follow the yellow blazes and loop sign.
2. At 0.18 miles, turn left, following signs for Echo Pond Trail.
3. At 0.28 miles, stay to the left to walk along the left side of Echo Pond.
4. At 0.6 miles, turn right, following the East/West Trail sign.
5. At 0.63 miles, bear left at the number 16 marked on the tree.
6. At 0.77 miles, bear right, following signs for June Pond Trail.
7. At 0.95 miles, turn right at the fork, following the blue blazes and Ridge Trail sign.
8. At 1 mile, bear left to continue following signs for Ridge Trail.
9. At 1.52 miles, turn right to continue following signs for Ridge Trail.
10. At 1.55 miles, bear left onto the actual Ridge Trail, which is marked with yellow blazes.
11. At 1.95 miles, bear left on the wide gravel path, then stay left again, following the signs for Tower Trail and Cedar Hill Overlook.
12. At 2.17 miles, bear left to follow the sign to Cedar Hill Vista (this is the steep section heading up to Cedar Hill).
13. At 2.25 miles, after taking in the view of Cedar Hill, continue on the wide path as it bends around to the right.
14. At 2.3 miles, turn right, then take a quick left following signs for Cedar Hill Trail.
15. At 2.5 miles, bear right, following signs for Noanet Trail.
16. At 2.72 miles, bear left on the gravel path, then stay to the right (away from the Private Property sign) and follow straight out to the parking lot, stopping for one last swim on the way.

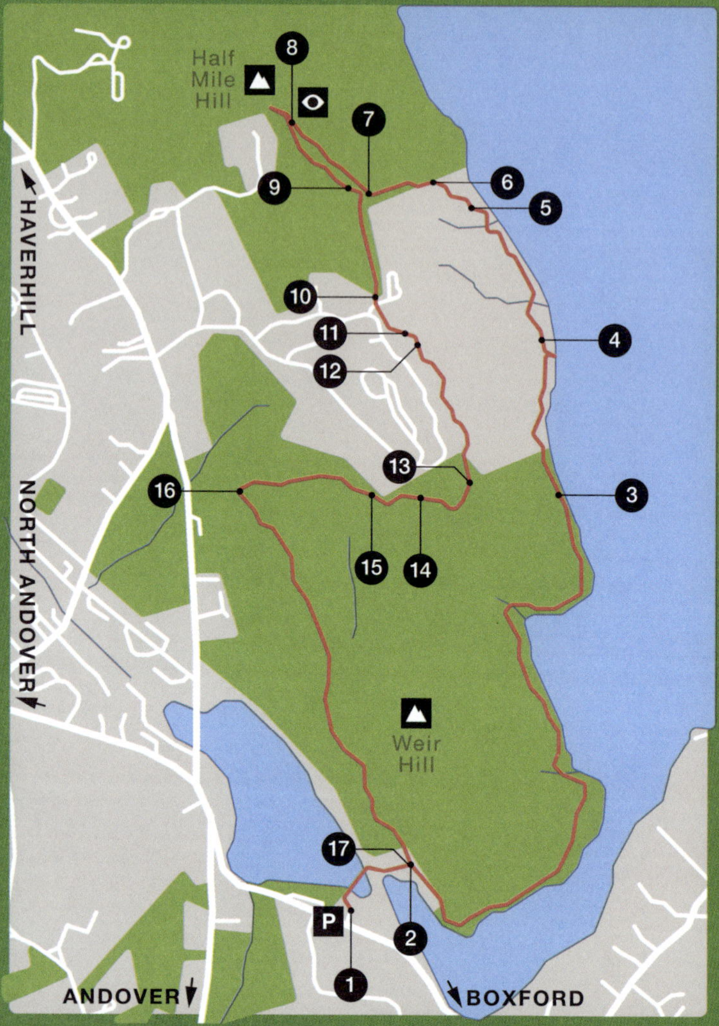

Half
Mile
Hill
Weir
Hill
HAVERHILL
NORTH ANDOVER
ANDOVER
BOXFORD
P
1
2
3
4
5
6
7
8
9
10
11
12
13
14
15
16
17

P Parking
Mountain
Viewpoint

ft
2500
2000
1500
1000
500
0
0.0
0.5
1.0
1.5
2.0
2.5
3.0
3.5
4.0 mi

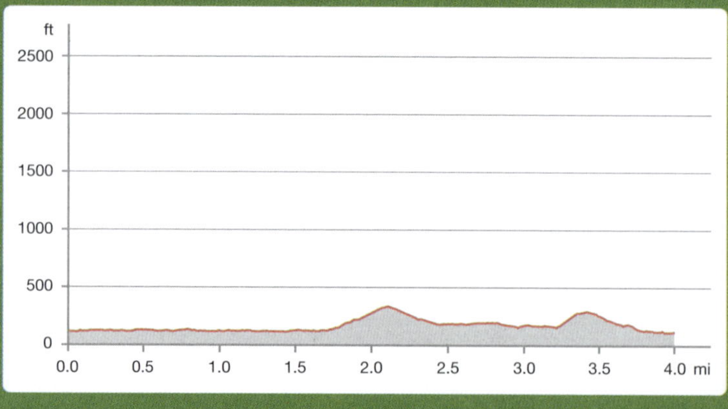

WEIR HILL RESERVATION TRAIL

SCENIC LAKE AND MEADOW VIEWS

NORTH ANDOVER, MA

30

LENGTH

4 miles (loop)

TIME & MONEY

1 hour 45 minutes; free

ELEVATION GAIN

387 feet

DIFFICULTY

Moderate

CONDITIONS

Soft trail, shaded along lake, open meadow views

HIGHLIGHTS

View over Lake Cochichewick, lake trail

ESSENTIALS

- **Find the trailhead:** From North Andover Town Common, head southeast on Massachusetts Avenue for one tenth of a mile. Enter the roundabout and take the third exit onto Great Pond Road. After 0.5 miles turn left onto Fox Hill Road, then right onto Pleasant Street, where you'll see the parking lot on your left after 0.04 miles.

- **Land manager:** The Trustees, 200 High Street, Boston, MA 02110; (617) 542-7696; info@thetrustees.org thetrustees.org

WHY YOU'LL LOVE IT

- Mostly wide paths
- Trails along water with lake views
- Wide-open meadow with views

Explore the pristine Weir Hill Reservation on a four-mile trail through diverse habitats. Enjoy the soft trails and views of Lake Cochichewick and Merrimack Valley from an open meadow.

Just 28 miles north of Boston is the town of North Andover. Established in 1646, it's one of the oldest towns in the state. Originally part of the town of Andover, North Andover was granted its independence in 1855.

North Andover has a picturesque New England downtown center alongside the grounds of the prestigious Andover and Exeter Phillips Academy schools. Minutes from downtown is a local treasure—Weir Hill Reservation, a 500-acre scenic conservation area with rolling hills and lakefront trails. The trail highlight is the view from Half Mile Hill's summit, rising 305 feet above wide-open grassy meadows, offering views of Lake Cochichewick and the surrounding Merrimack Valley.

Weir Hill Reservation is owned and cared for by The Trustees of Reservations. According to their website, Weir Hill, before being settled by Europeans, was likely a site of activity for Indigenous people. A 1968 archaeological survey found evidence of a campsite at the southeast end of the hill. It's believed that Indigenous groups burned parts of the hill, to make it better for hunting, and used underwater fish weirs. These woven fences, held up by stakes, caught alewives in Cochichewick Brook before the fish could reach Lake Cochichewick to lay their eggs. The reservation is named after these fish weirs.

This loop trail begins at the parking area along Pleasant Street. The path quickly guides you over a dam spanning Stevens Pond, beneath a beautiful, old, stone, arched railway bridge and into the forest. Going clockwise around the loop, the trail winds its way all along Lake Cochichewick, providing wide-open views of the lake at several points.

After the flat walk along the lake, there's a brief uphill which leads to the spectacular views atop Half Mile Hill.

We visited on a Saturday and ran into several happy hikers here with their dogs. Many were locals who visit almost every day, and almost all had their dogs off-leash on the open meadow and along the lake. We were surprised how dog-friendly this trail was!

TURN-BY-TURN DIRECTIONS

1. From the parking lot, find the start of the trail in the northern corner of the lot. Take a right at the fence with the Positively Dogs sign and walk toward and through the tunnel.
2. At 0.13 miles, the trail kiosk marks the start. Take a right to begin the loop here. Walk along the water with Lake Cochichewick on your right.
3. At 1.17 miles, at the Reservation Boundary sign, continue straight along the trail by the water.
4. At 1.45 miles, stay right and continue walking along the water's edge.
5. At 1.7 miles, continue straight, keeping the water on your right.
6. At 1.8 miles, turn left at the stone wall and start walking uphill.
7. At 1.9 miles, arrive at the open meadow and turn right to start walking up to the top of the hill.
8. At 2.1 miles, at the top of Half Mile Hill, enjoy the views of Lake Cochichewick from the lookout.
9. Afterwards, make your way down the meadow using the trail you just came up. Turn right at the bottom to walk on the narrow path, which is at about the 2.3-mile mark.
10. At 2.48 miles, cross a sidewalk area and find the gravel path with the Joyce's Trail sign. You'll be walking behind a condo area.
11. At 2.52 miles, bear right on the path behind the bench.
12. At 2.67 miles, at a fenced-in garden area, continue along the path behind the garden.
13. At 2.8 miles, bear right to walk on the yellow-blazed trail. Yellow circles are on the trees.
14. At 2.88 miles, bear right to continue on the yellow trail.
15. At 2.97 miles, continue straight on the yellow trail.
16. At 3.18 miles, turn left and start going uphill along the yellow trail.
17. At 3.81 miles, arrive back at the trail kiosk where you started. Turn right to exit the way you came in.

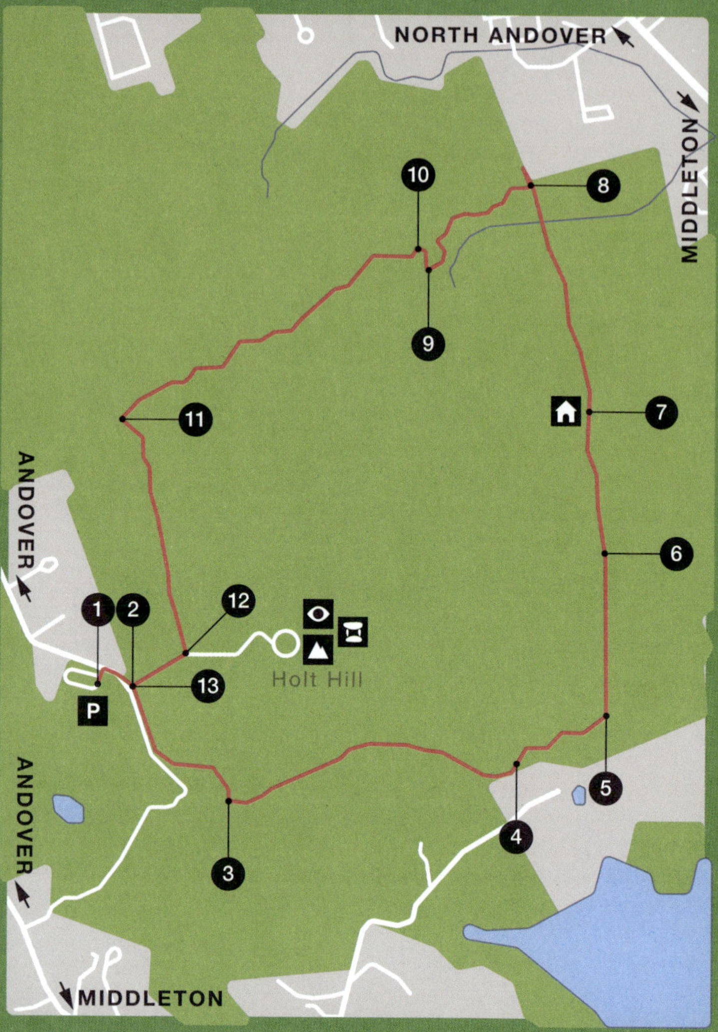

NORTH ANDOVER
MIDDLETON
ANDOVER
ANDOVER
MIDDLETON
Holt Hill
1
2
3
4
5
6
7
8
9
10
11
12
13
P

P Parking ▲ Mountain Viewpoint Solstice Stones Kiosk

ft
2500
2000
1500
1000
500
0
0.0
0.5
1.0
1.5
2.0
2.5
2.9 mi

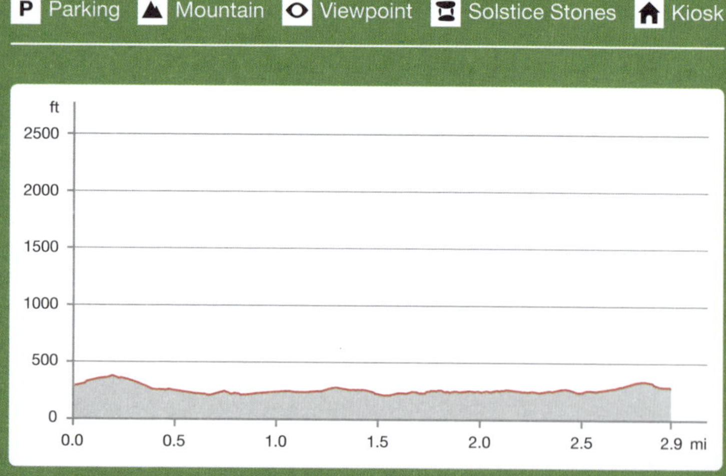

OLD PROSPECT ROAD TO WARD TRAIL LOOP

MEADOW VIEWS AND BOSTON SKYLINE

ANDOVER, MA

31

LENGTH

2.9 miles (loop)

TIME & MONEY

1 hour 14 minutes; $6 per vehicle (cards accepted)

ELEVATION GAIN

278 feet

DIFFICULTY

Moderate

CONDITIONS

Soft trail, mostly shaded in oak–pine woodlands

HIGHLIGHTS

Farm fields, rolling meadows, Boston skyline

ESSENTIALS

- **Find the trailhead:** From Memorial Hall Library, turn left toward Pearson Street and make a quick right onto Pearson Street. After 170 feet, turn right onto N Main Street (Route 28). After 0.9 miles, turn left onto Salem Street and go for 0.7 miles, then turn left onto Prospect Road. After 0.6 miles on Prospect Road, arrive at 65 Prospect Road. There is a large Ward Reservation parking lot on the right.

- **Land manager:** The Trustees, 200 High Street, Boston, MA 02110; (617) 542-7696; info@thetrustees.org
thetrustees.org

WHY YOU'LL LOVE IT

- Wide paths on old logging roads
- Holt Hill, highest point in Essex County
- Wide-open meadow with Boston-skyline views

Explore the trails of Ward Reservation, which features views atop an open meadow, a quaking bog and large beaver wetlands.

Just 24 miles north of Boston, Andover has a rich colonial history. Founded in 1646, it played a role in the abolitionist movement, hosting prominent figures like Frederick Douglass.

A natural gem in Andover is Ward Reservation, featuring 729 acres of woodlands, wetlands and sprawling meadows. A highlight of this stunning property is Holt Hill, the highest point in Essex County at 420 feet, which offers incredible 360-degree views, including toward the Boston skyline.

Managed by The Trustees of Reservations, strolling this sprawling property makes for an enjoyable outing for you and your pup. The Solstice Stones at the top of Holt Hill offer a unique landmark for photos with your pets and a beautiful place to rest and bask in the peaceful surroundings.

Beginning from the spacious parking area off of Prospect Road, head into the woods, picking up the red trail on Old Prospect Road, and take the loop counterclockwise. You'll encounter a small hill that quickly pays off with views facing southeast toward Boston.

The red trail loops around back to the beginning, where you have the option of walking up the paved driveway to Holt Hill to see the Solstice Stones before returning to the parking lot.

To Grassland Trails
Old Prospect

TURN-BY-TURN DIRECTIONS

1. Walk out of the entrance parking lot and turn right to walk onto Prospect Road for just a couple hundred feet to find the start of the trailhead and begin on the red trail.
2. Bear right on Rachel's Trail to begin the red trail loop going counterclockwise.
3. At 0.3 miles, Rachel's Trail becomes Old Prospect Road Trail. Stay straight on the red Old Prospect Road Trail.
4. At 0.78 miles, go straight to stay on the red trail.
5. At 0.85 miles, turn left onto the blue and red circle trail that is Old Chestnut Street.
6. At 1.1 miles, at the Old Chestnut Street sign, continue straight on the red trail.
7. At 1.26 miles, at the kiosk with a map, continue straight on the red trail.
8. At 1.6 miles, turn left onto Judy Family Trail, leaving the red trail.
9. At 1.83 miles, at the sign, take a right onto Ward Trail, leaving Judy Family Trail.
10. At 1.87 miles, take a left to continue on the red-circle-marked Ward Trail.
11. At 2.4 miles, turn left to continue on Ward Trail.
12. At 2.72 miles, walk up a small set of wooden stairs and then turn right onto the paved driveway. You are now on your way back to the parking lot. (If you'd like to see the Solstice Stones at the top of Holt Hill, take a detour here and go left up the paved driveway to Holt Hill, then back down to this spot.)
13. At 2.8 miles, turn right onto Prospect Road, where you started, and return to the parking lot.

15
14
12
13
10
11
9
16
19
20
21
Pearce Lake
8
17
22
23
Silver Lake
18
7
WAKEFIELD
LYNNFIELD, SAUGUS
6
Breakheart Hill
5
4
2
1
3
SAUGUS
LYNNFIELD
P Parking
Viewpoint
Toilet
Mountain
Bridge
ft
2500
2000
1500
1000
500
0
0.0
0.5
1.0
1.5
2.0
2.5
3.0
3.5
3.71 mi

BREAKHEART RESERVATION LOOP

BOSTON VIEWS AND LAKESIDE SERENITY

SAUGUS, MA

32

LENGTH

3.71 miles (loop)

TIME & MONEY

1 hour 48 minutes; free

ELEVATION GAIN

525 feet

DIFFICULTY

Moderate

CONDITIONS

Year-round; pine paths, small rocky scrambles

HIGHLIGHTS

Views, lakes and just enough challenge

ESSENTIALS

- **Find the trailhead:** From Saugus Public Library, head south on Central Street and after 151 feet take the first exit onto Main Street at the traffic circle. After 1.2 miles, turn right onto Forest Street. After 0.7 miles, turn left to stay on Forest Street and after 0.1 miles the destination, 177 Forest Street, is on your right.

- **Land manager:** Department of Conservation and Recreation, 10 Park Plaza, Suite 6620, Boston, MA 02116; (617) 626-1250; mass.parks@mass.gov
mass.gov

WHY YOU'LL LOVE IT

- Diverse trails and terrain, from rocky to padded pine
- Lake access for dogs and shade in second half
- Park-like setting in popular reservation on quiet trails

Exposed ridgeline views, a park-like setting and lakeside trails make this loop at Breakheart Reservation a scenic and varied hike right outside Boston.

Located in eastern Massachusetts, just 12 miles and under 20 minutes north of Boston, lies a perfect dog-friendly hike that offers a little bit of everything: ridge views, rocky terrain, pine paths, and a peaceful lakeside section.

Hiking all over New England, I was very impressed with the 652-acre Breakheart Reservation, which is managed by the MA Department of Conservation and Recreation. It offers a surprisingly peaceful escape just outside the city, with quiet paths through a hardwood forest, two freshwater lakes and multiple scenic ridge tops with views of Boston and the surrounding countryside.

Pulling into the crowded lot, you may wonder how it could be a quiet experience—especially on a weekend. Don't be discouraged! With over 18 miles of trails, it's easy to find solitude by sticking to the wooded loops instead of the paved paths that hug the lakes.

Parking is along Forest Road or in the small lot at the Breakheart Visitor Center. The visitor center is open Wed–Sun, 9 a.m. to 3:30 p.m., with bathrooms, vending machines, a fireplace room, and a water-filling station.

Start the hike on the paved road west of the visitor center between the playground and the brick garage building. The first part is all about the ridge, following the red-blazed Ridge Trail. There's not much shade on this section, so pack water for both you and the dogs. Expect small scrambles and a few ups and downs on your way to Castle Rock, but you won't need to drop the leash or use your hands.

After the view at Castle Rock, the trail begins to wind its way downward toward the lakes, leaving Ridge Trail and picking up Spruce Trail. You and your dog will appreciate the change to softer pine-needle trails and the cool, shaded respite after the ridge.

Streams and multiple opportunities for lake views and doggy dips (no swimming allowed for people) await on the second part of the hike as the trail makes its way along Pearce Lake, followed by Silver Lake. The trail around the lakes can be a little confusing to follow, but at 2.5 miles pick up the blue trail that hugs the southern portion of Pearce Lake, then cross to the north side of Silver Lake (see Upper Pond Trail sign). If you ever find yourself on a paved path, you can simply follow it back to the parking lot where you started.

Otherwise, soak in the shade and lakeside scenery in the second half of this hike, then stay on the blue trail to return to the lot. If your pup needs to burn off a little extra energy before or after the hike, head to The Barking Lot, a small off-leash fenced area located at the 177 Forest Street parking lot.

TURN-BY-TURN DIRECTIONS

1. Start on the paved road west of the visitor center between the playground and the brick garage building.
2. After about 100 feet or .05 miles, turn left on the red-blazed Ridge Trail.
3. At 0.43 miles, continue straight on red, following Ridge Trail. Continue following red up and over Ash Hill.
4. At 0.64 miles, continue straight on Ridge Trail.
5. At 0.73 miles, turn right to continue following the red-blazed trail.
6. At 1.08 miles, follow Ridge Trail as it bends to the left.
7. At 1.48 miles, keep left on the red trail. (You'll see red and white blazes to the right.)
8. At 1.67 miles, take a left on Castle Rock Trail for a short detour up to the Castle Rock view.
9. At 1.72 miles, on top of Castle Rock, take in the view then return down to the red trail the same way you came up. Continue straight on red.
10. At 1.96 miles, turn right following the red-and-purple-blazed Spruce Trail.
11. At 2.07 miles, take a left onto the paved road (Hemlock Road).
12. At 2.1 miles, turn right off the paved road following the white-blazed trail back into the woods.
13. At 2.16 miles, turn left on the yellow-and-purple-blazed trail.
14. At 2.22 miles, turn right, crossing the plank bridge. Soon, white blazes mark the trees.
15. At 2.30 miles, turn right and continue following the purple-blazed trail.
16. At 2.58 miles, after crossing the wooden bridge on the right over Pearce Lake, keep left on the blue trail.
17. At 2.78 miles, bear left on blue, continuing on the trail that hugs the lake. (If you arrive on the paved road, turn back around to get on the trail that stays along the right side of the lake.)
18. At 2.85 miles, stay to the left to continue on the path beside the lake.
19. At 3.03 miles, come to a large, exposed rock with the lake on the left. The dogs can swim or get a drink. Then take a sharp right uphill to continue on the blue trail, which rises just above the lake.
20. At 3.10 miles, continue straight up the stone steps and follow the blue-blazed trial.
21. At 3.17 miles, turn left onto the blue trail at the Upper Pond Trail sign. The water is on your right. Continue on the blue trail as it runs along the left of Silver Lake.
22. At 3.42 miles, turn left to cross the paved path, then continue straight on the gravel path following signs for Breakheart Hill Trail.
23. At 3.55 miles, either continue to stay straight on the blue-blazed gravel path, which leads all the way back to the parking lot, or take a detour to the right to check out the view of Breakheart Hill.

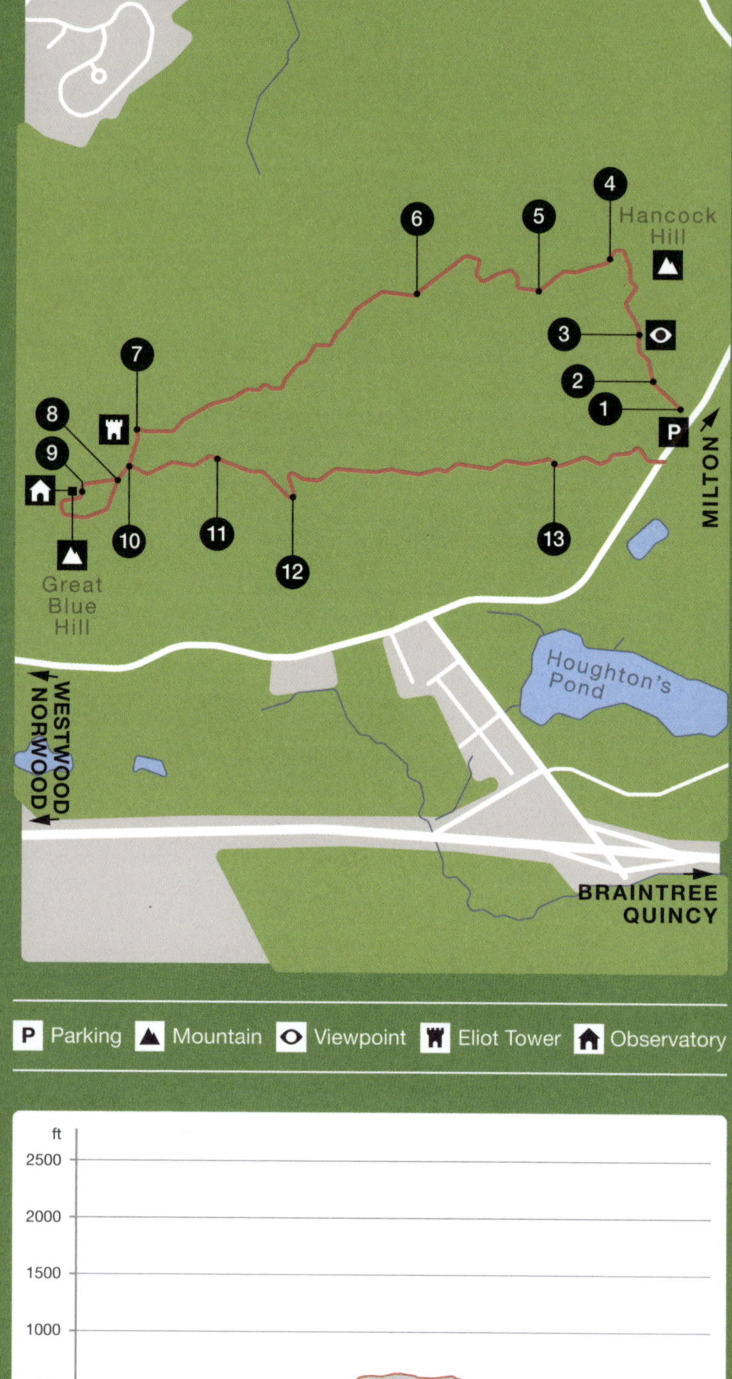

4
Hancock Hill
5
6
3
2
1
P
MILTON
7
8
9
10
11
12
13
Great Blue Hill
Houghton's Pond
WESTWOOD
NORWOOD
BRAINTREE
QUINCY
P Parking
Mountain
Viewpoint
Eliot Tower
Observatory
ft
2500
2000
1500
1000
500
0
0.0
0.5
1.0
1.5
2.0
2.5
3.07 mi

GREAT BLUE HILL VIA SKYLINE TRAIL

TOWER VIEWS OUTSIDE BOSTON

MILTON, MA

33

LENGTH
3.07 miles (loop)

TIME & MONEY
2 hours; free

ELEVATION GAIN
812 feet

DIFFICULTY
Moderate to strenuous

CONDITIONS
Year-round; rocky scrambles

HIGHLIGHTS
Multiple viewing points, challenging hike

ESSENTIALS

- **Find the trailhead:** From Milton Public Library, turn right onto Edge Hill Road, and after 0.8 miles continue on Pleasant Street. After 0.7 miles, turn right onto Reedsdale Road. After 0.1 miles, turn left onto Randolph Avenue (Route 28). After 1.7 miles, turn right onto Chickatawbut Road. After 1.2 miles, turn left onto Hillside Street. Parking is on the left after 0.4 miles.

- **Land manager:** Department of Conservation and Recreation, 10 Park Plaza, Suite 6620, Boston, MA 02116; (617) 626-1250; mass.parks@mass.gov
mass.gov

WHY YOU'LL LOVE IT

- Steep, rugged trails for high-energy dogs
- Panoramic views from Eliot Tower
- Varied landscapes across multiple scenic summits

Challenge yourself and your dog with this short but mighty hike just south of Boston, complete with steep scrambles and sweeping views from multiple hilltops and the historic Eliot Tower. A great test run for some of the bigger mountain hikes in this book.

Located just 12 miles south of Boston, Skyline Trail is part of the 7000-acre Blue Hills Reservation—the largest park, and one of the oldest, in metropolitan Boston. This hike offers a mountain-like climb while still being close to the city.

The reservation is home to towering eastern white pines, oaks and hickories—many of them well over a century old. On this hike, you'll find multiple hilltop views, lots of elevation change and 360-degree views from the historic stone Great Blue Hill Observation Tower, also known as Eliot Tower.

Though the distance is short—just under three miles—don't be fooled! It packs in a solid workout, with rocky ascents and technical scrambles that make it a fun and challenging hike for active dogs and humans alike.

Several times on the scramble sections, we had to drop the leash to use our hands to navigate up or down, and saw others do the same. According to a local hiker we met along the way, about 90 percent of dogs on this trail are off-leash, and most owners are friendly and respectful.

This hike is an excellent trail to build confidence and stamina before tackling some of the more demanding hikes in this book, especially those in New Hampshire's White Mountains. Another challenge to keep in mind is the limited parking: We were there on a rainy Saturday and found a spot, but there's room for less than 10 cars. The website notes to expect heavy use on weekends.

Begin at Houghton's Pond main parking area along Hillside Street right across from the MA State Police station and DCR State Parks South Office. Carefully cross Hillside Street, heading north on the crosswalk, following the blue-blazed N Skyline sign.

Once across, find the trailhead 200 feet up the driveway and to the left of the DCR building. Begin the loop counterclockwise, following the blue blazes and signs for Skyline Trail, which you'll stay on for most of this loop.

From the start, the trail climbs quickly up to Hancock Hill (509 feet) and Hemenway Hill (473 feet), where rewarding vistas await. After taking in these early views, continue following the blue-blazed N Skyline Trail to Great Blue Hill signs.

At 1.4 miles, arrive at Eliot Tower, which is named after Charles Eliot, a visionary landscape architect who helped establish Blue Hills Reservation and the Metropolitan Park System of Greater Boston. Walk up a few staircases and take in panoramic views of the Boston skyline, giving thanks to the man who "sought out hill, forest, shore for all to enjoy."

From here, follow the blue-blazed South Skyline Trail as it loops around Blue Hill Observatory and Science Center (open weekends 10 a.m. to 4 p.m.) before heading back down to the parking lot.

TURN-BY-TURN DIRECTIONS

1. Walk across the crosswalk on Hillside Street following the blue blazes and N Skyline Trail sign towards the DCR and MA State Police buildings. Find the trailhead on the DCR building's left. Start the hike here on the blue trail.
2. At .05 miles, turn right and walk up the stone steps, following the blue blazes and N Skyline Trail to Great Blue Hill sign.
3. At 0.18 miles, arrive at a viewpoint atop Hancock Hill, then continue following the blue trail to the left of the view.
4. At 0.4 miles, after the steep descent, continue straight following the blue-blazed trail.
5. At 0.57 miles, bear left on blue following N Skyline Trail to Great Blue Hill.
6. At 0.86 miles, at the four-way intersection, continue straight on blue following Skyline Trail to Great Blue Hill sign.
7. At 1.42 miles, continue following the blue trail up the stone staircase and arrive at Eliot Tower. When done, exit the front of the tower the way you came in and turn right on the gravel path, passing Charles Eliot monument.
8. At 1.47 miles, bear right onto the gravel loop.
9. At 1.53 miles, arrive at the Blue Hill Observatory and Science Center. Follow the gravel path along the left of the observatory and continue looping around on the gravel path to the left.
10. At 1.82 miles, turn right onto the blue-blazed trail following South Skyline Trail East sign.
11. At 2 miles, at the base of the steep scramble section, turn right to follow the wide path and blue-blazed trail.
12. At 2.15 miles, turn left to continue following the blue-blazed trail.
13. At 2.73 miles, bear right to continue following the blue trail all the way out to Hillside Street.

CONNECTICUT

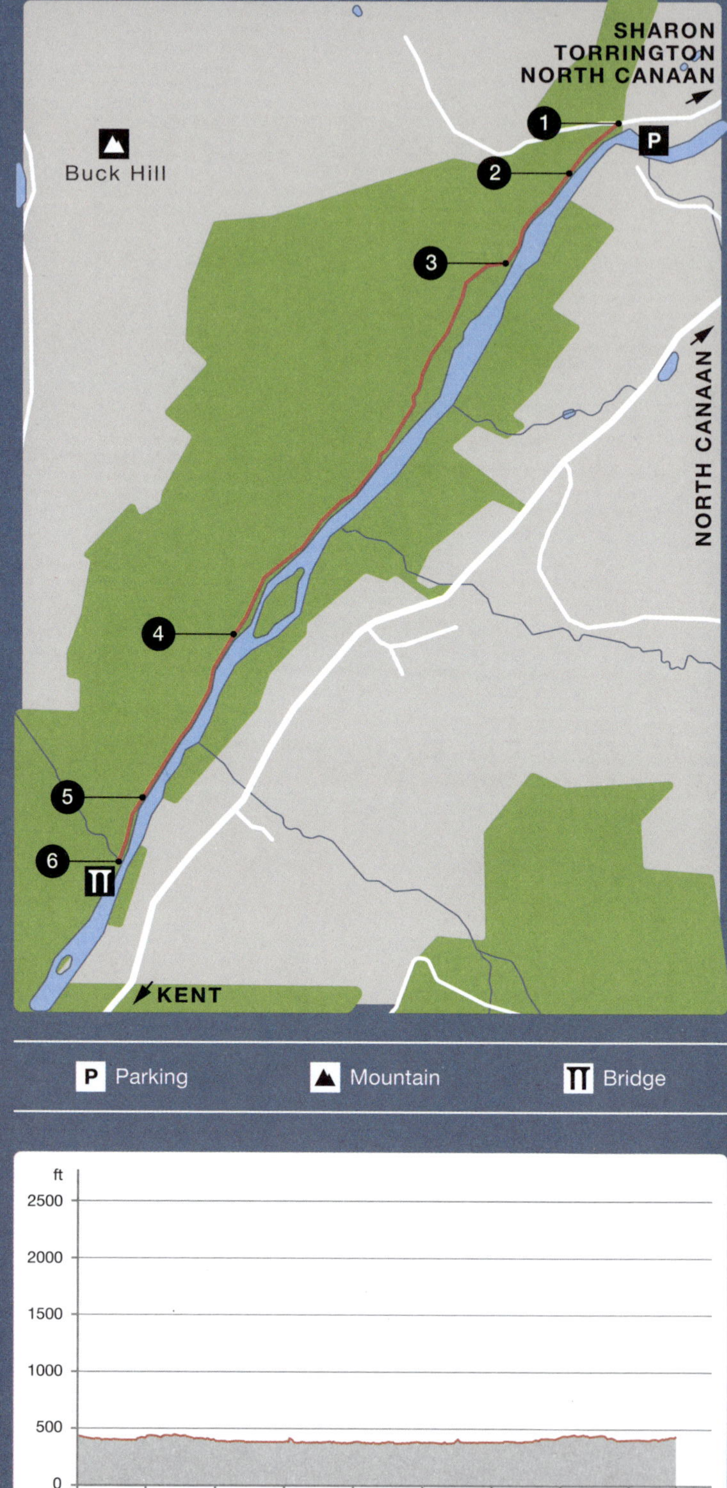
SHARON
TORRINGTON
NORTH CANAAN
1
P
2
Buck Hill
3
NORTH CANAAN
4
5
6
KENT
P Parking
Mountain
Bridge
ft
2500
2000
1500
1000
500
0
0.0
0.5
1.0
1.5
2.0
2.5
3.0
3.5
4.0
4.32 mi

HOUSATONIC RIVER TO APPALACHIAN TRAIL

SCENIC TRAIL ALONG THE HOUSATONIC RIVER

CORNWALL, CT

34

LENGTH

4.32 miles (in and out)

TIME & MONEY

1 hour 45 minutes; free

ELEVATION GAIN

95 feet

DIFFICULTY

Easy

CONDITIONS

Year-round; narrow and wide paths

HIGHLIGHTS

Views and access to the river, plus an open meadow

ESSENTIALS

- **Find the trailhead:** From Cornwall Library, head north on Pine Street and after 0.3 miles turn left on Furnace Brook Road (CT-4). After 3.3 miles, keep right to continue on Furnace Brook Road toward Sharon. After 0.3 miles bear right onto River Road (US-7). After 115 feet, turn right to stay on River Road and go for 1.1 miles until you see a small parking area on the left and an Appalachian Trail sign.

- **Land manager:** Appalachian Trail Conservancy, 799 Washington Street, PO Box 807, Harpers Ferry, WV 25425; (304) 535-6331; info@appalachiantrail.org appalachiantrail.org

WHY YOU'LL LOVE IT

- Scenic trail winding along Housatonic River
- Easy to follow, mainly flat
- Water access for the dogs

Hike for miles along this relatively flat Appalachian National Scenic Trail that winds along the Housatonic River.

Tucked away in rural Litchfield County, Cornwall is a quintessential New England town loaded with character, tons of hiking trails, charming cafes, and the longest covered bridge in Connecticut.

Though a little removed in the northwest corner of CT, this is the perfect place to take your pup for a ride with the windows down along winding country roads. Founded in 1740, Cornwall was shaped by its iron industry, farming roots and rugged landscape of steep hills and deep valleys.

With rolling hills on one side and the rambling river on the other, this trail provides endless scenery, water and fun for you and the dogs.

Following the white blazes of the Appalachian Trail the whole way, this hike is straightforward and easy to follow. While our hike here has you walk for a little more than 2 miles before turning around, you could extend it to be a 10.5-mile round trip if you wanted to.

Since it's easy to see ahead on this trail, we allowed the dogs to occasionally roam off-leash and called them back when we encountered other people. There are many spots for the dogs to walk right into the river to cool off, swim or take a drink.

From the parking on River Road, follow the Appalachian National Scenic Trail signs with the river on your left. At about half a mile in, the trail bends to the right, away from the river, where you'll emerge onto an expansive meadow. This is a great spot to let the dogs roam and explore.

After 2.1 miles, at the signs for Stony Brook Campsite and Stony Brook Falls, which tumble into the Housatonic River, turn back and walk out the way you came. This whole area is a known CT nesting spot for bald eagles in late winter and early spring, so keep your eyes peeled along the hike! I've spotted them a couple times here.

TURN-BY-TURN DIRECTIONS

1. From the parking area along River Road, walk north with the river on your left. The hike begins at the Appalachian National Scenic Trail sign.
2. At 0.18 miles, bear left onto the white-blazed Appalachian Trail.
3. At 0.42 miles, continue on the white-blazed trail as it curves to the right. You soon arrive at the open meadow with views facing west.
4. At 1.51 miles, bear right and continue on the white-blazed trail.
5. At 2 miles, with the Stony Brook Group Camping sign on your right, continue left on the white-blazed trail.
6. At 2.1 miles, walk across a little bridge with several cascading falls on your right. At this point, turn around and return back the same way. Or if you and your pup are feeling energetic, you can keep going for longer if you wish. The terrain stays relatively similar.

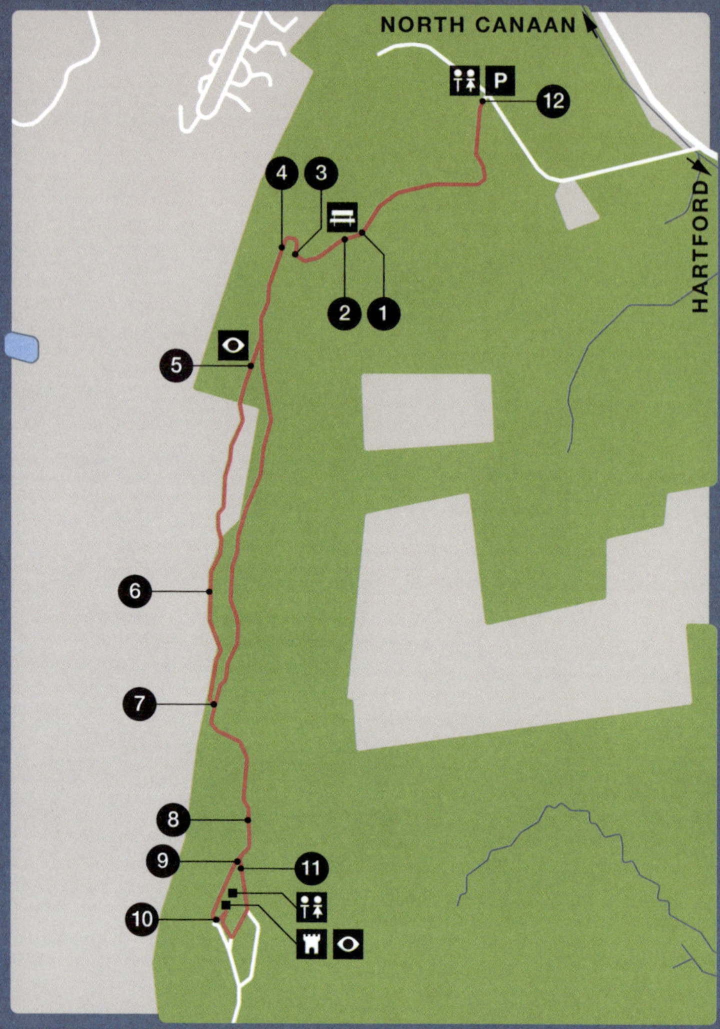

NORTH CANAAN
HARTFORD
P
1
2
3
4
5
6
7
8
9
10
11
12

P Parking | Toilet | Bench | Viewpoint | Heublein Tower

ft
2500
2000
1500
1000
500
0
0.0
0.5
1.0
1.5
2.0
2.59 mi

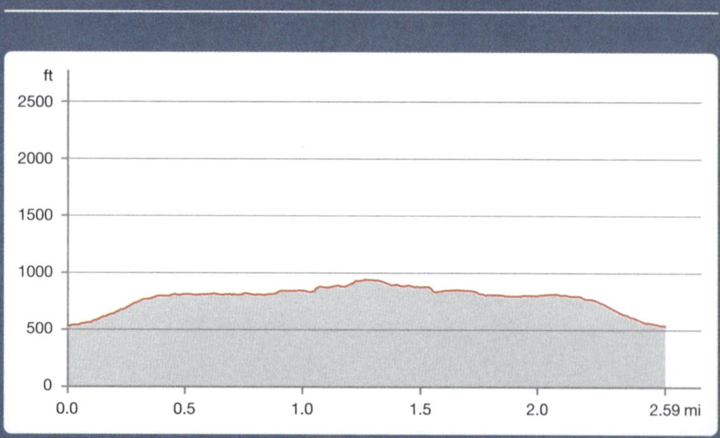

TALCOTT MOUNTAIN TRAIL

WIDE PATH TO ICONIC CT TOWER AND VIEWS

SIMSBURY, CT

35

LENGTH
2.59 miles

TIME & MONEY
1 hour 30 minutes; Interstate cars $15 on weekends, $10 weekdays

ELEVATION GAIN
427 feet

DIFFICULTY
Moderate

CONDITIONS
Year-round; leash required

HIGHLIGHTS
Historic Heublein Tower, multiple lookouts

ESSENTIALS

- **Find the trailhead:** From I-91 North or South: Take Exit 35B. Follow Cottage Grove Road heading west until Route 185. Follow Route 185 toward Simsbury. At the top of the hill, the state park entrance is on your left. From I-84 East or West: Take Route 44 Exit and head west until intersection with Route 218. Take a right on 218 and follow north to Route 185. Take a left on Route 185 toward Simsbury. At the top of the hill, the state park entrance is on your left.
- **Land manager:** CT Parks; (860) 424-3200; deep.stateparks@ct.gov ctparks.com/parks/talcott-mountain-state-park

WHY YOU'LL LOVE IT

- Wide-open path that's relatively flat
- Pet waste stations along the way
- Water station at the top (though always bring extra)

Hike up wide gravel paths through Talcott Mountain State Park to reach one of Connecticut's most impressive landmarks, located just minutes from Hartford.

Heublein Tower, a popular and iconic landmark in Connecticut, was built in 1914 by Gilbert F. Heublein, a wealthy member of Hartford's elite. He made a promise to his fiancée, Louise Gundlach, that he would build her "a castle on a mountain." Today, the 165-foot Bavarian-inspired Heublein Tower, high on the ridge, can be seen from many roads as you make your way through Simsbury. The path leading up to the tower takes you past several lookouts, all along Talcott Mountain Ridge.

Starting on the yellow trail off Summit Ridge Road, it's a moderately steep climb on a wide gravel path lined with tall oak, birch and maple trees. Designed to ensure you and your pup enjoy the adventure, there are benches to rest, plus pet waste stations, along this first steep section.

At the top of the ridge, enjoy the first west-facing view, with the towns of Simsbury and Avon below and Farmington River Valley in the distance. The steep, gravel path becomes a flat and narrow dirt trail along the ridge. Here, there are too many lookouts to count, culminating with one wide-open view before you head into the woods for the final stretch to the tower.

Once you reach Heublein Tower there are picnic tables, bathrooms and water available on the grounds. There are expansive views here, as well as views of this impressive tower. The tower is open Friday to Monday, 10 a.m. to 4 p.m. From the top, you can see into Massachusetts and New Hampshire. Dogs are, unfortunately, not allowed inside the tower. Once you're done exploring around the tower, take the yellow trail all the way back down to your car.

TURN-BY-TURN DIRECTIONS

1. From the parking lot, find the trailhead kiosk located on the south side of the parking lot toward the restrooms and start on the yellow trail, which is the wide gravel path.
2. At 0.3 miles, there's a pet waste station on your left and a bench on the right.
3. At 0.36 miles, at a fork in the trail, stay to the right.
4. At 0.4 miles, stay straight at the trail juncture.
5. At 0.42 miles, the dirt path on the ridge leads to the first lookout. Continue walking left along the ridge.
6. At 0.55 miles, enjoy the view. From here, to the left, take the narrow path that heads back into the woods. Continue walking along the ridge.
7. At 0.9 miles, avoid the path leading left and continue straight on the ridge trail.
8. At 0.98 miles, return to the wide gravel path again. Head to the right to continue on this trail, marked again with yellow blazes.
9. At 1.2 miles, blue markers are shown with the yellow. This is where Metacomet Trail intersects with the yellow trail. Take a right toward the ridge to stay on the blue/yellow trail.
10. At 1.25 miles, arrive at the tower, where there are restrooms and a water fountain.
11. At 1.3 miles, loop around the tower on the paved pathway and follow the yellow trail sign.
12. At 1.38 miles, the wide gravel path (yellow trail) takes you back down to the parking lot.

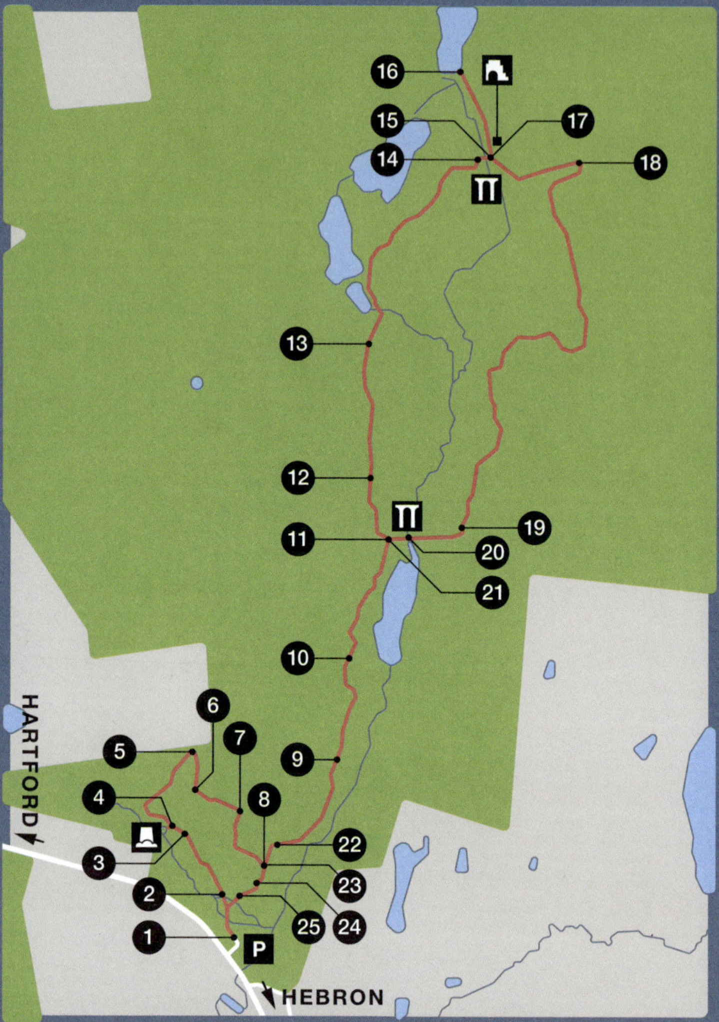

16
15
14
17
18
13
12
11
19
20
21
10
HARTFORD
6
5
7
4
9
8
3
22
23
2
24
25
1
P
HEBRON

P Parking
Waterfall
Bridge
Ruins

ft
2500
2000
1500
1000
500
0
0.0
0.5
1.0
1.5
2.0
2.5
3.0
3.5
4.0
4.5
5.0
5.44 mi

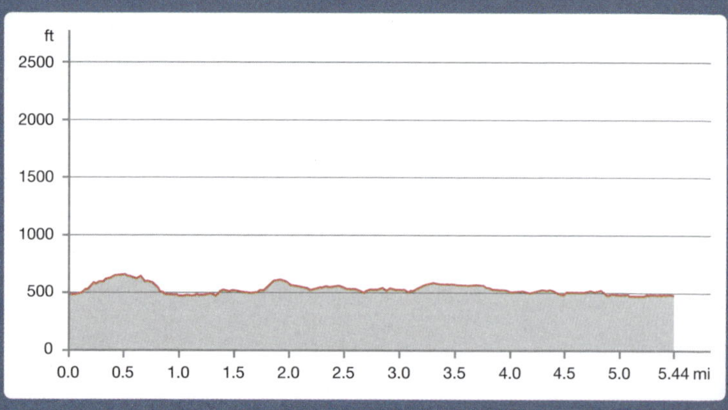

BLACKLEDGE FALLS AND GAY CITY STATE PARK

WATERFALL, PONDS AND MILL-TOWN RUINS

GLASTONBURY, CT

36

LENGTH
5.44 miles (loop)

TIME & MONEY
2 hours; free

ELEVATION GAIN
492 feet

DIFFICULTY
Moderate

CONDITIONS
Year-round; wide path, streams

HIGHLIGHTS
Blackledge Falls, ruins, ponds

ESSENTIALS

- **Find the trailhead:** From Welles-Turner Memorial Library in downtown Glastonbury, head southeast toward CT-94 W/Hebron Avenue. Continue following Hebron Avenue for 8.5 miles until you see the Blackledge Falls sign and entrance to the large parking lot on the left.

- **Land manager:** Connecticut Department of Energy and Environmental Protection (DEEP), 79 Elm Street, Hartford, CT 06106-5127; (860) 424-3000; deep.stateparks@ct.gov portal.ct.gov/deep/state-parks/recreation-information

WHY YOU'LL LOVE IT

- Waterfall; rivers and streams abound
- Stone walls, bridges and ruins along the way
- Mainly flat, wide paths

An adventurous hike through Gay City State Park with several spots for dogs to swim. Pass the 25-foot Blackledge Falls, several ponds and ruins from an abandoned mill town.

Less than 20 minutes east of Connecticut's capital, Hartford, the 1569-acre hiking oasis of Gay City State Park spans the towns of Glastonbury, Hebron and Bolton. The name Gay City comes from the numerous residents with the surname Gay who lived in the 18th-century mill town that once stood here.

This is a longer hike that's perfect for dogs of all ages, given the slight elevation change spread throughout the five-plus miles. The mostly flat trails, along with several opportunities for water and swimming along the way, make this a satisfying trek for you and your pup.

Aside from Blackledge Falls, which you encounter early in the hike, there's a lot more to see and appreciate on this hike, including foundations of the 1796 woolen mill and stone wall ruins.

From the left side of the large parking lot along Route 94/Hebron Avenue, pick up the blue-blazed trail. Do a short loop around Blackledge Falls, then pick up Blackledge Falls Connector Trail, leading you to a large loop through Gay City State Park.

At the loop's halfway point, dogs can take a dip at Gay City Pond. Note, there's a large parking lot here and a designated beach and swimming area in the summer. So while we let the dogs off-leash along stretches of this hike, they were leashed on approach to the pond. We visited on a spring weekend and encountered just a few people on the trail; however, with picnic tables and grills scattering the lawn around the pond, be prepared for more people when the weather's warmer.

TURN-BY-TURN DIRECTIONS

1. From the parking lot, with your back to Hebron Avenue, begin on the trail in the top left corner of the lot (on the opposite side of the trail kiosk).
2. At 0.06 miles, there are two stream crossings in a row. After crossing the second stream, bear left to start on the light-blue-blazed trail.
3. At 0.23 miles, take a left at the fork to continue on the light-blue trail.
4. At 0.28 miles, Blackledge Falls waterfall is on the left. Take a short detour down to see the waterfall up close. This is also a great spot for the dogs to cool off or get some water. After checking out Blackledge Falls, walk back up the little hill and continue straight on the blue-blazed trail with the waterfall on your left.
5. At 0.54 miles, bear right at the blue trail sign with an arrow pointing right.
6. At 0.61 miles, stay to the left on the blue trail and cross a small stream.

7. At 0.72 miles, atop the small hill, turn right to stay on the blue trail.
8. At 0.9 miles, turn left at the blue trail sign (which points to the right) and pass a sign that says Leaving Blackledge Falls.
9. At 1.13 miles, emerge from the woods into a powerline clearing. Continue on the path across the field and enter the woods on the other side.
10. At 1.4 miles, arrive at another open field. Cross the field and continue on the trail back into the woods.
11. At 1.68 miles, turn left onto the red trail, heading away from the creek. (There's an option here to turn right and cross the bridge if you want a shorter hike.)
12. At 1.82 miles, at the intersection, stay straight on the yellow trail.
13. At 2.18 miles, walk along a long boardwalk across the marshy area.
14. At 2.6 miles, at a junction, turn right on the yellow-blazed trail (there's a light-blue blaze on the tree, too) and cross the small wooden bridge.
15. After crossing the bridge, take an immediate left onto the white-blazed trail. The ruins of the old woolen mill are on your right.
16. At 2.8 miles, arrive at the large Gay City Pond. After exploring the pond, retrace your steps and walk back on the white trail.
17. At 3 miles, instead of crossing the bridge, turn left onto the blue trail to start the other side of the loop.
18. At 3.24 miles, at the trail juncture with a road up ahead and a road to your left, turn right. Stay on this red-blazed trail for the next mile plus.
19. At 4.28 miles, at a fork in the trail, keep right to stay on the red trail.
20. At 4.4 miles, cross the newly reconstructed wooden bridge over Blackledge River.
21. At 4.42 miles, after crossing the bridge, take a left onto the yellow-blazed trail (this is the trail from earlier).
22. At 5.23 miles, at the blue trail sign, continue straight on the blue-blazed trail.
23. At 5.28 miles, at the blue and white trail and Blackledge Falls signs, join the blue and white trail.
24. At 5.31 miles, bear left away from the blue and white trail toward the parking lot.
25. At 5.36 miles, take a left and eventually arrive at the parking lot.

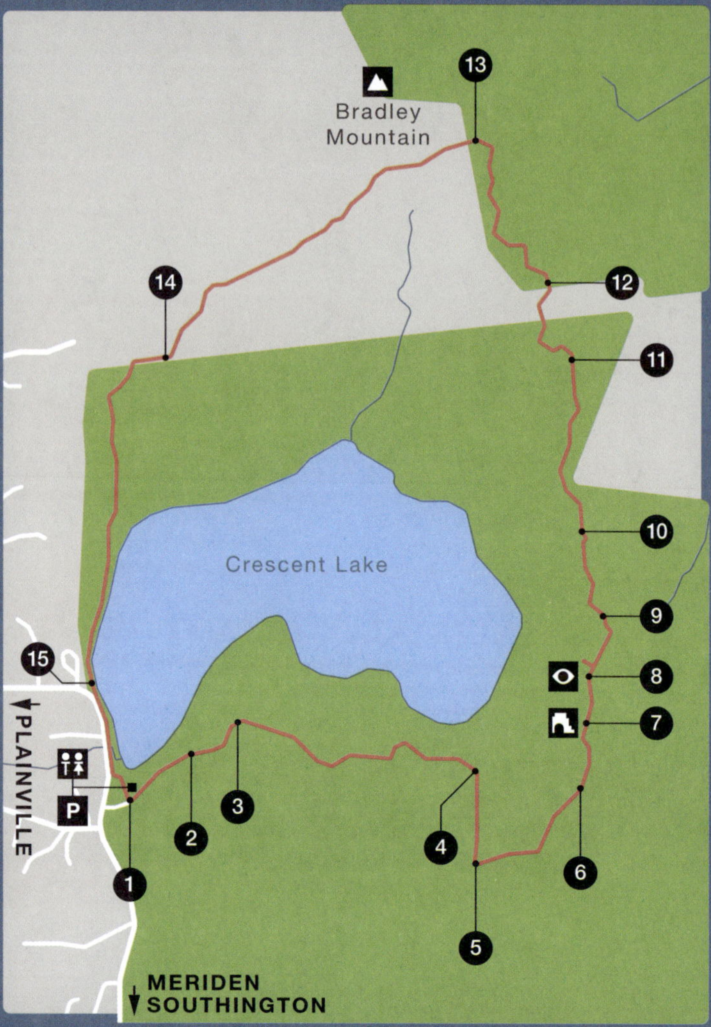

Bradley Mountain
Crescent Lake
PLAINVILLE
MERIDEN
SOUTHINGTON
1
2
3
4
5
6
7
8
9
10
11
12
13
14
15
P

P Parking
Toilet
Viewpoint
Ruins

ft
2500
2000
1500
1000
500
0
0.0
0.5
1.0
1.5
2.0
2.5 mi

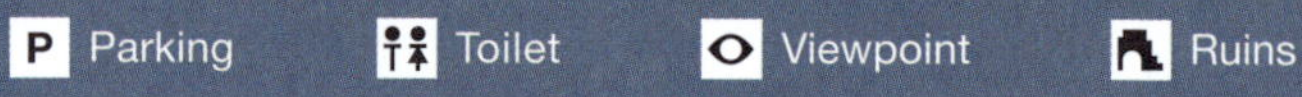

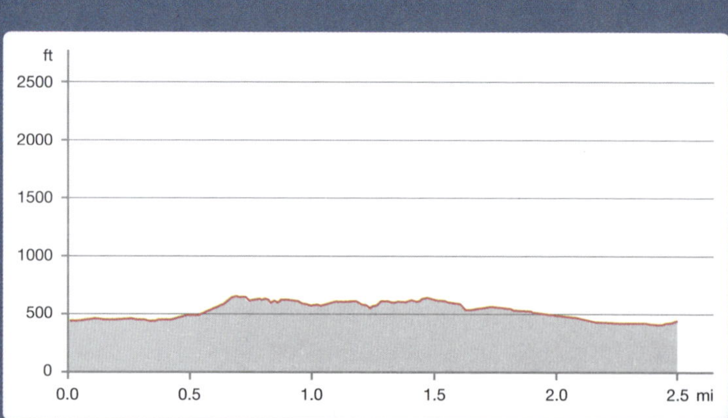

CRESCENT LAKE LOOP

OPEN SPACE WITH QUAINT LAKE VIEWS

SOUTHINGTON, CT

37

LENGTH

2.5 miles (loop)

TIME & MONEY

1 hour 15 minutes; free

ELEVATION GAIN

312 feet

DIFFICULTY

Moderate

CONDITIONS

Year-round; leash required

HIGHLIGHTS

Lake views, shaded forest trail

ESSENTIALS

- **Find the trailhead:** From I-84 East: Take Exit 32 (Queen Street). At the end of the ramp, turn left onto Queen Street/Route 10 S. Go through three traffic lights. At the fourth (Oak Hill Cemetery on your left), turn left onto Flanders Street. Continue straight to second stop sign (approx. 1.5 miles). Turn left onto Flanders Road. Go 0.6 miles and turn right onto Mine Hollow Road. Travel approx. 1 mile on Mine Hollow Road, passing Rogers Orchards store, and make a sharp left onto Shuttle Meadow Road. Crescent Lake will be about 0.8 miles further on your right. From I-84 West: Take Exit 32 (Queen Street). At the end of the ramp, turn right onto Queen Street/Route 10 S. Go through four traffic lights. At the fifth (Oak Hill Cemetery on your left), turn left onto Flanders Street. Follow directions above the rest of the way.

- **Land manager:** Southington Recreation Department, 388 Pleasant Street, Southington, CT 06489; (860) 276-6219 southington.org/departments/recreation/index.php

WHY YOU'LL LOVE IT

- Dogs can swim at Crescent Lake before and after the hike
- Short, shaded trail leading to a spectacular view
- Normally quiet on the mountain top, as most people just come for the lake

Wander the 2.5-mile loop around Crescent Lake, where dogs can swim, up to a spectacular lookout. Arrive at sunset to witness the inspiration behind the name Sunset Rock State Park.

Crescent Lake loop hike within Sunset Rock State Park is located in a quiet residential area of Southington just minutes off I-84. Crescent Lake (aka Plainville Reservoir) sits at the western base of Bradley Mountain—a traprock mountain that's part of southern New England's Metacomet Ridge and Connecticut's Metacomet Trail. Here you'll get a sample of the 62.3-mile blue-blazed Metacomet Trail, as this loop merges with the Metacomet during the first portion of the loop up and over Bradley Mountain.

There's ample parking at Crescent Lake Park on Shuttle Meadow Road, as well as amenities like picnic areas and bathrooms. The blue and orange trail starts just to the right of the lake, entering a lush forest of hardwoods and evergreens and offering a cool, shaded canopy even on warm summer days.

At the start of the trail, short paths lead down to the lake should your dog need to hydrate in the first half mile before the climb begins. There are several mountain biking trails here, too, so be sure to follow the turn-by-turn directions to get to the view.

A steep but wide gravel path takes you to the top of Bradley Mountain and once there you'll notice the rocky trail turn to padded pine, as well as the remains of a tall, stone fireplace that was likely part of the farmland in the late 1800s.

Take in the expansive views facing west over Crescent Lake and Quinnipiac River Valley from multiple rocky escarpments. After leaving the views, begin the gentle descent heading toward the other side of the lake; the end of the loop provides more opportunities for dogs to take a dip on the other (quieter) side, too.

TURN-BY-TURN DIRECTIONS

1. Find the trailhead kiosk to the right of the lake behind the porta-potty and begin the hike here on the blue/orange-blazed trail.
2. At 0.08 and 0.11 miles, stay to the left to follow the blue/orange trail.
3. At 0.14 miles, bear right to stay on the blue/orange trail.
4. At 0.4 miles, continue to stay to the right and start walking away from the reservoir.
5. At 0.52 miles, take a sharp left at the juncture to stay on the blue/orange trail and begin the ascent along the wide, rocky path.
6. At 0.68 miles, reach the top of the hill with a Metacomet Trail sign to the left on a tree. Turn left here to merge with Metacomet Trail (blue blaze) and continue on the blue/orange trail.
7. At 0.78 miles, there's a large stone fireplace. Bear left to continue on the blue/orange trail.
8. At 0.82 miles, arrive at the west-facing lookout for spectacular views over Crescent Lake and surrounds.
9. At 0.93 miles, bear left to stay on the blue/orange trail and start descending toward the lake.
10. At 1 mile, stay to the left on the trail with the orange marker.
11. At 1.23 miles, come to a juncture and stay straight onto the blue/orange trail.
12. At 1.35 miles, stay left and follow the blue/red trail.
13. At 1.60 miles, turn left onto the lime-green trail and start another gentle descent toward the lake.
14. At 2.03 miles, bear right onto the orange trail. The lake is on the left through the trees. Make sure the dog is leashed here, as the road is nearby.
15. At 2.37 miles, reach Shuttle Meadow Road. The parking lot is on the left. Turn left to walk along Shuttle Meadow Road for the last tenth of a mile to your car.

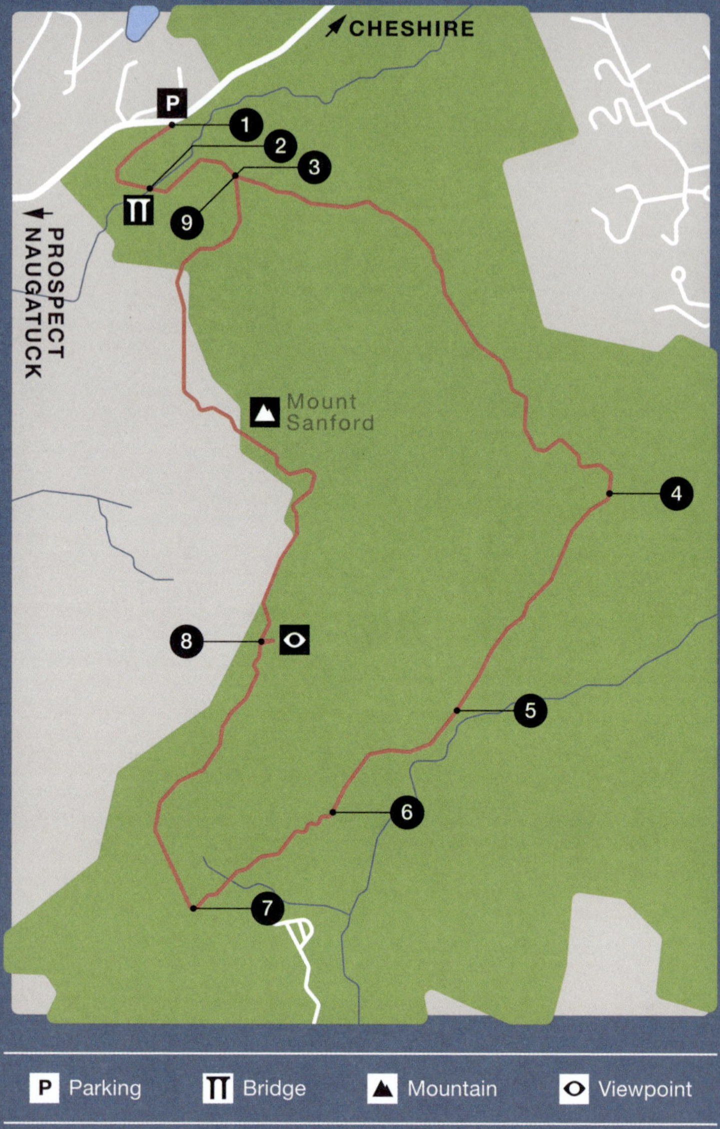
CHESHIRE
P
1
2
3
9
PROSPECT
NAUGATUCK
Mount
Sanford
4
8
5
6
7
P Parking
Bridge
Mountain
Viewpoint

ft
2500
2000
1500
1000
500
0
0.0
0.5
1.0
1.5
2.0
2.5
3.0
3.49 mi

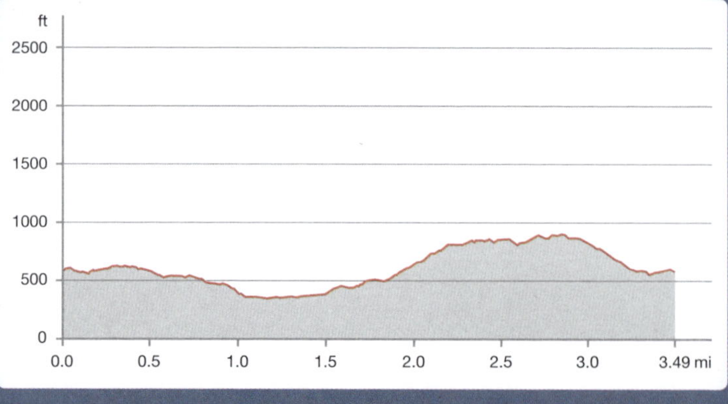

MOUNT SANFORD LOOP

WIDE-OPEN, WEST-FACING VIEWS

CHESHIRE, CT

38

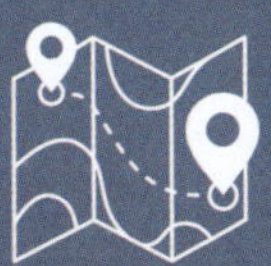

LENGTH

3.49 miles (loop)

TIME & MONEY

1 hour 40 minutes; free

ELEVATION GAIN

643 feet

DIFFICULTY

Moderate

CONDITIONS

Year-round; shaded forest, stone steps

HIGHLIGHTS

Long, flat portion and views

ESSENTIALS

- **Find the trailhead:** From Cheshire Public Library, turn left on Main Street (CT-68/CT-70) and after 0.1 miles turn right on Highland Avenue (CT-10/CT-68/CT-70). After 1.3 miles, turn right onto N Brooksvale Road (CT-42). After 1.8 miles, turn right onto Bethany Mountain Road (CT-42). After 0.7 miles, the parking lot is on the left.

- **Land manager:** Connecticut Department of Energy and Environmental Protection (DEEP), 79 Elm Street, Hartford, CT 06106-5127; (860) 424-3200; deep.stateparks@ct.gov portal.ct.gov/DEEP/State-Parks

WHY YOU'LL LOVE IT

- Wide-open views atop Mount Sanford
- Varied terrain and forest setting
- Easy-to-follow loop

Hike past streams and stone walls and under a canopy of trees leading to a scenic west-facing overlook along Quinnipiac Trail.

At just 15 miles (about 25 minutes) from New Haven, Mount Sanford Loop in the 5000-acre Naugatuck State Forest is a tranquil forest escape where you and your pup can enjoy some peaceful time on the trails.

Tucked into the Cheshire side of this sprawling CT State Forest, this hike offers a mix of wide forest roads and narrower wooded paths that wind through a shaded canopy of oak and maple trees, along gentle streams and up to a scenic overlook.

Aside from the views, there's a half-mile stretch along a wide gravel path where you can see a long way ahead—this is a great spot to let the dogs have a little room and run a bit.

This 3.49-mile Mount Sanford Loop is part of the 20-mile blue-blazed Quinnipiac Trail. While it is not too challenging, it has a steady uphill section leading to the lookout, which is great for energetic dogs. There is nothing technical about the short incline, and rocks serve as steps for the walk up.

From the parking lot on Bethany Mountain Road, walk with the trailhead on your left to begin on the blue-blazed trail. After almost 0.2 miles, there's a stream for the dogs to hydrate before the hike.

After 0.3 miles, the loop portion begins. Bear left to go clockwise. This blue-blazed trail is easy to follow, meaning you can really relax.

About 1.5 miles in, you may notice, and hear noise from, a YMCA camp property in the distance through the trees.

The incline up to the lookout starts at the 1.68-mile mark. The view from Mount Sanford faces west, making it a perfect spot to enjoy the sunset with your dog and take some great photos.

TURN-BY-TURN DIRECTIONS

1. From the parking lot, find the trailhead in the western corner of the lot and begin the blue-blazed trail. After about 50 feet, there's a Quinnipiac Trail sign.
2. At 0.18 miles, cross a wooden bridge over a creek.
3. At 0.32 miles, bear left to start the loop going clockwise on the blue-and-red-blazed trail.
4. At 1.08 miles, at the bottom of a hill, turn right to continue on the blue-and-red-blazed trail.
5. At 1.4 miles, the trail becomes an old logging road. Continue following the blue and red blazes.
6. At 1.68 miles, come to a gate and Naugatuck State Forest sign. Turn right off the path and onto the blue and red trail at the Sanford Trail sign.
7. At 1.92 miles, turn right on the blue trail to pick up Quinnipiac Trail heading up toward the ridge.
8. At 2.35 miles, arrive at Mount Sanford Overlook, facing west, then continue on the blue trail.
9. At 3.19 miles, the loop portion is finished. Turn left to walk on the trail you came in on, following the blue blazes back to the parking lot.

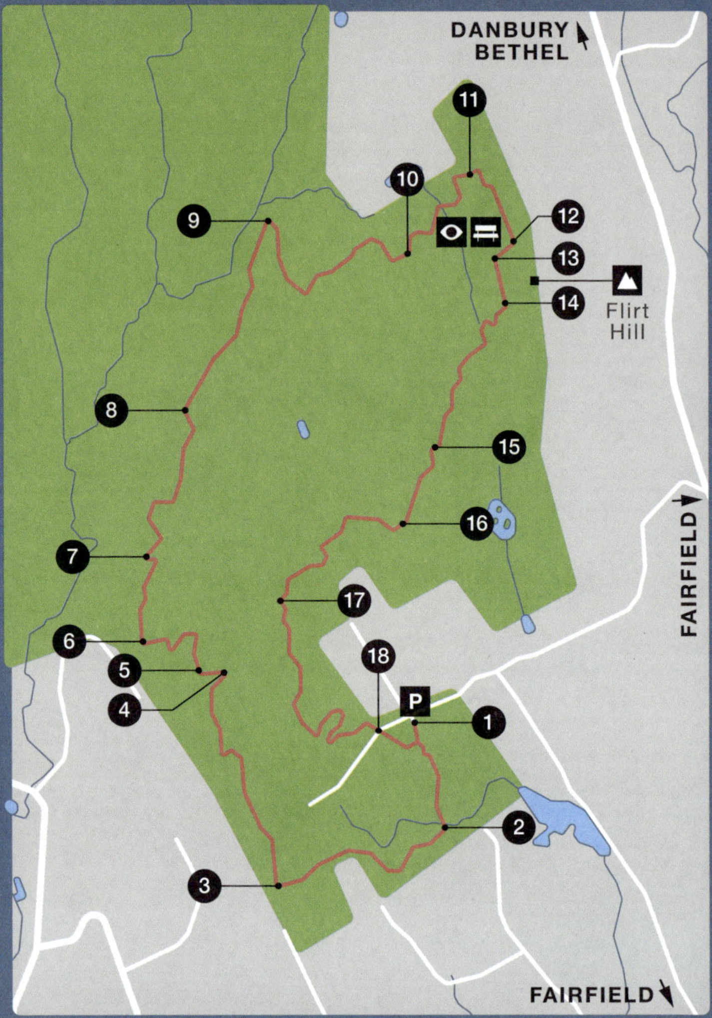

DANBURY
BETHEL

Flirt Hill

FAIRFIELD

FAIRFIELD

P Parking   Bench   Viewpoint   Mountain

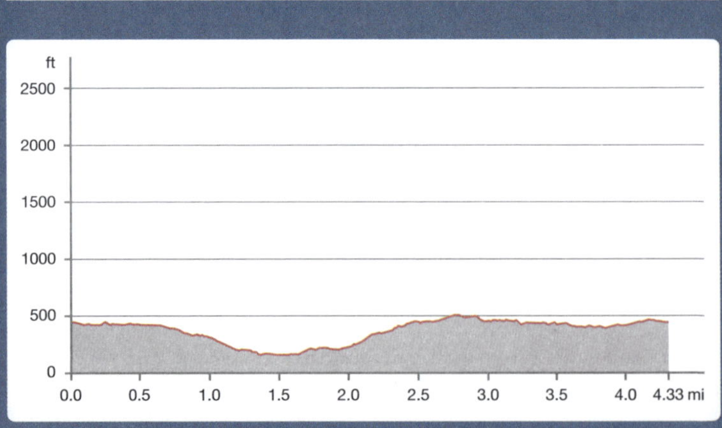

TROUT BROOK VALLEY PRESERVE LOOP

OFF-LEASH SECTION AND MEADOW VIEWS

EASTON, CT

39

LENGTH
4.33 miles (loop)

TIME & MONEY
2 hours 2 minutes; free

ELEVATION GAIN
436 feet

DIFFICULTY
Easy

CONDITIONS
Year-round; smooth forest and farm trails

HIGHLIGHTS
Off-leash portion, wide paths, relatively flat

ESSENTIALS

- **Find the trailhead:** From Easton Public Library, turn left onto Morehouse Road and after 154 feet turn left onto Center Road. After 1.3 miles, turn right onto Black Rock Turnpike (CT-58). After 0.1 miles, turn left onto Freeborn Road. After 0.7 miles, the parking lot is on the right.

- **Land manager:** Aspetuck Land Trust, PO Box 444, Westport, CT 06881; (203) 331-1906; administration@aspetucklandtrust.org aspetucklandtrust.org

WHY YOU'LL LOVE IT

- Designated off-leash portion
- Varied terrain, from forest to meadow
- Streams for dogs

Scenic views from Flirt Hill, peaceful forest trails and a dog-friendly off-leash area make Trout Brook Valley Preserve a must-do hike for dogs in CT.

Less than nine miles (15 minutes) from Fairfield and 20 miles (30 minutes) from Stamford, Trout Brook Valley Preserve in Easton offers a peaceful escape and hike with your pup. Managed by the Aspetuck Land Trust, this 1000-acre preserve features over 20 miles of well-marked trails winding through meadows and hardwood forests, passing by stone walls and quiet streams.

What makes this hike special is it's one of the very few with a designated off-leash section, during the first mile. If you had a long drive to get here, now's a good time to let the dogs blow off some steam!

I spoke with a few locals who come here regularly and they said that the off-leash boundary is a bit unclear. A sign denotes where it ends, but we ran into a few people who continued to have their dogs off-leash, yet under control, and they called them back before we approached.

Aside from being a place you can let your pup run free, another highlight of Trout Brook Valley is the meadow and view from the top of Flirt Hill. With a bench at the top, you can sit with your dog, have a snack and take in the views of the rolling meadow and farmland.

Though over four miles, there is nothing technical about this hike and there are no steep sections to navigate, which is great for dogs of all ages.

Begin from the parking lot on Freeborn Road, starting on the trail's off-leash section, known as Crow Hill Preserve within Trout Brook Valley. From there, follow the blue trail to connect with the pink trail, taking you up through the orchard to the top of Flirt Hill. After enjoying the view, loop back down and return to Crow Hill Preserve area.

TURN-BY-TURN DIRECTIONS

1. From the parking area, find the trailhead and begin the trail, bearing left after 50 feet to follow the pink blazes with black arrows.
2. At 0.2 miles, bear right at the 42 sign to continue on the pink trail.
3. At 0.5 miles, turn right at sign 44.
4. At 0.95 miles, at a stream and several rock walls, turn left onto the blue-blazed trail.
5. At 1 mile, reach the end of the off-leash loop. Turn right onto the blue-blazed trail.
6. At 1.23 miles, at sign 41, turn right to continue on the blue trail.
7. At 1.4 miles, turn right at sign W26, then bear left on the blue-and-green-blazed trail.
8. At 1.7 miles, at sign 30, turn right to continue following the blue trail.
9. At 2.05 miles, take a sharp right onto the blue trail and begin walking uphill.
10. At 2.4 miles, with vernal pools on the right, turn left to go up a small hill on the purple-blazed trail with white arrows.
11. At 2.65 miles, go through the gate with the Aspetuck Land Trust sign, then turn right to walk to the top of the meadow with the orchard on your left.
12. At 2.8 miles, reach the top of Flirt Hill, where there's a bench and view across the meadow. After taking in the view, continue walking southwest down the hill.
13. At 2.88 miles, take a left to walk along the fence.
14. At 2.95 miles, go through the gate and bear left, heading back into the woods toward the pink blazes.
15. At 3.25 miles, bear left and then, in about 50 feet, bear right to pick up the blue trail.
16. At 3.42 miles, walk straight across the gravel road (Norton Road) and continue on the blue trail.
17. At 3.71 miles, bear left on the pink trail where you will see an Off Leash Loop sign.
18. At 4.2 miles, walk across Freeborn Street and enter the trail back into the woods. Find the parking lot on your left in a couple hundred feet.

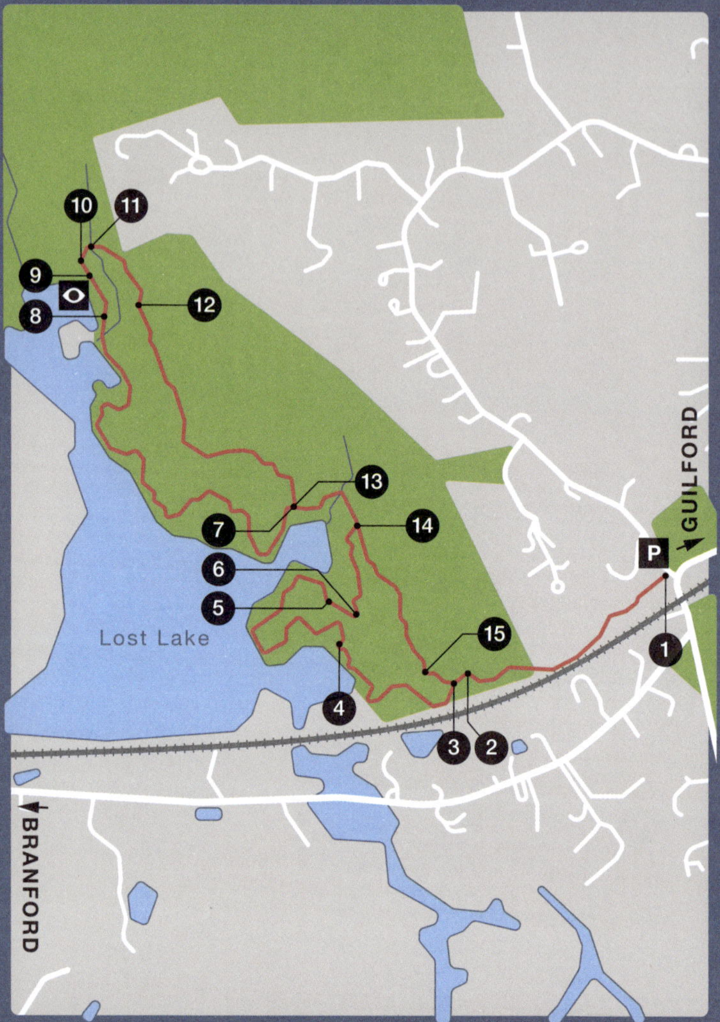

Lost Lake
GUILFORD
BRANFORD
P
1
2
3
4
5
6
7
8
9
10
11
12
13
14
15

P Parking
Viewpoint

ft
2500
2000
1500
1000
500
0
0.0
0.5
1.0
1.5
2.0
2.5
3.0 mi

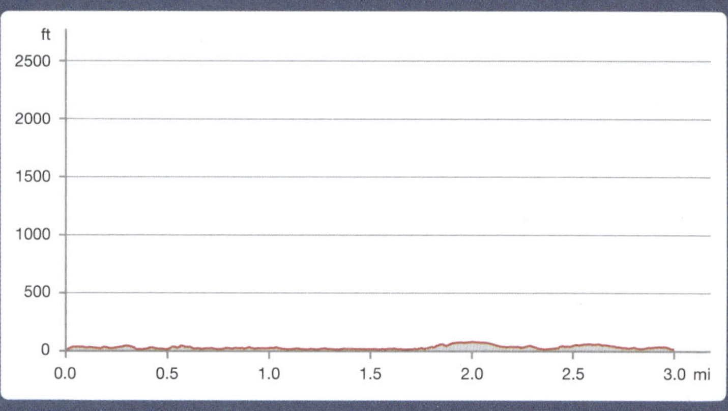

WESTWOODS TRAIL

LAKESIDE AND WOODS WALK CLOSE TO TOWN

GUILFORD, CT

40

LENGTH

3 miles
(loop)

TIME & MONEY

1 hour 24 minutes;
free

ELEVATION GAIN

197 feet

DIFFICULTY

Easy to moderate

CONDITIONS

Year-round;
rocky paths

HIGHLIGHTS

Views and access
to the lake

ESSENTIALS

- **Find the trailhead:** From Guilford Free Library, head west on Broad Street and after 0.1 miles turn left onto Whitfield Street (CT-77). After 0.2 miles, turn right onto Water Street (CT-146) and after 1.3 miles turn right onto Sam Hill Road. The parking lot is on the left after 115 feet.
- **Land manager:** Guilford Land Conservation Trust, P.O. Box 200, Guilford, CT 06437; (203) 457-9253; info@guilfordlandtrust.org guilfordlandtrust.org

WHY YOU'LL LOVE IT

- Scenic views all along Lost Lake
- Varied terrain and landscape
- Water access for the dogs

Hike all along the shore of Lost Lake, with scenic water views during the whole first portion of the loop, plus marshes, unique rock formations and water access for the dogs.

Just 1.5 miles from Guilford Green, and under 20 minutes from New Haven and the bustling Yale University Campus, lies a hiking oasis within Guilford's Westwoods. Part of the Guilford Land Trust, Westwoods is a 1200-acre property with 32 miles of trails.

What makes Westwoods special is the variety of interesting sites: saltwater and freshwater marshes, an inland tidal lake, unique rock formations, and the almost-constant views across expansive Lost Lake. All of this provides the dogs with plenty of stimulating scents, areas to explore and water to dip in.

From the parking lot off Sam Hill Road, pick up the white-blazed trail for almost the entire hike—it alternates between the white-circle trail and white-square trail. There's an active railroad so keep the dogs close until you move away from the tracks after about 0.4 miles.

After a half mile on the white-square trail, a 1.5-mile stretch begins along Lost Lake, offering continuous views throughout. We were here in spring, before the leaves filled in, which meant the lake was in view the whole time. We stopped several times for photos, and there are also opportunities for the dogs to explore the shoreline.

This first part of the loop along the lake is not only scenic, but also the most challenging section because of the rocky shoreline. While there are no steep inclines, the stones create large, uneven steps along the way.

At 1.8 miles, at the northern tip of Lost Lake, take in one last sweeping view before picking up a short connector trail to get back onto the white-trail system. Soon, you're in the woods on the back portion of the loop. This trail is much smoother, and everyone will be glad you saved the easy part for last!

TURN-BY-TURN DIRECTIONS

1. From the parking area, find the trailhead and begin on the white-blazed trail following the sign for Sam Hill Road.
2. At 0.3 miles, bear left on the white-circle trail.
3. At 0.31 miles, bear left on the white-square trail.
4. At 0.6 miles, continue on the white-square trail, which bends to the right, away from the lake.
5. At 0.9 miles, stay on the white-square trail as it bends to the left.
6. At 0.91 miles, take a sharp left onto the white-circle trail.
7. At 1.2 miles, bear left onto the white-square trail.
8. At around 1.7 miles, there are white-circle blazes on the trees as the two white trails merge.
9. At 1.8 miles, arrive at the expansive view facing southwest over Lost Lake.
10. At 1.82 miles, bear right on the orange-circle trail.
11. At 1.9 miles, turn right onto the orange-and-white-blazed trail and stay to the right.
12. At 2 miles, the path merges with the white-circle trail. Continue on the white-circle trail.
13. At 2.35 miles, bear left to stay on the white-circle trail. The lake is on the right.
14. At 2.45 miles, bear left onto the white-square trail.
15. At 2.65 miles, turn left and continue following the white-circle trail, which leads out to the parking lot.

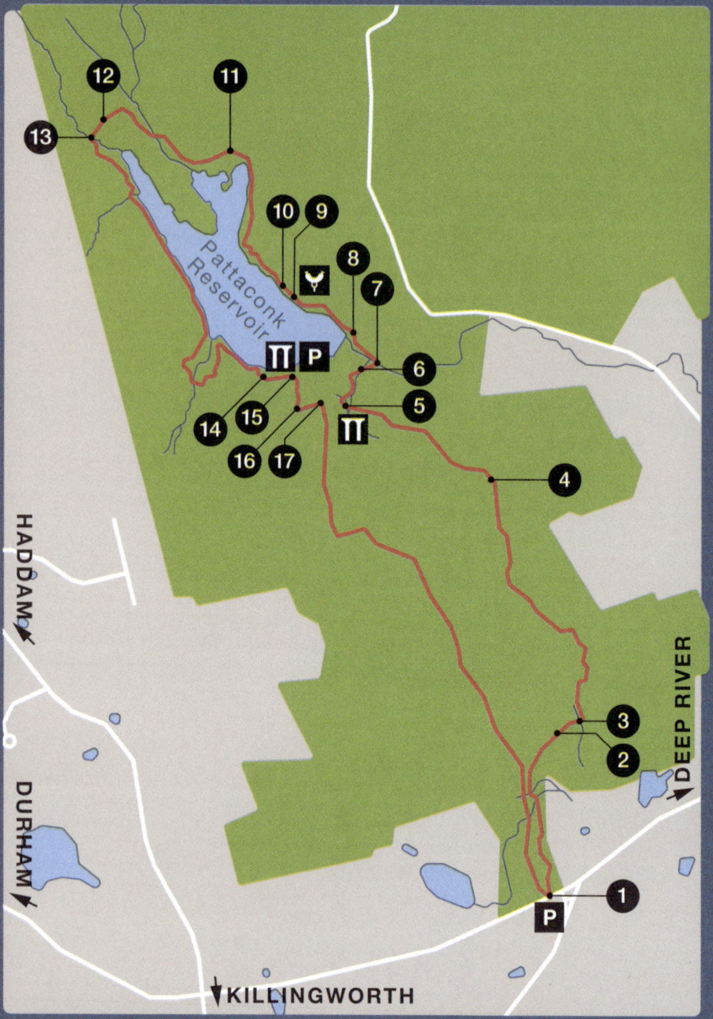

Pattaconk Reservoir
HADDAM
DURHAM
KILLINGWORTH
DEEP RIVER

COCKAPONSET TO PATTACONK RESERVOIR

SCENIC LOOP WITH WATER VIEWS

CHESTER, CT

41

LENGTH

5.39 miles (loop)

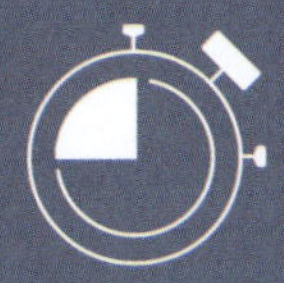

TIME & MONEY

2 hours 23 minutes; free

ELEVATION GAIN

453 feet

DIFFICULTY

Moderate

CONDITIONS

Year-round; soft, forested trails

HIGHLIGHTS

View over Pattaconk Reservoir Dam, mainly flat trail

ESSENTIALS

- **Find the trailhead:** From Chester Public Library in downtown Chester, turn left, heading west on W Main Street (CT-148). Drive for 3.6 miles southwest on W Main Street (CT-148) until you arrive at the trailhead and parking at 269 W Main Street.
- **Land manager:** Cockaponset State Forest, 18 Ranger Road, Haddam, CT 06438; (860) 345-8521; deep.stateparks@ct.gov portal.ct.gov/deep/state-parks/forests/cockaponset-state-forest

WHY YOU'LL LOVE IT

- Trails along water with lake views
- Plenty of drinking and swimming spots
- Dogs allowed off-leash on the beach

Walk along trails that hug the 56-acre Pattaconk Reservoir with views of the water and plenty of swimming opportunities for the dogs.

The charming town of Chester, settled in the late 1600s and incorporated in 1836, has a rich history in shipbuilding and milling, given its location along the Connecticut River. Today, its quaint downtown and natural beauty draw visitors year-round. It's particularly dog-friendly, too, with water bowls placed outside many shops. After this hike we ate outside with the pups at Pattaconk 1850 Bar & Grill.

One of Chester's nearby outdoor gems is Blue Cockaponset Trail, winding through Cockaponset State Forest's 17,000+ acres and along the coastline of Pattaconk Reservoir. A distinct highlight, aside from the many dips the dogs will enjoy, is the serene reservoir itself, where hikers can enjoy peaceful waterfront views surrounded by forested hills.

Blue Cockaponset Trail, beginning from a parking area off the north side of Route 148, quickly takes you into scenic woodland trails and diverse forest landscapes; this is a quieter atmosphere perfect for exploring with pets. The trail features diverse terrain, including pine forests, rocky outcrops and the reservoir shoreline where your pups can cool off on warmer days.

Cockaponset is named after a Native American chief, and this trail is part of Connecticut's extensive, blue-blazed system, spanning over 16 miles through the state's second-largest forest.

The trail begins with a 1.5-mile walk into the forest that leads to Pattaconk Reservoir. The next 2.3 miles hug the reservoir, looping around counterclockwise and providing lovely water views. There are several opportunities for the dogs to swim before walking the 1.5 miles back to the car.

TURN-BY-TURN DIRECTIONS

1. From the parking lot, walk north across W Main Street to find the start of the trail. Enter the trail on the right side to walk the loop counterclockwise.
2. At 0.4 miles, bear right on the blue and yellow trail (both markers are on the trees).
3. At 0.5 miles, cross another stream and follow the blue trail blazes on the trees.
4. At 1.2 miles, at an intersection with mountain biking trails, continue straight on the blue-blazed trail.
5. At 1.57 miles, turn right onto the yellow trail and cross the wooden bridge.
6. At 1.67 miles, turn right onto the paved State Forest Road, and walk for just a couple hundred feet.
7. At 1.72 miles, turn left on the yellow-blazed trail and head back into the woods.
8. At 1.8 miles, arrive at Pattaconk Reservoir Dam, continuing uphill, walking closely along the right side of the water. Yellow blazes are on the trees.
9. At 2.05 miles, picnic tables and a lean-to for camping are on your left.
10. At 2.2 miles, continue along the yellow-blazed trail.
11. At 2.4 miles, bear left to walk on the wide gravel path, which is still the yellow trail.
12. At 2.71 miles, bear left to stay on the yellow trail. The loop starts around to the other side of Pattaconk Reservoir.
13. At 2.8 miles, stay left again to take the trail closest to the reservoir.
14. At 3.77 miles, walk across the bridge and bear left toward the water on the blue-and-red-blazed trail.
15. At 3.85 miles, turn right to walk toward a small parking lot and find the yellow-blazed trail entrance on the right side of the lot.
16. At 4 miles, turn left to start walking on the blue-blazed trail.
17. At 4.05 miles, turn right onto the paved Filley Road, an old logging road, and take it all the way back to the start of the trail.

RHODE ISLAND

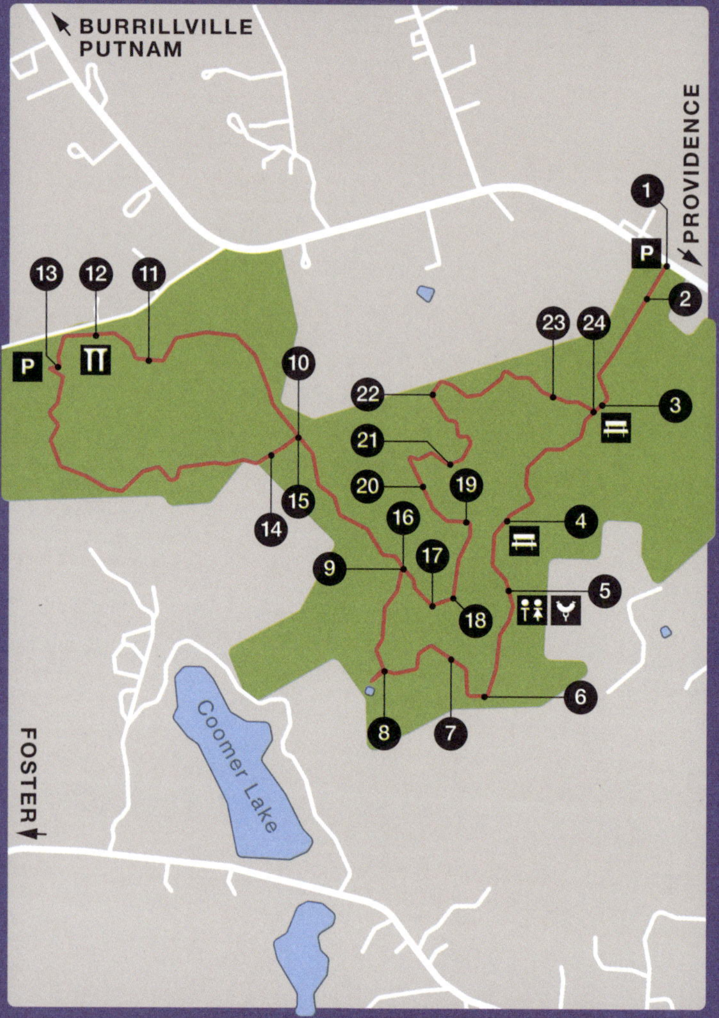

BURRILLVILLE
PUTNAM
PROVIDENCE
FOSTER
Coomer Lake
P
P
1
2
3
4
5
6
7
8
9
10
11
12
13
14
15
16
17
18
19
20
21
22
23
24

P Parking   Bench   Picnic tables   Toilet   Bridge

ft
2500
2000
1500
1000
500
0
0.0
0.5
1.0
1.5
2.0
2.5
3.0
3.5
4.0
4.5
4.78 mi

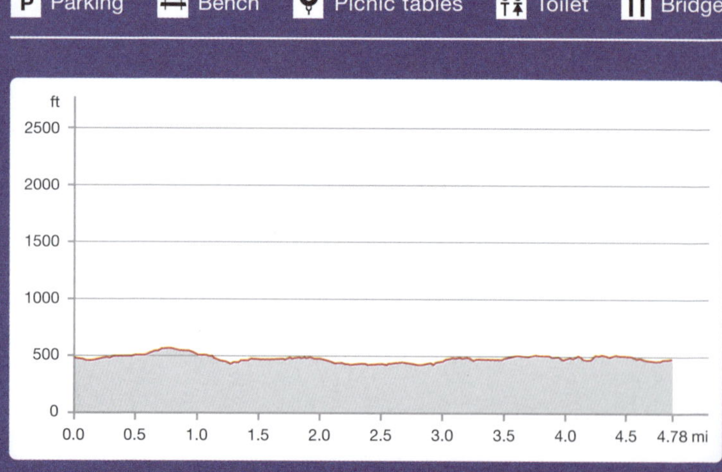

STEERE HILL AND HERITAGE HILL LOOP

WIDE PATHS THROUGH WOODLANDS AND FIELDS

CHEPACHET, RI

42

LENGTH

4.78 miles (loop)

TIME & MONEY

1 hour 55 minutes; free

ELEVATION GAIN

344 feet

DIFFICULTY

Easy

CONDITIONS

Year-round; relatively flat

HIGHLIGHTS

Elevated gazebo, open meadows, wide paths

ESSENTIALS

- **Find the trailhead:** From Glocester Manton Public Library, turn left on Putnam Pike (US-44). After 0.3 miles, bear left to stay on Putnam Pike (US-44). After 3.3 miles, the large parking lot and entrance to Glocester Land Trust is on your right.
- **Land manager:** Glocester Land Trust, PO Box HH, Chepachet, RI 02814; w.morin@glocesterlandtrust.org glocesterlandtrust.org

WHY YOU'LL LOVE IT

- Wide forested trails
- Minimal incline
- Expansive 448-acre preserve

Discover the scenic charm of Steere Hill's 448-acre trail network: a blend of historic farmsteads, diverse habitats and meadow views.

Chepachet, a village in Glocester, Rhode Island, dates back to the early 1700s and is known for its rural charm and pivotal role in the 1842 Dorr Rebellion, a movement for expanded voting rights. This historic village retains much of its 19th-century character, thanks to landmarks like the Old Stone Mill and traditional town center.

Nature enthusiasts and dog lovers frequent the nearby Steere Hill Farm Conservation Area, a preserved expanse of meadows and woodlands well cared for by the Glocester Land Trust. At the summit of Steere Hill is an elevated gazebo with views of the surrounding hills and forest.

The Glocester Land Trust allows deer and turkey hunting on various dates between November and May. We visited out of season but had the dogs wear their orange vests as a precaution.

The property, with its expansive meadows, is perfect for leashed dogs to explore the open space. The trails wind through a mix of woodlands and grassy fields, providing plenty of sensory stimulation for curious pups. Additionally, the wide paths make it easy to navigate, even with larger dogs, and there are numerous shady spots for water breaks.

Starting from the large parking lot on Route 44 (Putnam Pike), make your way into the forest and onto the red-blazed Steere Hill Trail, taking the loop around Steere Hill clockwise.

At 0.77 miles, there's an elevated gazebo with picnic tables and meadow views. This is a great spot to offer water to the dogs if it's a hot day. There are also porta-potties off to the side here.

Continuing on the wide path through the meadow, enter back into the woods and at 1.8 miles pick up Heritage Park Loop heading counterclockwise. When completed, pick up the white trail again to finish Steere Hill Loop.

While there are no big views on this hike, it's a very serene and scenic walk in the woods, with classic New England features like stone walls, vernal pools, fens, and old foundations. The minimal elevation change is perfect for dogs of all ages!

TURN-BY-TURN DIRECTIONS

1. From the parking lot, walk behind the gate onto the wide gravel path to begin the trail. A trailhead sign is straight ahead.
2. At 0.1 miles, arrive at the trailhead and stay to the right on the red-rectangle-blazed trail.
3. At 0.3 miles, at the bench and Steere Hill Trail sign, stay straight on the red-blazed trail, going clockwise to begin the loop.
4. At 0.6 miles, pass the bench on the left and stay straight on the red trail.
5. At 0.77 miles, at the gazebo with meadow views on the right, there are porta-potties.
6. At 0.9 miles, pass the sign for Woodworth Trail on your left and continue on the wide path as it bends to the right.
7. At 1.06 miles, bear to the left onto the orange-blazed trail. The path goes from the open meadows back into the woods now.
8. Optional: At 1.21 miles, bear to the left to visit a little pool of water for the dogs, just 100 feet ahead. After visiting the water, get back on the trail, turning left onto the orange-blazed trail.
9. At 1.45 miles, take a left at the Andrews Trail sign and walk along the white-blazed trail.
10. At 1.8 miles, at a fork, begin a small loop around Heritage Park. Turn right onto the red-dot trail to begin this loop counterclockwise.
11. At 2.2 miles, bear right to continue on the red-dot trail. Big rock formations are on your right.
12. At 2.3 miles, bear right to continue on the red-dot trail and walk across a small bridge.
13. At 2.42 miles, there's a gate and parking area to the right. Stay straight and join the blue-triangle-blazed trail.
14. At 3.04 miles, the trail curves around to the right.
15. At 3.08 miles, Heritage Park Loop is complete. Turn right to walk back on the white-rectangle-blazed trail.
16. At 3.4 miles, stay straight at the Andrews Trail sign to continue on the white-rectangle-blazed trail.
17. At 3.47 miles, back at the large meadow, stay left.
18. At 3.5 miles, turn left at the Heritage Trail sign to join Beech Trail, marked by green blazes.
19. At 3.7 miles, the trail curves around to the left. At the fork shortly after, bear left at the Ridge Trail sign. Ridge Trail has purple-dot blazes.
20. At 3.83 miles, continue straight on Ridge Trail.
21. At 3.93 miles, stay left at a trail fork on the purple-blazed Ridge Trail.
22. At 4.12 miles, take a right to continue on Ridge Trail.
23. At 4.4 miles, continue straight onto the orange-triangle-blazed trail.
24. At 4.44 miles, arrive back at the main trail where you began the first loop. Turn left onto the Steere Hill red-blazed trail and pass the bench ahead. Follow the path out to the parking area to complete the hike.

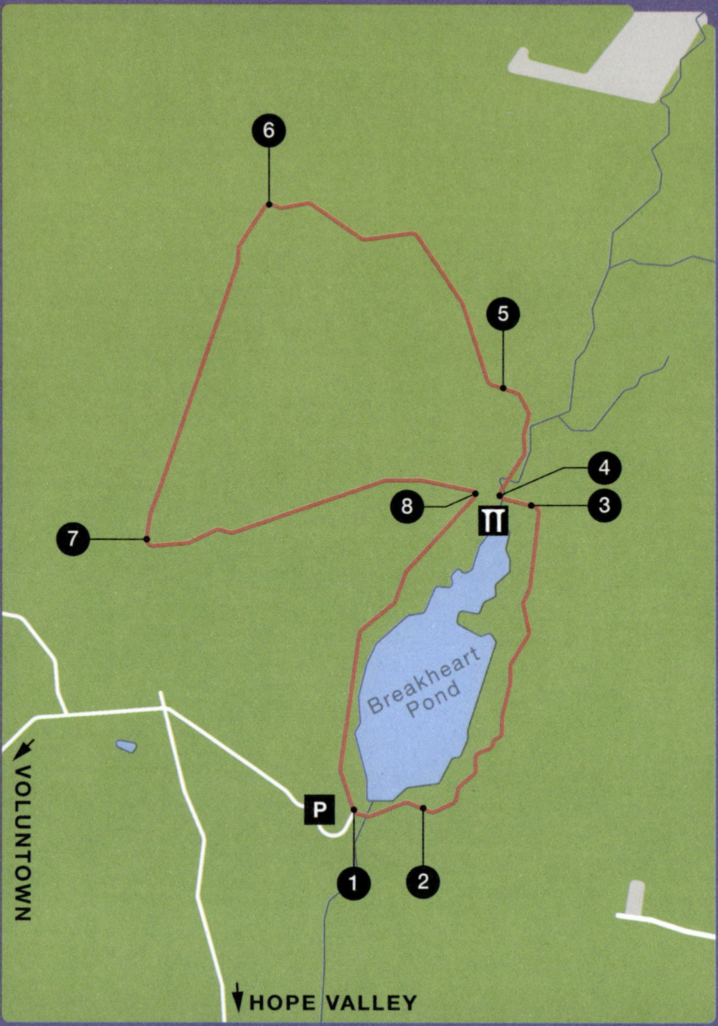

6
5
4
8
3
7
Breakheart Pond
P
VOLUNTOWN
1
2
HOPE VALLEY

P Parking

Bridge

ft
2500
2000
1500
1000
500
0
0.0
0.5
1.0
1.5
2.0
2.5
3.0
3.6 mi

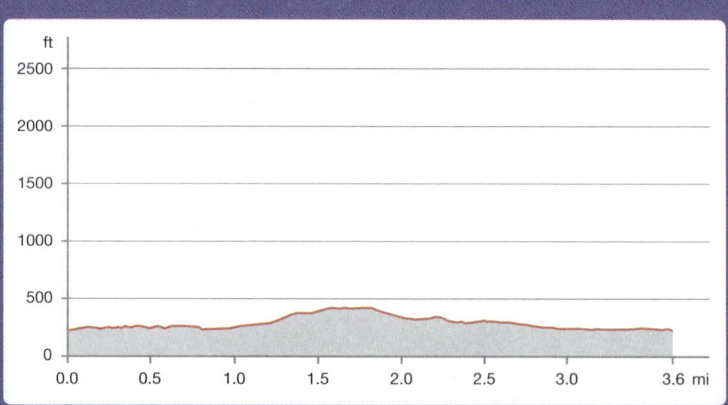

BREAKHEART TRAIL LOOP

QUIET POND LOOP THROUGH TALL PINE FOREST

WEST GREENWICH, RI

43

LENGTH

3.6 miles (loop)

TIME & MONEY

1 hour 20 minutes; free

ELEVATION GAIN

240 feet

DIFFICULTY

Moderate

CONDITIONS

Year-round; smooth forest trails, wide trails

HIGHLIGHTS

44-acre pond in RI's largest protected forest

ESSENTIALS

- **Find the trailhead:** From I-95 north or south take Exit 5A for Route 102 south. After 0.7 miles, turn right onto Nooseneck Hill Road/ Route 3 south. After 1.3 miles, turn right onto Route 165/Ten Rod Road. After 2.8 miles, turn right onto Frosty Hollow Road—it's directly opposite the clearly marked Summit Road sign and just before West Exeter Baptist Church (the Frosty Hollow sign is hard to spot until you're already turning). After 1.5 miles, turn right at the T-junction, then go 0.5 miles to the pond, with Lillibridge Lot parking on your left. *Note: Both Frosty Hollow Road and the final road are dirt.*

- **Land manager:** Arcadia Management Area Headquarters, 260 Arcadia Road, Hope Valley, RI 02823; (401) 539-2356; dem.riparks@dem.ri.gov
riparks.ri.gov/other-state-lands

WHY YOU'LL LOVE IT

- Towering pine forest with a remote feel
- Mix of woodland trails and wide paths
- Water access for the dogs

With towering pines, a large lake and a quiet, secluded atmosphere, Breakheart Trail Loop stands out as one of the most peaceful dog-friendly hikes in Rhode Island.

Located within the expansive Arcadia Management Area—Rhode Island's largest protected forest with over 14,000 acres—this trail offers a deeply immersive woodland experience that feels more like northern New England than southern Rhode Island.

Breakheart Trail around Breakheart Pond is located just 25 miles southwest of the busy city of Providence and 25 miles northeast from the popular beach town of Narragansett.

Surrounded by a thick canopy of white pines and hemlocks, you'll quickly forget how close you are to the coast as you and your pup wander through a landscape that feels both remote and wild.

This loop is a great option for dogs who enjoy shaded, soft terrain, access to water, and the occasional wide-open stretch to roam. Most of the trail is under the cover of tall pines, offering a sense of being completely enveloped by the forest. The woods are quiet, serene and varied—alternating between narrow singletrack paths and wide-open, old logging roads—along the shore of Breakheart Pond and over small brooks.

There are a couple things to keep in mind with this hike:

1. Hunting is allowed in parts of Arcadia Management Area. During Rhode Island's hunting season (typically mid-September–February and late April–May), hikers must wear at least 200 square inches of solid daylight fluorescent orange (a hat or vest).

2. During shotgun season (usually early December–early January), 500 square inches is required (both a hat and vest). We stopped at a nearby Ocean State Job Lot to purchase lightweight and cheap vests and neon T-shirts.

3. Narragansett Gun Club is outside the Arcadia Management Area, but you may hear shots during the first part of the loop. The sound was far away and didn't bother the dogs, but it's good to know that these aren't from hunters, in case you visit on a weekend, like we did, when the club is open.

Park at the large Lillibridge Lot east of Breakheart Pond. Start on the yellow-blazed Breakheart Trail at the southern tip of the pond and loop counterclockwise (pond on your left). Follow Breakheart Trail for about 1.8 miles until Matteson Plain Road, an old logging road, and follow it for about 0.7 miles before turning left onto Newman Trail (there aren't any signs or obvious markings for Newman Trail, so keep your eyes out for the trail leading back into the woods).

After 0.6 miles on Newman Trail, turn right onto Hicks Trail, which leads back to the parking lot, with Breakheart Pond on your left. There will be opportunities for the dogs to pop into the water here before the hike is done (unfortunately people aren't allowed to swim!).

TURN-BY-TURN DIRECTIONS

1. From Lillibridge Lot, walk to the southern tip of the pond by the dam to start the loop, counterclockwise, on the yellow trail.
2. At 0.14 miles, at the Breakheart Trail sign, bear left on yellow.
3. At 0.82 miles, turn left on the yellow trail and soon cross Breakheart Brook, with water for the dogs.
4. At 0.9 miles, after crossing the bridge over the creek, turn right to continue on yellow.
5. At 1.13 miles, continue straight on the yellow trail.
6. At 1.76 miles, turn left onto Matteson Plain Road.
7. At 2.4 miles, keep an eye out for the wide trail on your left, leading back into the forest. There are no obvious blazes here, but blue spray paint soon marks some of the trees.
8. At 3 miles, turn right onto Hicks Trail. There are no obvious blazes here, but the water will be on your left. Follow this trail back to the parking lot.

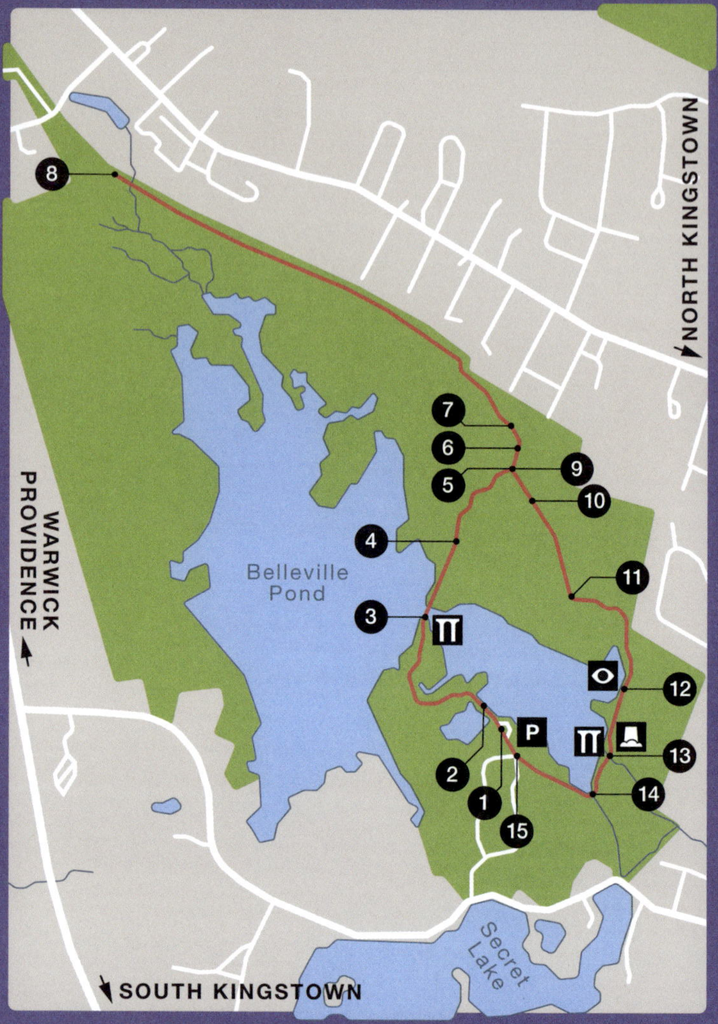

NORTH KINGSTOWN
WARWICK
PROVIDENCE
Belleville Pond
Secret Lake
SOUTH KINGSTOWN
1
2
3
4
5
6
7
8
9
10
11
12
13
14
15
P

P Parking Bridge Waterfall Viewpoint

ft
2500
2000
1500
1000
500
0
0.0
0.5
1.0
1.5
2.0
2.5
2.92 mi

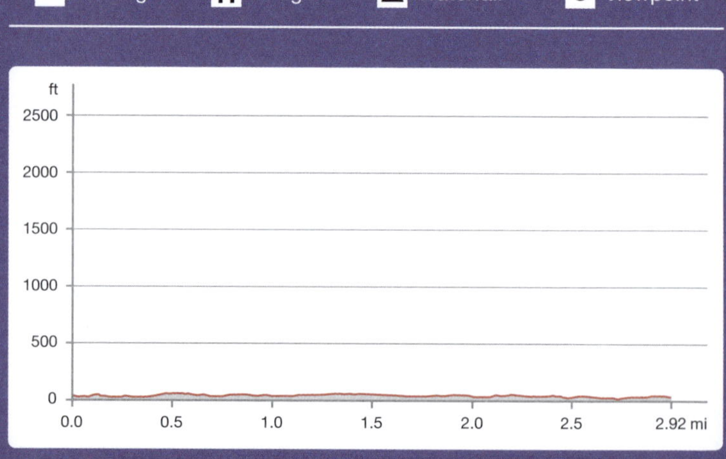

BELLEVILLE POND

WATER VIEWS ABOUND ON A QUIET, FLAT PATH

NORTH KINGSTON, RI

44

LENGTH
2.92 miles
(out and back)

TIME & MONEY
1 hour 5 minutes;
free

ELEVATION GAIN
79 feet

DIFFICULTY
Easy

CONDITIONS
Year-round

HIGHLIGHTS
Views of Belleville Pond, bridges, waterfall

ESSENTIALS

- **Find the trailhead:** From North Kingston Town Hall, turn right toward Fairway Drive and turn left onto Fairway Drive. After 0.3 miles, turn right onto Annaquatucket Road. After 0.8 miles, turn left onto Tower Hill Road. After 0.3 miles, turn right onto Oak Hill Road. After 0.5 miles, the parking for Belleville Pond trails is on your right, at 291 Oak Hill Road.

- **Land manager:** The Town of North Kingstown, 100 Fairway Drive, North Kingstown, RI 02852; (401) 294-3331; recreationsecretary@northkingstownri.gov northkingstownri.gov

WHY YOU'LL LOVE IT

- Scenic shoreline trails
- Walk along large 100-acre pond
- Relatively flat

Belleville Pond is a serene escape in Ryan Park, where flat, peaceful trails, stunning water views, access to water, and quiet natural beauty offer the perfect dog-friendly adventure.

North Kingstown, established in 1674, has a history rooted in maritime trade, agriculture and industry. Early settlers capitalized on the region's coastal location, building shipyards and participating in the rum trade, among other ventures.

Belleville Pond offers a quiet retreat within Ryan Park, where trails loop around the water's edge and along long-forgotten locomotive lines. The shallow waters of the pond support a rich ecosystem, making it a great spot for wildlife, especially birds.

A distinct highlight of this hike are the many views across the pond. With calm reflections of the surrounding woodlands, it's a peaceful and rewarding spot for a walk with your best furry friends.

The trails loop gently through dense woodlands and open fields, and around Belleville Pond, providing several miles of hiking paths. The mostly flat terrain makes it accessible for dogs of all sizes and ages, allowing you both to enjoy a leisurely hike without strenuous inclines.

Weaving right along the pond's edge, the trails give dogs plenty of natural sights and smells to explore. Enjoy the occasional access points to the pond where they can cool off on warmer days.

With its easy trails, beautiful views and tranquil setting, Belleville Pond is an ideal spot for a relaxed day of hiking, allowing both you and your dogs to enjoy nature's beauty at a comfortable pace.

TURN-BY-TURN DIRECTIONS

1. After parking, find the blue blazes on trees to the left if facing the water. (Walk northwest to find the start of the trail.)
2. At 0.1 miles, walk between two bodies of water with a small pond on your left and Belleville Pond on your right.
3. At 0.34 miles, walk across the little bridge that spans the pond.
4. At 0.4 miles, there will be a few trails branching off to the left and right; continue to stay straight on the light-blue-blazed trail.
5. At 0.6 miles, bear left.
6. At 0.62 miles, bear left again then continue straight.
7. At 0.67 miles, walk behind a barn and small residential area. Follow the straight path.
8. At 1.33 miles, the straight path ends. Turn around and walk back the way you came.
9. At 2.1 miles, bear left at the fork to start the left side of the loop portion.
10. At 2.18 miles, where a trail branches off to the right, stay left.
11. At 2.4 miles, stay to the left. Blue blazes appear on trees behind a residential area with a couple of houses.
12. At 2.57 miles, enjoy the view across the pond to the bridge.
13. At 2.65 miles, emerge at a wide-open meadow by the pond. There's a small waterfall on the right. Walk across the wooden bridge here.
14. At 2.74 miles, at a parking area, stay right.
15. At 2.84 miles, turn right and return to your car.

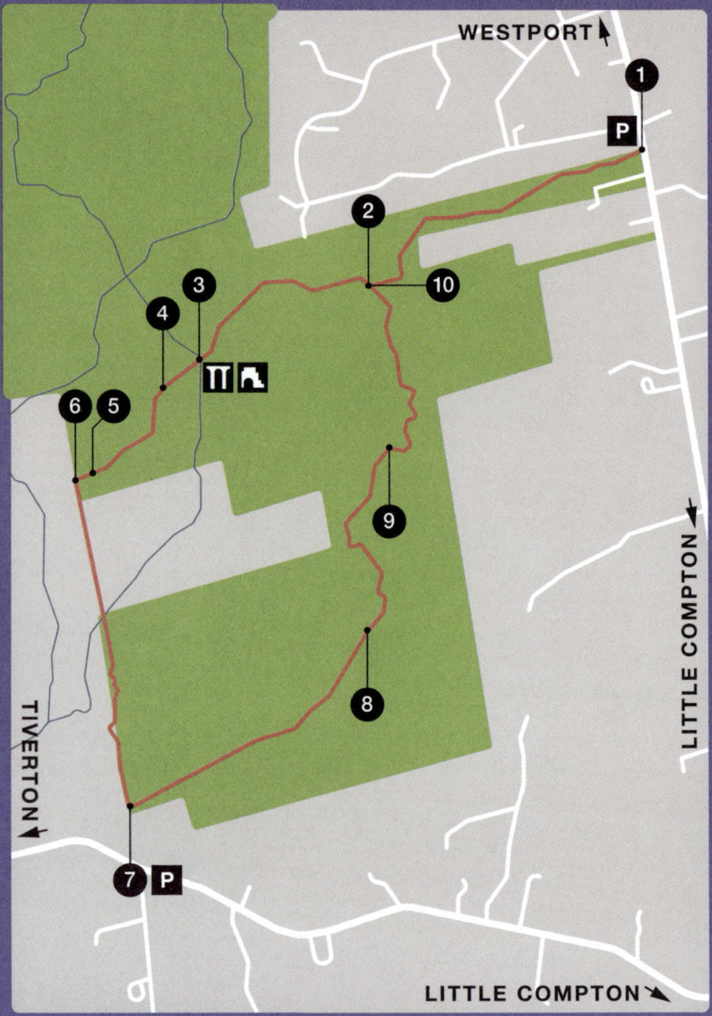

WESTPORT
LITTLE COMPTON
TIVERTON
LITTLE COMPTON
1
2
3
4
5
6
7
8
9
10
P
P

P Parking | Bridge | Ruins

ft
2500
2000
1500
1000
500
0
0.0
0.5
1.0
1.5
2.0
2.5
3.0
3.34 mi

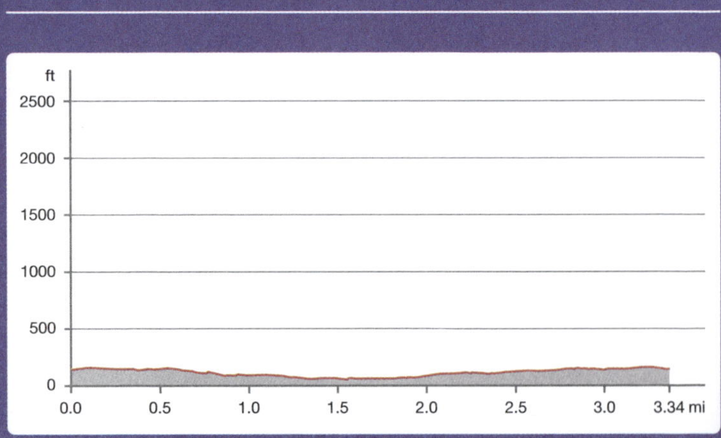

WEETAMOO WOODS LOOP

OFF-LEASH PORTION AND MEADOW VIEWS

TIVERTON, RI

45

LENGTH
3.34 miles (loop)

TIME & MONEY
1 hour 22 minutes; free

ELEVATION GAIN
157 feet

DIFFICULTY
Easy

CONDITIONS
Year-round; smooth, wide forest trails

HIGHLIGHTS
Off-leash, meadow views, multiple streams, historic ruins

ESSENTIALS

- **Find the trailhead:** From Tiverton Library, turn right on Roosevelt Drive and after 360 feet, turn right on Bulgarmarsh Road (RI-177). After 0.2 miles, turn right onto Crandall Road (RI-81). After 1.4 miles, turn right onto King Road. After 1.2 miles, continue on Lake Road and the parking lot is on the left after 0.8 miles.
- **Land manager:** Tiverton Open Space Commission, 343 Highland Rd, Tiverton, RI 02878; (401) 625-6700
tiverton.ri.gov

WHY YOU'LL LOVE IT

- Off-leash trails in large, forested setting
- Historic mill sites and stone walls
- Multiple streams for the dogs

Wide woodland trails, rich colonial history and a dog-friendly off-leash policy make Weetamoo Woods a top hiking destination for pups and their people in Rhode Island.

Just 30 minutes southeast of Providence and west of Newport, Weetamoo Woods offers over 650 acres of beautiful, varied terrain featuring oak forests, open meadows and peaceful wetlands.

It's a fantastic place to explore with your dog, especially since it's one of the few approved off-leash hiking spots in the area. With more than seven miles of well-maintained trails and several brooks along the way, it's easy for dogs to stay entertained and hydrated as they roam.

The area is named after Weetamoo (c. 1635–1676), a respected female sachem of the Pocasset Wampanoag Indigenous people. Traces of the land's rich history and Colonial-era farmland past are evident along the wooded trails—most following wide cart paths bordered by old stone walls and scattered with remnants like cellar holes and stone foundations. This hike crosses Borden Brook several times and passes a historic 1800s sawmill.

Managed by the town of Tiverton, the trail system is clearly marked and easy to follow. With little elevation gain, it's a great option for dogs (and people) of all ages. On our way out, we passed a couple walking two dogs, off-leash, who told us they visit almost every day—and their dogs were 16 and 17 years old!

About half a mile from the parking area, pick up the red trail to begin the loop counterclockwise. After about a mile, turn left onto the yellow trail, and then close out the loop on the orange trail.

TURN-BY-TURN DIRECTIONS

1. Find the trailhead and start the hike.
2. At 0.53 miles, begin the loop portion, bearing right onto the red trail.
3. At 0.83 miles, continue straight on the red trail, crossing the bridge and passing the old sawmill.
4. At 0.9 miles, bear left to stay on the red trail.
5. At 1.1 miles, bear left to pick up the yellow trail.
6. At 1.15 miles, bear left to continue on the yellow trail. (There are two different trails on the left, both marked in yellow: Take either one, as they meet after a couple hundred feet.)
7. At 1.72 miles, turn left onto the orange trail at the trailhead kiosk, after passing the barn on your right.
8. At 2.15 miles, continue straight on the orange trail.
9. At 2.5 miles, continue on the orange trail as it curves to the right.
10. At 2.85 miles, arrive back at the loop's start. Turn right to return to the parking lot, the same way you came in.

ACKNOWLEDGMENTS

I dedicate this book to my husband, Tim: You've always believed in me and encouraged me to follow my dream of being a writer. Thank you for supporting my hiking research by joining my travels or holding down the fort at home. I couldn't ask for a more supportive partner and I couldn't have written this book without you! I love you so much.

To my kids, Finn and Henry: You inspired all the hikes we took on backyard trails during the COVID-19 pandemic, which led to my first book. You convinced us to get a dog, which led to my second book. In reality, you are the inspiration for everything I do! Thank you for your understanding when I spent many evening hours on the couch—our family time—writing on my laptop. Thank you for supporting me as I followed my dreams; I'll always be here to support you in following yours. I'm so proud of you both and love you beyond words.

To my parents, Jan Stover, Doug Tallaksen and Gail Frisch: Thank you for loving me through the winding path of life. I'm thankful to have inherited your love of adventure, writing and dogs (respectively). To Jack and Elaine McMahon: Thank you for your unwavering support. To Matt: Growing up with you and your friends gave me the grit and humor I use in this work. I'm so glad you're my brother.

To my friends: Becca, you've been my greatest cheerleader as I juggled writing a book, working full-time and raising a family. Thank you for encouraging me when I needed it most. Anna and Brian, thank you for finding and bringing Romy home. This book wouldn't have happened without her or you! Sharing sister dogs has been the greatest gift. And Jaime, thanks for being the best hiking partner a girl could ask for.

This book would not exist without the incredible Helvetiq team: Thank you to Richard Harvell for giving me the opportunity to write about dogs and hiking, two things that bring me so much joy. I appreciate your idea to co-author the book, which lightened my workload and introduced me to Kristen. Heartfelt thanks to Angela, our wise and witty editor. Your expert guidance and ability to fine-tune my writing never cease to amaze me. Thank you to Ela for your brilliant illustrations, layout and design—the final product is more beautiful than I could've imaged—and to Theresa for your sharp eye and attention to detail. And Kristen, thank you for your heart and thoughtfulness every step of the way—I'm grateful we shared this journey together.

I would like to thank Carey Kish for introducing me to Helvetiq, Marc Lesperance for connecting me with Carey, and Lori Uhland for recommending me to Marc when he asked if she knew any dog folk who could write a trail guide. I'm grateful for our Portland dog-walking community.

And to the land managers, trail-maintenance workers and all the friendly folks on the trails: You make the hiking community one I am proud to belong to. If I've forgotten anyone, know that I am grateful for everyone whose ideas influenced this book and for those who support it moving forward. I hope you enjoy this guide and discovering new hikes with your dog!

Jill McMahon
outdoormovementproject.com

I dedicate this book to Jared, Captain and Bruin, and the people in the dog community who only want to go when their dogs can come too.

Jared: Thank you for making hiking with our dogs part of everyday life, for giving me the courage to chase my dreams, and for always finding a way to help. And for joining me on every single hike for this book! I couldn't have done it without you.

To Mom and Dad: Thank you for your love and unwavering support and for always sharing in the excitement of my various projects! You're truly the best parents and I owe my love of dogs, photography and nature to you both.

To my sister Gina, brother-in-law John, and nieces Ava and Caila and nephew Johnny: Having you in my life means the world. Your kindness to Captain and Bruin and the way you fill my life with love means so much. And thanks to the rest of my family—lifelong dog lovers, every one!

To Alison, Jon and John: Thank you for always being there for us and for sharing in the hiking fun. Your adventurous spirits continue to inspire me and I love how much you love our dogs! To Kristy and Derek: I loved our camping trip where we got to do several of these hikes together with Charlie and Lucy—the best trail models! Thank you to all my friends for being in my corner—you help me be brave!

To Helvetiq: Richard, thank you for asking me to be a part of this amazing project. When you first mentioned a book about dogs and hiking, it felt like the stars had aligned! I'm so grateful for the opportunity. Angela, thank you for your thoughtful edits, sharp eye and patience. You pushed me to dig deeper and grow as a writer, and I'm so grateful for your guidance. Jill, you've been a source of calm and inspiration in this process—I'm so glad you were my partner and I look forward to future projects together!

And to the two souls who can't read this but have shaped my heart and trail life in the most meaningful way: Captain and Bruin. Captain, no matter what anyone says, you made me a mom; you gave me purpose and companionship and reignited my love of hiking. Seeing the back of your head as we head down a trail will always be my favorite view. And Bruin, the ultimate little brother—you keep us on our toes as you fly down the path.

Also, a heartfelt thank you to the land managers, conservation groups and volunteers who maintain these trails and help protect the beautiful outdoor spaces we're so lucky to explore: Your work makes adventures like these possible. I also want to acknowledge that many of the trails featured in this book pass through lands originally cared for and inhabited by Indigenous peoples. I am grateful to walk them.

Finally, a huge thank you to everyone who picks up this book and finds joy in exploring the outdoors with their dog. Dog people truly are the best people, and I'm grateful to be part of this community. Don't hesitate to reach out—I'd love to hear all about your trail experiences!

Kristen Valenti
earlybirdonthetrail.com

NOTES